Editors
Brent L. Fox, M. Ed.
Erica N. Russikoff, M.A.

Editor in Chief
Karen J. Goldfluss, M.S. Ed.

Creative Director
Sarah M. Smith

Cover Artist
Barb Lorseyedi

Imaging
James Edward Grace
Craig Gunnell
Amanda R. Harter

Publisher
Mary D. Smith, M.S. Ed.

DAILY WA...

Reading

GRADE 7

- Over 150 nonfiction and fiction passages
- Follow-up questions for each passage target essential comprehension skills.
- Ideal for test preparation!

Teacher Created Resources

Author
Tracie Heskett, M. Ed.

CORRELATED TO COMMON CORE STANDARDS

For Common Core State Standards correlations, visit
http://www.teachercreated.com/standards.

Teacher Created Resources
6421 Industry Way
Westminster, CA 92683
www.teachercreated.com
ISBN: 978-1-4206-3658-1
© 2014 Teacher Created Resources
Made in U.S.A.

Teacher Created Resources

Table of Contents

Animals 9

A Forest Secret—Animal Intelligence—Long-Distance Travelers—The Jumping Spider—Swimming with the Turtles—The Rare Dolphin—Blue Dragons—Pippi—Nature's Helicopters—The African Generuk—Deadly Delicacy—The Climbing Rodent—Panda Ants—Cave Dwellers—Animals and Humans

Biographies 24

The Unknown Winston Churchill—Lawrence of Arabia—Sir Thomas More—Olympic Inspiration—Harry S. Truman, U.S. President—Man of Finance—Stronger Than Steel—Just an Ordinary Guy—Woman of Justice—The Father of Public Libraries—Margaret Thatcher, Prime Minister—Author of Adventure—Pelé—Harland David Sanders—Walt Disney's Greatest Storyman—Barbara McClintock, Nobel Prize Winner

History 40

Washington's Crossing of the Delaware—Animated Cartoons—Handheld Calculators—The Emancipation Proclamation—Prohibition—The Great American Dessert—The History of Airships—Pirates of the South China Sea—The Beginnings of Fountain Drinks—The Louisiana Purchase—Julius Caesar, Kidnapped—That Phone in Your Pocket—Livestock Reduction—Salt of the Earth—Claiming the South Pole for Mankind—Braces

Science 56

Microbursts—Invasive Plant Species—Twins—"Beam Me Up"—The Science of Color—Audiology—How Are Mountains Formed?—Telling Time Without a Clock—Physics for Our Amusement—Antarctic Ice Sheet—Garbage to Good—The Exciting Field of Engineering—How We Use Corn—International Space Station—Geothermal Energy

Current Events 71

Football for Kids—Men on Mars?—The Philippines—United States Spy Agencies—Word of the Year—Global Warming—3D Printing—Is Recycling Worth It?—The Homework Debate—Meteorites on Earth—Electric Cars—Tree Climbing: Not Just for Kids—Weather Is a Current Event—Travel of the Future—The State of Hawaii—Virtual Learning

Table of Contents *(cont.)*

Introduction

The goal of this book is to improve students' reading and comprehension skills. The more experience a student has with reading and comprehending, the better reader and problem-solver he or she will be. *Daily Warm-Ups: Reading* contains a variety of passages to be read on a daily basis. Each passage is followed by comprehension questions. The questions that follow the passages are based on Bloom's Taxonomy and allow for higher-level thinking skills. Making this book a part of your daily classroom agenda can help your students' reading and comprehension abilities improve dramatically.

Nonfiction and Fiction

Daily Warm-Ups: Reading is divided into two sections: nonfiction and fiction. It is important for students to be exposed to a variety of reading genres and formats. The nonfiction section is divided into five categories. These categories are animals, biographies, history, science, and current events. By reading these nonfiction passages, your students will be exposed to a variety of nonfiction information, as well as questions to stimulate thinking on these subjects.

The fiction section of the book is also divided into five categories. These categories are fairy tales/folklore, historical fiction, contemporary realism, mystery/suspense/adventure, and fantasy. Each story is followed by questions to stimulate thinking on the plot, characters, vocabulary, and sequence.

Comprehension Questions

Comprehension is the primary goal of any reading task. Students who comprehend what they read perform better on both tests and in life. The follow-up questions after each passage are written to encourage students to improve in recognizing text structure, visualizing, summarizing, and learning new vocabulary. Each of these skills can be found in scope-and-sequence charts as well as standards for reading comprehension. The different types of questions in *Daily Warm-Ups: Reading* are geared to help students with the following skills:

- Recognize the main idea
- Identify details
- Recall details
- Summarize
- Describe characters and character traits
- Classify and sort into categories
- Compare and contrast

- Make generalizations
- Draw conclusions
- Recognize fact
- Apply information to new situations
- Recognize sequence
- Understand vocabulary

Introduction *(cont.)*

Readability

Each of the reading passages in *Daily Warm-Ups: Reading* varies in difficulty to meet the various reading levels of your students. The passages have been categorized as follows: below grade level, at grade level, and above grade level. (See the Leveling Chart on page 6.)

Record Keeping

Use the Tracking Sheet on page 176 to record which warm-up exercises you have given to your students, or distribute copies of the sheet for students to keep their own records.

How to Make the Most of This Book

Here are some simple tips to supplement your educational strategies. They are only suggestions to help you make your students as successful in reading as possible.

- Read through the book ahead of time so you are familiar with each portion. The better you understand how the book works, the easier it will be to answer students' questions.

- Set aside a regular time each day to incorporate *Daily Warm-Ups* into your routine. Once the routine is established, students will look forward to and expect to work on reading strategies at that particular time.

- Make sure that any amount of time spent on *Daily Warm-Ups* is positive and constructive. This should be a time of practicing for success and recognizing it as it is achieved.

- Allot only about 10 minutes a day to *Daily Warm-Ups*. Too much time will not be useful; too little time will create additional stress.

- Be sure to model the reading and question-answering process at the beginning of the year. Model pre-reading questions, reading the passage, highlighting information that refers to the questions, and eliminating answers that are obviously wrong. Finally, refer back to the text once again to make sure the answers chosen are the best ones.

- Create and store overheads or interactive-whiteboard slides of each lesson so that you can review student work, concepts, and strategies as quickly as possible.

- Utilize peer tutors to assist struggling students.

- Offer small-group time to students who need extra enrichment or opportunities for questions regarding the text. Small groups will allow many of these students, once they are comfortable with the format, to achieve success independently.

- Adjust the procedures, as you see fit, to meet the needs of all your students.

Leveling Chart

NONFICTION   ▲ = below grade level   ● = at grade level   ■ = above grade level

Animals		Biographies		History		Science		Current Events	
Page 9	■	Page 24	■	Page 40	■	Page 56	■	Page 71	■
Page 10	■	Page 25	■	Page 41	●	Page 57	■	Page 72	■
Page 11	●	Page 26	■	Page 42	■	Page 58	■	Page 73	●
Page 12	●	Page 27	▲	Page 43	■	Page 59	■	Page 74	■
Page 13	■	Page 28	■	Page 44	■	Page 60	●	Page 75	●
Page 14	■	Page 29	●	Page 45	●	Page 61	■	Page 76	■
Page 15	●	Page 30	●	Page 46	●	Page 62	▲	Page 77	■
Page 16	●	Page 31	▲	Page 47	▲	Page 63	●	Page 78	■
Page 17	●	Page 32	■	Page 48	■	Page 64	■	Page 79	■
Page 18	▲	Page 33	●	Page 49	■	Page 65	▲	Page 80	●
Page 19	▲	Page 34	■	Page 50	▲	Page 66	●	Page 81	●
Page 20	▲	Page 35	●	Page 51	■	Page 67	■	Page 82	■
Page 21	▲	Page 36	●	Page 52	■	Page 68	▲	Page 83	●
Page 22	●	Page 37	■	Page 53	▲	Page 69	■	Page 84	●
Page 23	●	Page 38	▲	Page 54	●	Page 70	●	Page 85	●
		Page 39	●	Page 55	▲			Page 86	■

FICTION   ▲ = below grade level   ● = at grade level   ■ = above grade level

Fairy Tales/ Folklore		Historical		Contemporary Realism		Mystery/ Suspense/Adventure		Fantasy	
Page 89	▲	Page 104	▲	Page 120	▲	Page 136	●	Page 151	▲
Page 90	▲	Page 105	●	Page 121	●	Page 137	▲	Page 152	▲
Page 91	▲	Page 106	▲	Page 122	▲	Page 138	▲	Page 153	▲
Page 92	●	Page 107	▲	Page 123	●	Page 139	▲	Page 154	▲
Page 93	●	Page 108	●	Page 124	●	Page 140	●	Page 155	▲
Page 94	●	Page 109	■	Page 125	●	Page 141	●	Page 156	▲
Page 95	●	Page 110	●	Page 126	▲	Page 142	▲	Page 157	●
Page 96	●	Page 111	●	Page 127	▲	Page 143	▲	Page 158	▲
Page 97	▲	Page 112	▲	Page 128	▲	Page 144	▲	Page 159	●
Page 98	▲	Page 113	▲	Page 129	▲	Page 145	▲	Page 160	▲
Page 99	▲	Page 114	▲	Page 130	●	Page 146	▲	Page 161	■
Page 100	▲	Page 115	▲	Page 131	▲	Page 147	●	Page 162	■
Page 101	●	Page 116	▲	Page 132	●	Page 148	▲	Page 163	●
Page 102	▲	Page 117	●	Page 133	▲	Page 149	●	Page 164	●
Page 103	▲	Page 118	●	Page 134	●	Page 150	■	Page 165	●
		Page 119	▲	Page 135	▲			Page 166	■

Nonfiction

8

Name_____

A Forest Secret

Until recently, saolas remained one of Earth's best-kept secrets. Upon discovering this animal in the wild, scientists just as quickly recognized this unique species as endangered. Immediate steps are being taken, in the form of establishing national parks, to ensure the survival of the species.

Villagers in Vietnam and Laos have spotted saolas only on rare occasion. Although saolas physically resemble miniature antelopes, DNA testing confirmed they are a separate species, previously unknown to mankind. Biologically, saolas are related to cows and bison. Their name means "spinning wheel posts," referring to the animals' long horns that sweep back over the neck. Their most distinguishing feature, aside from the horns, are massive scent glands in their cheeks. Saolas mark their territory with musk from these glands. Scientists are uncertain exactly how many of the animals exist today.

Nearly twenty years ago, an adult female was captured and sent to a zoo in Laos. The saola stood about waist-high with 18-inch horns. This interesting mammal appears to have little fear of humans and was observed to be approachable in zoo settings. Their reaction to dogs, however, gives a clue as to possible predators. Unfortunately, observations of saolas have been limited, as those captured have died shortly thereafter. Causes of each death have not been fully determined, although at least two have succumbed to infection.

Scientists disagree as to the best course of action for saving saolas. Some believe that leaving the saola alone to roam the few remaining patches of their native habitat—wet evergreen forests—will ensure their survival. Others argue for a more direct approach, such as captive breeding. Either way, if saolas become extinct, it will represent another failure in protecting Earth's fragile ecosystems.

Text Questions

1. What is the main idea of the last paragraph?
   a. It provides examples of keeping a saola in captivity.
   b. It offers ways to save saolas.
   c. It describes how saolas are unique.
   d. It gives a description of the saola's appearance.

   90

2. What does the word *distinguishing* mean as it is used in the second paragraph?
   a. different   c. infamous
   b. separated   d. unknown

3. Why is this passage titled "A Forest Secret"?
   a. Saolas were not known about until recently.
   b. Saolas are a unique species.
   c. Saolas are afraid of dogs, but scientists do not know why.
   d. Saolas are endangered.

4. Which information about saolas is not included in the passage?
   a. their habitat   c. their diet
   b. their appearance   d. their possible predators

5. What are some reasons scientists might want to keep saolas from becoming extinct?   —5

   It will represent another failure in protecting Earth's fragile ecosystems.

   ? food chain?

   1/2

Name_____

Animal Intelligence

Did you know that animals can spy and retrieve information? People have trained animals to perform useful tasks, do entertaining tricks, and provide information as spies during wartime.

Often, the techniques and principles used to train animals for useful tasks have their roots in behavioral conditioning, as first described by B.F. Skinner. Subjects are trained to do things voluntarily based on cues in the environment. Rewards or consequences shape the likelihood of repeated behavior in the future. In classic experiments, animals learn to associate an action with a reward.

During the Cold War, ravens were trained to deposit and retrieve objects. The birds could recognize characteristics of objects and would be instructed accordingly. For example, a raven could be taught to always fly to a large or small table. Ravens are also able to carry quite a bit of weight, so they could transport objects that contained a message.

Intelligence agencies have also experimented with training cats. In one such instance, each feline was fitted with a wire, battery, and instruments to create a transmitter. While directing the cat remotely with ultrasonic sound, operators could eavesdrop on critical communications.

Advocates of such programs cite animals' low profiles as a benefit. People are less likely to pay attention to an animal arriving and leaving. In addition, animals can get into places people can't. On the downside, animals require ongoing training, care, and maintenance.

The details of specific intelligence programs actually put into use are relatively unknown. Many documents and records are classified information or have since been destroyed. It's safe to say, though, that studies in animal training for intelligence and security tasks continue. K-9 dog police units are one such example.

Text Questions

1. What is the main idea of the second paragraph?
   a. It describes the types of animals that are used as spies.
   b. It explains the principles used to train animals for intelligence work.
   c. It states the reason the author wrote the article.
   d. It states the author's conclusion.

   70%

2. Which animals are not mentioned in the article as potential subjects for animal intelligence tasks?
   a. birds
   b. cats
   c. dogs
   d. rats

3. What does the word *associate* mean as it is used in the second paragraph?
   a. to be a companion with
   b. to connect in your mind
   c. to be a member with less than full status
   d. to ignore

4. What is one benefit of using animals for intelligence work?
   a. They can come and go without attracting attention.
   b. They require training.
   c. They need care and maintenance.
   d. They can understand critical communications.

   for
   for

5. How do we use trained animals today? Give examples and evidence to support your answer.
   Policemen have K-9 dogs and disabled people sometimes have guard dogs.

   -10

   Canine 10 assistants

Name_____

Long-Distance Travelers

Arctic terns migrate farther than any other animal on the planet. They travel from their native habitat in the Arctic to Antarctica and back. During the migration season, terns nest in open tundra, rocky beaches, and boreal forests along the Pacific and Atlantic coasts. They have been observed migrating south along the coast of South America and as far south as New Zealand and Australia. They winter in the northernmost part of Antarctica. Arctic terns may migrate as far as 25,000 miles round trip every year!

How did researchers track such long-distance migratory routes? They attached locaters to terns in Greenland and discovered the birds flew south along the coast of Africa in the fall, spent winter on the north coast of Antarctica, and then returned to their Arctic habitat in the spring. Given a life span of about thirty years, this adds up to over one million miles traveled in a tern's lifetime. That's the equivalent of three trips to the moon and back!

Researchers find it difficult to observe and study Arctic terns due to their remote habitats. Scientists have learned a few things, though. Terns hover in mid-air before plunging into the water to catch fish. Occasionally, they may steal fish from other birds in mid-flight.

Along with many other species, Arctic terns will be affected by possible global warming. They winter on pack ice in the Antarctic and rely on Arctic ecosystems for breeding, habitat, and feeding. During the winter, they molt and lose most of their feathers. If feathers are lost faster than they can be replaced, the birds are rendered flightless for a time. Perhaps this is nature's way of giving them a rest before they make the long trek back north for the summer breeding season.

Text Questions

1. What is the main idea of the text?
   a. how global warming will affect Arctic terns
   b. the migratory routes and patterns of Arctic terns
   c. why scientists study Arctic terns
   d. to compare Arctic terns to other birds

2. Which title would be a good alternative for this text?
   a. "Breeding Habits of Arctic Terns"
   b. "All About Arctic Terns"
   c. "The Longest Flight"
   d. "Fishers of the Arctic"

3. What does the word *remote* mean as it is used in the text?
   a. distant
   b. wireless
   c. temperate
   d. tropical

4. Which statement from the text best describes the migratory route of the Arctic tern?
   a. They travel from their native habitat in the Arctic to Antarctica and back.
   b. This adds up to over one million miles traveled in a tern's lifetime.
   c. The birds flew south along the coast of Africa in the fall.
   d. Arctic terns will be affected by possible global warming.

5. How can learning about the migration routes of Arctic terns benefit people?
   This may want someone to go to the Arctic to see some Arctic Terns.

Name_____

The Jumping Spider

Nature photographers have captured on film a spider jumping from one flower to another. Using its large eyes, the jumping spider follows its prey. Then, the jumping spider set its sights, spins out a "safety line," and jumps.

A common variety in the United States, the Daring Jumping Spider makes its home in woods, fields, and gardens. Its distinctive, big-eyed appearance makes it easy to recognize. Four of its eight eyes are located on its face, and the other four are on top of its head. The spider is black with gray or white stripes, and it has spots on its abdomen.

Jumping spiders feast on a variety of insects, as well as other spiders. Some varieties climb as well, giving them a wide range of potential prey. These arachnids do not build webs to catch prey. They hunt on foot by sneaking up and pouncing on their victims. Even though jumping spiders only grow to be between one-quarter and one-half inches long, they can leap amazing distances for their size. Additionally, their excellent eyesight makes them very accurate. Jumping spiders are also one of the fastest arachnids. Scientists claim they are very smart.

In addition to using silk for safety lines when jumping, jumping spiders also use this thread to create shelter under leaves and to encase eggs until hatching.

Insects should be wary of this spider without a web that can stealthily approach, keenly observe, and leap.

Text Questions

1. Why does the author say these spiders are distinctive?
   a. They have large eyes to observe their prey.
   b. They spin out a line to construct a web and catch prey.
   c. They enclose their eggs in a silk sack.
   d. They create a shelter under a leaf.

2. Which is a synonym for the word *stealthily* as it is used in the text?
   a. awkwardly
   b. unreliably
   c. privately
   d. slyly

3. Which paragraph gives details about the spider's jumping abilities?
   a. the first paragraph
   b. the second paragraph
   c. the third paragraph
   d. the fourth paragraph

4. Which title would be a good alternative for this text?
   a. "The Spider Without a Web"
   b. "Life Cycle of the Jumping Spider"
   c. "A Beautiful Web"
   d. "Ready, Set, Jump!"

5. Describe what makes the jumping spider's tactics so effective. Use evidence from the text to support your answer.

   In paragraph 3 it says that they hunt on foot by sneaking up and pouncing on their victims. They will get it almost every time

Name_____

Swimming with the Turtles

Imagine swimming through refreshing ocean waves with a graceful prehistoric animal. Many people hope to do just this when they snorkel off the shores of the tropical islands where green sea turtles make their home.

The Hawaiian sea turtle (or "Hono") is a symbol of peace and good luck to the Hawaiian people. Out of respect for this ancient creature, laws have been enacted to protect them. It is illegal to touch or harass them.

Green sea turtles have smooth shells with shades of black, brown, gray, green, or yellow. The soft bottom shell is yellowish-white. So why are they called green sea turtles? The largest of all hard-shelled sea turtles, green sea turtles feed exclusively on plants, such as seaweed and algae. Scientists believe their diet contributes to their green fat, for which they are named. They are the only herbivorous marine turtle.

Habitats of green sea turtles include nesting beaches, the open ocean, and coastal areas for feeding. Females return to the same beaches where they were born to lay their eggs. Hatchlings swim to offshore areas for feeding for several years. Once they reach a certain age, they return to coastal areas to live as adult sea turtles.

Green sea turtles are not overly fearful of people, although they can swim up to 35 miles per hour to escape perceived danger. They are endangered in many areas of the world due to the harvesting of eggs and adult turtles. Turtles also face the danger of becoming accidentally trapped in gillnets and other fishing gear. They are subject to a disease that causes tumors that interfere with the animals' swimming, vision, feeding, and ability to escape from predators.

Ongoing research and legislation seek to ensure that green sea turtles will remain part of the tropical ecosystem for many years to come.

Text Questions

1. Which context clue from the text helps define the meaning of *herbivorous*?
   a. Laws have been enacted to protect green sea turtles.
   b. They return to coastal areas to live as adult sea turtles.
   c. Green sea turtles feed exclusively on plants.
   d. Hatchlings swim to offshore areas for feeding for several years.

2. Which pair of words from the text best describes the author's opinion of green sea turtles?
   a. tropical, endangered
   b. harass, escape
   c. fearful, prehistoric
   d. graceful, respected

3. What is the main idea of the second paragraph?
   a. Treat green sea turtles with respect.
   b. Green sea turtles are endangered.
   c. It describes details about the turtles' habitat.
   d. It describes the life cycle of a green sea turtle.

4. Which of the following is <u>not</u> an example of a threat to green sea turtles?
   a. Green sea turtles can swim up to 35 miles per hour to escape perceived danger.
   b. People harvest turtle eggs and adult turtles.
   c. Green sea turtles can become trapped in gillnets and other fishing gear.
   d. Green sea turtles are subject to a disease that causes tumors.

5. What can people do to protect sea turtles and other endangered species?

_____

_____

Name_____

The Rare Dolphin

We don't always think of dolphins as being a rare species; however, the Chinese River Dolphin is considered by scientists to be the rarest of all marine mammals, to the point of possibly being extinct.

This rare dolphin makes its home in the freshwater of the Yangtze River. Its low dorsal fin and light color have given it the alternate name of "white-flag dolphin." As with other species of river dolphins, it originally came from the ocean.

Decreasing numbers have made this species of dolphin difficult to research and study. The dolphins are shy and do not expose much of themselves when surfacing for air. They feed mostly on freshwater fish. Due to the murky waters of the Yangtze, they rely on sound for feeding, orientation, and communication. Based on studies of similar species, scientists think the Chinese River Dolphin uses two main types of sounds: clicks and whistles. They use the clicks for navigation and identifying prey. Whistles are used for communication.

Currently, its habitat is limited to the Yangtze River in China. Habitat loss due to development along the river has further reduced its range. River development includes the construction of dams and other water management devices along the river. This affects the dolphins' movements within the river ecosystem. Fish resources have also declined.

Reserves have been established for the preservation of the species. However, these attempts do not prevent accidental deaths. Little, if any, effort has been made to breed the dolphins in captivity.

A survey team conducted an extensive study in 2006 using visual and acoustic measures. They failed to locate any individual animals within the species' range. The National Marine Fisheries Service has concluded that the Chinese River Dolphin may now be extinct.

Text Questions

1. Which of the following threats to Chinese River Dolphins is specifically mentioned in the passage?
   a. river development
   b. entanglement in fishing gear
   c. pollution
   d. underwater explosions

2. Which is a synonym for the word *declined* as it is used in the text?
   a. settled
   b. rejected
   c. decreased
   d. failed

3. Which statement from the text provides the best explanation for why scientists have difficulty researching the Chinese River Dolphin?
   a. Habitat loss due to development along the river has further reduced its range.
   b. The dolphins are shy and do not expose much of themselves when surfacing for air.
   c. Due to the murky waters of the Yangtze, they rely on sound for feeding, orientation, and communication.
   d. They use the clicks for navigation and to identify prey.

4. What is the probable current status of the Chinese River Dolphin?
   a. common
   b. threatened
   c. endangered
   d. extinct

5. How might the extinction of this species of river dolphin affect people?

_____

_____

_____

Name_____

Blue Dragons

Do dragons exist today? Although often dismissed as a mythical creature, we actually live among several different types of "dragons." For example, you may have seen a dragonfly hovering in a summer garden or read about a Komodo dragon lizard. The ocean has its share of dragons, too.

The blue dragon is a marine snail without a shell. It is commonly known as a blue sea slug. This particular species of marine snail can swallow a bubble of air (which it holds in its stomach) that enables it to float upside down on the surface of the ocean. The underside of the slug is blue, and its back is a grayish color. This helps to conceal it from birds flying overhead and from fish swimming below.

Blue dragons feed on poisonous man-of-war jellyfish and other similar species. When food is scarce, they will eat each other. They collect toxins from the jellyfish and store it in many finger-like structures. This ability to store poison gives them a much stronger sting than the jellyfish itself. They use this poison as a defense against predators. The sting can also be felt by people.

These creatures are rarely visible for study and observation except for when they approach land during times of onshore winds. They have been sighted in Hawaii and in tropical waters around the world. Beware of the blue dragon's sting!

Text Questions

1. What is the purpose of the first paragraph?
   a. to give details about the topic
   b. to introduce the subject
   c. to introduce the author
   d. to give examples of mythical monsters

2. What is the blue dragon's main defense against predators?
   a. It floats upside down in the water.
   b. It stores poison and stings predators.
   c. It feeds on poisonous jellyfish.
   d. It moves to coastal waters during times of onshore winds.

3. What does the word *conceal* mean as it is used in the text?
   a. discover
   b. reveal
   c. protect
   d. hide

4. How does the coloring of the blue sea slug provide camouflage?
   a. It floats right side up so the blue faces down in the water.
   b. Its blue coloring makes it blend in with ocean waves.
   c. The blue blends in with the ocean as seen from above, and the gray blends in with the ocean as seen from below.
   d. It squirts blue poison into the water to conceal it from predators.

5. Why do you think this animal has the word *dragon* as part of its name?

   _____

   _____

   _____

Name_____

Pippi

Pippi, a golden retriever and Labrador retriever mix, lives a life of purpose. Her meticulous training is called into action daily by Micah Nash and his parents, Andy and Heather Nash.

On one particular day, Micah dropped to the floor and stared at the ceiling of a small grocery store in Missouri. Heather commanded Pippi to "nudge." Immediately, Pippi used her nose to remind Micah to stand up and resume his position at her side. Micah laughed as he got up and again grasped his part of Pippi's leash.

Why is a dog in a grocery store? Pippi is not a pet dog. She is a skilled companion dog, trained by Canine Companions for Independence. Her job is to assist Micah in dealing with his autism. She wears a blue and gold vest proclaiming her status as a service dog whenever she is in public.

People often ask to pet her. Pippi is trained to take the attention in stride, responding promptly to Heather's commands. Heather answers most questions now, but

in the future, Micah will be given more opportunities to interact verbally with the people around him.

One of Pippi's duties is to accompany Micah to restaurants. She curls into a ball under his table, ready to help Micah focus on the world around him. At the command "visit," she will lay her head in Micah's lap. This grounds him in the reality of the present.

During every family outing, Micah will increase his hard-earned verbal skills by giving Pippi commands, such as "sit" and "down." But Pippi's job doesn't end when the family goes home. Over time, Micah will become more responsible for Pippi's care. This will help him expand his conversation skills with peers and family.

When Pippi is "off duty," Micah and his brother chase her wildly through the house. And Pippi, released from her duties, behaves like any dog loved by two rambunctious boys.

Text Questions

1. What does it mean to say that Micah will *resume* his position at Pippi's side?
   a. He will start walking again.
   b. He will take his place next to her again.
   c. He will summarize what he is supposed to say to her.
   d. He will continue to lie on the floor.

2. What is the theme or moral of the text?
   a. how to train a Labrador retriever
   b. what it is like to have autism
   c. why service dogs are allowed in public places
   d. how trained dogs can help people with autism

3. Which of the following is not a place where Pippi will likely be on duty for Micah?
   a. in the car
   b. at home
   c. at the store
   d. at a restaurant

4. Which statement from the text shows one way in which Pippi interacts with Micah?
   a. Pippi lives a life of purpose.
   b. Pippi uses her nose to remind Micah to stand up and resume his position at her side.
   c. She wears a blue and gold vest proclaiming her status as a service dog whenever she is in public.
   d. Pippi is trained to take the attention in stride, responding promptly to Heather's commands.

5. Based on what you read, what is one part of his life in which Pippi will assist Micah?

   _____

   _____

Name_____

Nature's Helicopters

Nature offers spectacular examples of "true flight." This refers to the ability to lift and hover above the ground without forward motion to provide these forces. People have long been intrigued with the concept of vertical flight, and as we've observed the hummingbird and the dragonfly, we've been able to develop technology (such as the helicopter) that mimics their behavior. The hummingbird hawk-moth is another animal that has the same flight dynamics.

Although this moth gets the first part of its name from its flight patterns, it resembles a hummingbird in other ways as well. The moth has a long, straw-like mouth, which it uses to gather nectar from flowers. While hovering, it emits an audible humming noise. Its constant wing movement requires large amounts of food, similar to hummingbirds. Hummingbird hawk-moths keep track of flowers they have already visited. This conserves energy since the moth doesn't return to empty flowers. The need for calories is so strong, they

may even feed while mating. As the second part of this animal's name implies, it is a moth, not a bird. As an insect, it pollinates various garden flowers such as honeysuckle.

The hummingbird hawk-moth is native to warm climates. It makes its home in parts of Europe, North Africa, and Asia. It is a strong flier, particularly during the summer months. The moth does not tolerate cold weather well, and adults typically spend winter in crevices of rocks, trees, and buildings. Although in a different group, a similar moth known as a "bee moth" can be found in various parts of North America.

Hummingbird hawk-moths have good vision and are able to learn colors. The moth has the ability to fly during the day, at dawn and dusk, and even in the rain.

As we continue to study these unusual creatures, there is the potential for even more technological developments and benefits to humans.

Text Questions

1. According to the text, what characteristics are found in "true flight"?
   a. The animal or craft flies in a straight line.
   b. The animal or craft requires large amounts of fuel.
   c. The animal or craft has the ability to lift and hover above the ground without forward motion to provide these forces.
   d. The wings of the animal or craft move constantly.

2. What does it mean to say the moth *emits* a humming noise?
   a. It utters words.
   b. It transmits a signal.
   c. It puts into circulation.
   d. It gives off sounds.

3. Why do the moths require such large amounts of food?
   a. Their wings are in near constant motion.
   b. They do not tolerate cold weather well.
   c. They migrate long distances in the winter.
   d. They do not eat very much at one time because their mouths are small.

4. What is the text structure in the second paragraph?
   a. cause and effect
   b. problem solution
   c. descriptive
   d. compare and contrast

5. How has observing nature helped humans develop new technology?

   _____

   _____

   _____

Name_____

The African Generuk

Giraffes aren't the only animals with long necks. The African generuk's name means "giraffe-necked" in the Somali language. They stand on their hind two legs and extend their necks to reach leaves on tall shrubs. They also use their front legs to pull down branches. This enables them to feed from bushes six to eight feet in height. The generuk's diet consists of leaves from thornbushes. They also eat buds, flowers, fruit, and climbing plants. They do not require water as they get all the moisture they need from their food.

The generuk has a small head with large eyes and ears. Males have stout, ringed horns. Related to gazelles, they have scent glands in front of their eyes and on their knees. They use the glands to mark territory.

Small groups of female generuks may live together with their young or with unattached males. Females range over a territory of one to two miles, traversing the males' territory. Fawns are born in thickets apart from the group. The mother keeps the fawn hidden for a time. She leaves to feed but returns for nursing. The mother removes scents that would attract predators by cleaning or eating the fawn's waste.

One way that generuks warn others in the group of danger is by making a loud bleat. They communicate with their young with soft bleats. These antelopes make buzzing sounds when alarmed, and they may whistle when annoyed.

Predators of the generuk include lions, cheetahs, and leopards. Wild dogs and jackals also prey on generuks. Habitat loss and destruction threaten generuks. This makes it difficult for them to find food and shelter from predators. Conserving the thickets is one way to maintain the survival of this long-necked antelope.

Text Questions

1. Which title would be a good alternative for this text?
   a. "The Giraffe's Cousin"
   b. "The Long-Necked Antelope"
   c. "Leaf Eaters"
   d. "Hidden Fawns"

2. What are two unusual features of this animal?
   a. It eats leaves and has a small head.
   b. It has natural predators and can whistle when annoyed.
   c. It has a long neck and does not need water.
   d. The mother cares for the young, and the males have horns.

3. What does the word *traversing* mean as it is used in the third paragraph?
   a. opposing
   b. surveying
   c. turning
   d. crossing

4. How would you summarize the fourth paragraph?
   a. Generuks are very vocal.
   b. Generuks warn group members when there is danger.
   c. Generuks are silent animals.
   d. Generuks communicate with their young.

5. What can we learn from studying animals with unusual characteristics?

_____

_____

Name_____

Deadly Delicacy

Imagine a fish that swallows water to inflate itself like a balloon. The pufferfish does just that as a defense against predators. Its slow, clumsy swimming ability makes it hard for it to escape. However, once the pufferfish expands its size, it becomes an inedible ball. The fish can puff up to two or three times its normal size. Quick-acting predators that manage to eat the fish before it inflates will receive a lethal poison. The poison is also toxic to humans; one fish contains enough poison to kill thirty people.

However, in Japan, people consider the meat of the pufferfish a delicacy. Chefs undergo special training to learn how to prepare the fish in such a way that it is safe to eat. It takes two years to complete this training. Thin slices of the flesh are served with all traces of toxins from the organs removed. Still, as many as two hundred people a year are poisoned from the fish, and about half of them die.

Many species of pufferfish exist. Most make their homes in tropical or subtropical waters, but some are freshwater fish. Pufferfish have rough or spiny skin in place of scales. Some have bright coloring to warn predators of the poison. Others have coloring that blends in with their environment.

Pufferfish consume mostly invertebrates and algae. Some species eat clams, mussels, and other shellfish. Perhaps they derive toxins from the bacteria in the food they eat. The toxin acts on victims by affecting the nervous system. Paralysis begins from the outermost parts and works inward.

Why would anyone wish to eat such a food? Some people like to live on the edge. There's a thrill in doing something daring. Others want to experience the tingling sensation that can occur on the tongue and lips. The best approach, though, is to beware of the pufferfish.

Text Questions

1. What does the word *lethal* mean as it is used in the first paragraph?
   a. authorized by law
   b. slow
   c. deadly
   d. harmful

2. What do other fish have that pufferfish lack?
   a. gills
   b. scales
   c. skin
   d. poison

3. What is the purpose of the second paragraph?
   a. It describes how chefs prepare pufferfish to make it safer to eat.
   b. It gives details about a chef's training.
   c. It explains why pufferfish are poisonous.
   d. It tells why people like to eat pufferfish.

4. What does the idiom "live on the edge" mean in the fifth paragraph?
   a. to be different from other people
   b. to do unusual things
   c. to participate in dangerous activities
   d. to have a house built on a cliff

5. Why do you suppose people like to eat poisonous fish?

   _____

   _____

Name_____

The Climbing Rodent

At first glance, it's hard to tell if vizcachas are related to rabbits or rodents. The large ears and long hind legs of a vizcacha resemble those of a rabbit. However, it has a bushy tail similar to a chinchilla. Rodents and rabbits have specific physical differences. The vizcacha has two incisors, as do other rodents. Unlike some rodents, however, it is an herbivore, feeding on almost any type of plant.

Vizcachas live in colonies that range from a few members to hundreds. They use many different methods to communicate. The position of their tails indicates anxiety or relaxation. An extended tail shows the animal is anxious, and if the tail is curled, the animal is at ease. The animals chatter to one another within the colony. They give loud warning calls to alert others of danger. One advantage of colony living is protecting the young. A female gives birth to one fully developed baby, which is weaned at two months. But the young is small and vulnerable.

Mountain vizcachas live in rocky mountain areas of South America. Unable to dig well enough to escape predators, the animal has adapted to its habitat by developing superb climbing skills. It uses its powerful hind legs to jump quickly among the rocks. Their speed and harsh living environment keep the vizcacha safe from most predators, such as pumas and foxes. But speed cannot fully protect it from its worst enemy: humans. People hunt vizcachas illegally for their meat and fur. Habitat loss also threatens them.

We group things in our environment to help us understand the world in which we live. Most often, we use visual cues to help us categorize plants and animals. However, sometimes things are not what they seem. Not all furry creatures with large ears, long hind legs, and fluffy tails are rabbits. Not all rodents burrow to escape predators. Each animal adapts to its unique environment.

Text Questions

1. What is the vizcachas' main defense against predators?
   a. digging
   b. climbing
   c. attacking
   d. hiding

2. Which statement does <u>not</u> describe a communication behavior of vizcachas?
   a. They extend their tails to show anxiety.
   b. They chatter within the colony.
   c. They move their ears to communicate food sources.
   d. They give loud warning calls to alert others of danger.

3. What is one purpose of this passage?
   a. to show how one species is different from another
   b. to describe the habitat of a chinchilla
   c. to explain how animals communicate
   d. to describe how animals survive in rocky mountain environments

4. Which is a synonym for the word *categorize* as it is used in the text?
   a. classify
   b. characterize
   c. describe
   d. attribute

5. How can scientists help people understand differences between species?

   _____

   _____

Name_____

Panda Ants

Is it a wasp or is it an ant? Meet the panda ant—a wasp that looks like a hairy ant! The black and white panda ant is so named due to its appearance. It is covered with coarse, short hair. Panda ants are part of a much larger family of wasps known as "velvet ants." Females in this wasp family do not have wings, however, which makes them look more like ants. Some species make their home in arid areas of the southern and western United States. The panda ant, however, is found specifically in Chile.

Young velvet ants are parasites, feeding on the mature larvae and pupae of other species. They have an unusually tough exoskeleton, which likely helps them invade the nests of their prey. Although only the female is capable of inflicting a sting, they are known to be quite painful. This powerful sting has earned them the name "cow killer."

We often associate wasps with their stings. Wasps also bring to mind colonies of angry insects. However, they are more beneficial to humans than harmful. They prey on other insects we consider pests. However, many species, including the panda ant, are solitary. Solitary wasps use their sting to hunt rather than for defense.

Very little is known about this particular species of wasp. Other related species have been observed and studied in the United States. Scientists want to learn more about any harmful effects and benefits to people.

Text Questions

1. What does the word *parasites* mean as it is used in the second paragraph?
   a. animals that live in multiple locations
   b. people who live at the expense of others without paying
   c. animals that live on an organism from which they receive nourishment
   d. animals that spread bacteria to other organisms

2. What can you infer about this insect from its name?
   a. It lives in China.
   b. Its black and white color resembles a panda bear.
   c. It is an ant that eats bamboo leaves.
   d. It has a lot of fur.

3. Based on the text, how do solitary wasps differ from social wasps?
   a. They are never seen around people.
   b. They sting to defend themselves.
   c. Their sting is used to hunt.
   d. They do not build nests.

4. What organizational structure does the author use to help the reader understand the information?
   a. compare and contrast
   b. sequential
   c. problem and solution
   d. cause and effect

5. Why might farmers place wasps near crops?

   _____

   _____

   _____

   _____

Name_____

Cave Dwellers

Amphibians are cold-blooded vertebrates that live in water and breathe with gills when they are young. As they mature, they develop lungs and live on land. However, not all species go through this common metamorphosis. The olm, or cave salamander, retains external gills and a tail fin throughout its life. The amount of time it takes for the young to mature depends on water temperature.

Found mostly along the Adriatic Sea, the olm dwells in underwater caves. It also lives in underground freshwater lakes and streams in the mountains. These bodies of water contain high amounts of oxygen. The temperature of the water ranges from 40 to 60 degrees. The animals generally live almost 1,000 feet below the surface of the water.

The relatively inaccessible habitat of olms makes studying them difficult. Much of what we know about this animal has been learned from those in captivity. Scientists expect the life span to be around 100 years, making olms the longest-lived amphibian species.

Olms prey mostly on insects and spiders. They will also eat crustaceans and mollusks. Due to their underwater environment, the salamanders' eyes are not well developed, although their eyes do have some sensitivity to light. Olms can sense chemicals, sound vibrations, and electric fields. They use these abilities to orient themselves as well as to detect prey. They have no known predators. As with many species, they are vulnerable due to loss of habitat and pollution.

Text Questions ....

1. Why might olms have poorly developed vision?
   a. They do not lose their juvenile underwater characteristics.
   b. They can detect their prey using other senses.
   c. There is nothing to look at underwater.
   d. They need to develop senses that will enable them to survive in permanently dark environments.

2. What does the word *inaccessible* mean as it is used in the text?
   a. impossible to reach
   b. cannot be seen
   c. cannot be obtained
   d. cannot be influenced by the environment

3. What can you infer about olms that makes them different from most amphibians?
   a. They do not swim well.
   b. They do not have gills.
   c. They do not venture onto land.
   d. They are not vertebrates.

4. What is the main idea of the second paragraph?
   a. where cave salamanders live
   b. why cave salamanders are considered amphibians
   c. the senses of olms
   d. how people study olms

5. What can we learn from studying cave salamanders?

   _____

   _____

   _____

Name_____

Animals and Humans

Animal behavior is a fascinating study. Scientists divide animal behavior into categories that are similar to those we use to describe human behavior, such as diet and habitat. Scientists study the strategies animals use to hunt, capture, or forage for their food. They research the defenses animals use against predators and which animals prey on other animals. All of this helps us understand how animals can benefit us.

Each country or cultural group raises certain animals for food. In the United States, people mainly eat meat from cows, chickens, and pigs. In other countries, people might raise sheep or buffalo for meat. The differences arise in part from climate and other environmental factors. People around the world eat a variety of fish and shellfish from oceans and freshwater sources. In the United States, we don't always consider some animal groups as valid options for food as readily as others. For instance, you might not have thought about eating insects. But people in other countries regularly consume insects. Amphibians for dinner? In specific regions such as West Africa, yes.

Animals provide humans with more than food. They have been helping people with daily tasks for thousands of years. Horses, oxen, and other work animals pull loads. Harnessed, they can move machinery to do work such as grinding grain. Elephants, camels, and other animals transport people and goods from place to place. Carrier pigeons have been used to deliver messages.

People also receive companionship and other health benefits from animals. For instance, dogs and cats can have a calming effect on people. This is helpful for people fighting various diseases. Animals can also lower stress, making it easier for people to concentrate on learning new information, such as reading. When people interact with dogs or horses, it encourages exercise.

Animals and humans share space on Earth. Maintaining a healthy relationship with our fellow inhabitants is in our best interest.

Text Questions

1. Which of the following would be a good summary sentence for this text?
   a. We study animal behavior to help us learn how to find food.
   b. Animals provide us with food, work, and companionship.
   c. Animals make great companions for people.
   d. People and animals should learn to work together.

2. Why did the author include the information in the first paragraph?
   a. to summarize the passage
   b. to give details about how animals help us with work
   c. to explain why people eat animals
   d. to introduce the topic and provide an overview

3. What does the word *forage* mean as it is used in the text?
   a. to search for food
   b. to search for what you want
   c. to take food from others
   d. to provide with provisions

4. Which statement explains one way in which animals benefit people?
   a. We divide animal behavior into categories that are similar to those we use to describe human behavior.
   b. In the United States, we don't always consider some animal groups as valid options for food as readily as others.
   c. Animals have been helping people with daily tasks for thousands of years.
   d. Animals and humans share space on Earth.

5. What can studying animal behavior teach us about the world in which we live?

   _____

   _____

Name_____

The Unknown Winston Churchill

Sir Winston Churchill is known as one of the greatest leaders in world history. His courage rallied England during World War II at a time when Germany was conducting nighttime bombing raids over British cities, killing thousands of civilians and destroying tremendous amounts of property. But the private Winston Churchill was a man of varied hobbies who lived an exciting life outside of his major political role in saving Europe from Nazi Germany.

During the Boer War in 1899, a train he was traveling on was stopped when Boer commandos blocked the train rail with a massive boulder. He fought bravely but was captured and taken as a prisoner to Pretoria in enemy territory. He escaped by jumping a wall and hitching rides on trains. His dangerous escape made him a national hero.

He suffered from depression and painted to help overcome it. He mostly painted landscapes with oil paints. He once entered and won a painting contest for anonymous painters. Many of his paintings hang today in galleries, and he is considered a very accomplished artist.

Churchill was also a world-renowned writer. Over the course of his life, he wrote many books and articles for magazines and newspapers. His most famous writings had to do with history. He was awarded the Nobel Prize in Literature in 1953, which is the highest award an author can receive.

In addition to being a famous writer and painter, he was also a bricklayer and built many structures. Although built sixty years ago or more, many of the buildings and walls still stand today. He also bred butterflies and loved small animals.

Soldier, escaped prisoner of war, statesman, artist, writer, and bricklayer—Winston Churchill is not only known for his abilities as a world leader but also because he was an amazing man of numerous talents.

Text Questions

1. What does the word *structures* mean as it is used in the fifth paragraph?
   a. organizations
   b. arrangement of parts
   c. buildings
   d. the parts of an organism

2. What is one of Churchill's greatest accomplishments as an author?
   a. He wrote mostly about history.
   b. He won the Nobel Prize in Literature.
   c. He wrote articles for newspapers.
   d. He wrote about his accomplishments during World War II.

3. When was Churchill captured by the Boers?
   a. in 1953
   b. during World War II
   c. during World War I
   d. in 1899

4. What is Winston Churchill most known for?
   a. He was a great leader in world history.
   b. He rallied England during World War I.
   c. He escaped from capture in Pretoria.
   d. He was an accomplished painter.

5. Who do you consider to be one of the greatest leaders in history? Give reasons to support your answer.

   _____

   _____

   _____

Name_____

Lawrence of Arabia

The person referred to as "Lawrence of Arabia" was actually a British World War I army officer named Thomas Edward (T.E.) Lawrence. A movie made about his adventures won seven Academy Awards.

Lawrence was an archeologist and had traveled extensively in the Middle East prior to World War I. When the war broke out, he joined the British army to do some survey work, including some intelligence work spying for the British.

During the war, Lawrence fought with Arab troops in guerilla operations against the armed forces of the Ottoman Empire. He helped develop strategies that were vital to an Arab revolt in the area.

In addition to guerilla operations, Lawrence arranged and fought in three major battles, including the Battle of Aqaba—the first major victory for the Arab guerilla forces. Other major battles include the battle of Tafileh and the Fall of Damascus. He was awarded medals and promoted to Colonel.

Despite his heroic exploits, Lawrence was mostly unnoticed. Even the Turks, who had a bounty for his death, did not know what he looked like. It wasn't until an American war correspondent gave a lecture series about Lawrence's achievements in the war that he became known as "Lawrence of Arabia."

After the war, Lawrence refused a knighthood by the King of England. He became a close adviser to Winston Churchill and joined the Royal Navy under an assumed name due to all the publicity he received. Eventually, he had to resign due to spy activities attributed to him.

Lawrence had a love of motorcycles and owned many, but a motorcycle accident in 1935 took his life. He is considered the most famous British military figure in history.

Text Questions

1. What background knowledge would be helpful for understanding this text?
   a. an understanding of what it means to be a knight
   b. an understanding of events during World War I
   c. knowledge about motorcycles
   d. a viewing of an Academy Award-winning movie

2. What does the word *exploits* mean as it is used in the fifth paragraph?
   a. deeds
   b. speeches
   c. profits
   d. advertisements

3. According to the text, which of the following was <u>not</u> one of Lawrence's roles in the British military?
   a. spy
   b. colonel
   c. developer of strategies
   d. archaeologist

4. What can you infer about Lawrence in this biographical sketch?
   a. He was a courageous person.
   b. He didn't believe in fighting for the cause of the war.
   c. He was loyal to the King of England.
   d. He was a recluse.

5. Based on what you read, what do you think was Lawrence of Arabia's biggest contribution to history?

   _____

   _____

Name_____

Sir Thomas More

Sir Thomas More lived during a time of political change in England. The king had declared himself head of the Church of England, and More refused to acknowledge this transfer of power within the church. Instead, he stood up for his beliefs.

Prior to the King's declaration, Thomas More served as counselor, secretary, and confidant for Henry VIII. He practiced law but was also a scholar and a journalist. More had a good education and studied spiritual texts while preparing for his law career. Finally, he felt he must make a choice between a life of civil service and the monastic life. He moved to a monastery outside of London in 1503 and participated in the community as much as his legal career would allow. After a time, he once again felt the calling to civil service. More wanted to serve his country, so he left the monastery to enter Parliament just one year later. Eventually, he was elected as speaker of the House of Commons. During the course of his career, he published novels as well as papers defending the Catholic church and lashing out against Martin Luther and the protestant revolution.

After the king disclosed his plans to divorce Catherine of Aragon to marry Anne Boleyn, More resigned from the House of Commons. He cited ill health as his reason, but most likely his decision came as much from his disapproval of the king's actions as anything else. More subsequently did not attend the coronation of the new queen, and the king did not view this favorably. The king's ire was further raised when More refused to swear to the Oath of Supremacy, which effectively declared King Henry as the head of the Church of England. He was found guilty of treason, sent to the tower, and beheaded a year later.

More's final words were, "The king's good servant, but God's first."

Text Questions

1. What words could be used in the first paragraph in place of the phrase "stood up for his beliefs"?
   a. defended his persuasion
   b. defended his doubt
   c. defended his convictions
   d. defended his guilty sentence

2. Which title would be a good alternative for this text?
   a. "The King's Good Servant"
   b. "A Monastic Life"
   c. "A Man of Principle"
   d. "Servant to All"

3. What is the significance of More's choices?
   a. He considered others less important than himself.
   b. He made decisions based on what other people wanted him to do.
   c. He thought only of what would serve his best interests.
   d. He tried to stand up for what he thought was right.

4. Which of the following does not describe a way in which Thomas More served Henry VIII?
   a. He was secretary to the king.
   b. He refused to support the king's declarations.
   c. He was an adviser to the king.
   d. He was the king's confidant.

5. What significance do More's last words hold for people today?

   _____

   _____

Name_____

Olympic Inspiration

The 2012 Olympic Games in London was a year for gold. Katie Ledecky, the youngest member of the United States Olympic swim team, took gold in the 800m freestyle. She credits her win, in part, to being inspired by watching Michael Phelps and Missy Franklin win gold.

Katie worked diligently the year prior to the Olympic Games. She balanced training and ninth grade, winning the 800m in two pre-Olympic Games events. Katie gained confidence and speed during training camp prior to the Olympic Games.

During the games, Katie focused her thoughts on world records and the medals her teammates won. She wanted to do well for her country. In an interview, Katie said watching Phelps and Franklin win was very exciting, but she kept it to herself and "just used it as extra energy."

During the race, Ledecky got off to a dynamic start and soon was an entire body-length ahead. Phelps summed up the race by commenting that Katie had fun, nearly broke a world record, and won the gold. He felt that was pretty impressive for a fifteen-year-old.

Katie continues to swim and train at swim clubs near her home in Maryland. She recently won the 2013 U.S. Olympic Committee Sportswoman of the Year award. In addition, she has won four gold medals at the World Championships and broken two world records. Some news reports have called Katie a "hometown hero."

Text Questions

1. On which aspect of Katie's career does this passage focus?
   a. her training
   b. details of every race she has won
   c. her experience at the 2012 Olympic Games in London
   d. her hopes and goals for the future

2. How did Phelps and Franklin inspire Katie to win gold?
   a. They cheered her on during the race.
   b. Their wins excited her and gave her extra energy.
   c. They helped her during training.
   d. They showed her how to have an edge over the competition.

3. Which paragraph summarizes Katie's Olympic Games race?
   a. the first paragraph
   b. the second paragraph
   c. the third paragraph
   d. the fourth paragraph

4. What does it mean in the second paragraph to say that Katie worked *diligently*?
   a. She persevered and kept working.
   b. She worked carefully.
   c. She made sure everything was done correctly.
   d. She studied to learn everything she could about swimming.

5. Why might news reporters call Katie a "hometown hero"? In what ways do you agree or disagree with this opinion?

   _____

   _____

   _____

Name_____

Harry S. Truman, U.S. President

When people think of a United States president, they typically think of someone who is highly educated and from a family of successful people. Harry Truman, the 33rd president, lived a humble life until thrust into the United States Senate at age 50 without a formal college education. He became vice president in 1945 and then president that same year after President Franklin Roosevelt died in office. He was the last president not to have a college degree.

Truman was born into a farming family in Missouri. As a child, he loved the piano, becoming proficient and playing regularly the rest of his life. After graduating high school, he started working and had a succession of jobs that included being a railroad timekeeper and a mailroom clerk for a newspaper. After his military service, he started a business, which ultimately failed.

In 1917, Truman joined the army to serve in World War I. He was captain of an artillery unit and showed exceptional leadership and courage. One time during battle, the Germans attacked, and his men began to turn and flee. He was able to rally them to turn and fight. After that, he had undivided loyalty from his men.

He showed that same determination as president. Taking over during World War II, he immediately faced immense difficulties. Through courage and homespun wisdom, he was able to help guide the war to a successful end. His decision to use atomic weapons against Japan was perhaps the single most difficult decision a president has ever had to make. He led the world in the post-war era providing food, clothing, and hope to much of Europe.

Harry Truman serves as a reminder that difficulties in life can be overcome and that one can achieve great things in spite of setbacks and trials.

Text Questions ···

1. What is one fact from Truman's life that sets him apart from other presidents in recent history?
   a. He had a job before becoming president.
   b. He served in the U.S. Senate.
   c. He did not have a college degree.
   d. He served in the military.

2. What is one example of Truman's leadership abilities?
   a. He inspired his men to turn and fight while under German attack.
   b. He played the piano well.
   c. He was not accepted into West Point.
   d. He had a successful business after the war.

3. Which statement from the text best explains Truman's success as president?
   a. He became vice president in 1945.
   b. He became president that same year after President Franklin Roosevelt died in office.
   c. Taking over during World War II, he immediately faced immense difficulties.
   d. Through courage and homespun wisdom, he was able to help guide the war to a successful end.

4. Which is a synonym for the word *exceptional* as it is used in the third paragraph?
   a. uncommon
   b. unbelievable
   c. rare
   d. outstanding

5. What do you think made Truman's decision to use atomic weapons so difficult?

   _____

   _____

Name_____

Man of Finance

Many Americans seek success, but very few make it into the history books. Even fewer become known and remembered for their positive contributions to the development of their country. John Pierpont ("J.P.") Morgan was considered a master of finance and is still considered one of America's leading businessmen.

Morgan got a glimpse into his future early in life, as he learned the language of banking and studied at a leading private financial house in New York. The son of a banker, he followed his father into the family business. He went on to become a well-known financier. In 1871, he founded a private banking company, which later became known as J.P. Morgan & Company. Over time, Morgan learned to make wise financial decisions, including investing in the emerging electricity industry. During times of depression and financial crisis, the government requested help from Morgan's company.

During the period in which Morgan lived, people scrutinized the few who had wealth and power. They accused J.P. Morgan of creating monopolies, which made it difficult for other businesses to compete in the market. It's true that he invested heavily in the railroad industry, as well as founding the U.S. National Steel Corporation.

Finance didn't consume Morgan's entire life, however. An avid sailor, he was a member of a yacht club and a participant in America's Cup races. As one of the founders of the Metropolitan Museum of Art, Morgan also enjoyed collecting art, eventually donating his collection to the museum. He also played a role in organizing the Museum of Natural History. Morgan made private donations as well, in one instance donating money toward the construction of a new hospital building.

At the time of his death in 1913, Morgan was considered an influential financier. His influence continues even today, not only in the finance company that bears his name, but also in the concept of corporate power and wealth.

Text Questions

1. Which of the following is <u>not</u> an industry in which J.P. Morgan invested?
   a. electricity
   b. railroads
   c. steel
   d. plastic

2. Which statement from the text gives a clue about a major influence in Morgan's career?
   a. The son of a banker, he followed his father into the family business.
   b. During times of depression and financial crisis, the government requested help from Morgan's company.
   c. During the period in which Morgan lived, people scrutinized the few who had wealth and power.
   d. He invested heavily in the railroad industry, as well as founding the U.S. National Steel Corporation.

3. What is the main idea of the fourth paragraph?
   a. It describes Morgan's early life.
   b. It explains Morgan's role in the development of corporate business in America.
   c. It describes Morgan's interests outside of finance.
   d. It explains what made J.P. Morgan so successful.

4. Which is a synonym for the word *crisis* as it is used in the second paragraph?
   a. dilemma   c. plight
   b. emergency   d. decision

5. Based on what you read, what might be considered J.P. Morgan's greatest contribution to our economy?

   _____

   _____

Name_____

Stronger Than Steel

Many inventions are renowned for their role in improving quality of life or for helping people. Stephanie Kwolek contributed to both with her invention of Kevlar®. At first, Kwolek wanted to study medicine. After earning a degree in chemistry, she took a temporary research position. Kwolek became so intrigued, she decided to pursue a career in the area of chemical research.

Her work and discoveries with polymers led to the creation of a material five times stronger than steel. The material was named Kevlar. It came about through a combination of experimenting with polymers, heat, and spinning various substances. When tested, the new polymer proved to be very lightweight, yet extremely strong. Resistant to fire and other types of corrosion,

it is the primary component of bulletproof vests. As such, it helps save the lives of countless soldiers and law enforcement officers. Many people don't realize, however, that Kevlar is also used in other products. Safety helmets, skis, and hunting and camping gear all make use of Kevlar. Not surprisingly, it is also used in suspension bridge cables, and in sea and space technology as well.

Kwolek has received numerous awards for her work and patents. Today, she is retired and enjoys her hobbies, as well as speaking with students about her invention. Kwolek likes to tell her audiences, "Every person has value, no matter what you do. This is what you have to remember."

Text Questions

1. What does the word *corrosion* mean as it is used in the second paragraph?
   a. extreme heat sources
   b. wearing away due to chemical reactions
   c. a substance formed from a long chain of simple molecules
   d. multiple liquids stirred together

2. Which was not one of Kwolek's goals in life?
   a. to study medicine
   b. to work in chemical research
   c. to help people and improve their quality of life
   d. to build suspension bridges

3. Why might Kevlar be a good material for safety helmets?
   a. It is bulletproof and fire resistant.
   b. It has a smooth, shiny finish.
   c. It is inexpensive to manufacture.
   d. It can withstand heat.

4. Which of the following was a key factor in the invention of Kevlar?
   a. Some important people walked into the lab on the right day.
   b. It passed military tests.
   c. It resulted from a combination of experimenting with polymers, heat, and spinning various substances.
   d. Kwolek was a research intern at a chemical company.

5. What might a student find significant about Kwolek's quote, "Every person has value, no matter what you do"?

   _____

   _____

   _____

Name_____

Just an Ordinary Guy

Louis Sachar, the author of *Holes*, is just an ordinary person. He spent part of his childhood in New York, but his family moved to California while he was still in elementary school. While living in New York, his father worked on the 78th floor of the Empire State Building. Sachar says this may have been the inspiration for the Wayside School.

Sachar studied economics in college. He received a flier on campus one day that offered college credit in exchange for helping out as a teacher's aide at a local elementary school. Sachar thought it sounded like a good way to obtain free credit, so he signed up. It quickly became his favorite college class. He helped in classrooms and on the playground as a lunch supervisor. Sachar says that the kids in his books are based on kids he knew while working at that school.

After college, Sachar got a job at a warehouse. During this time he wrote his first book, *Sideways Stories from Wayside School*. It took him almost a year to write the book, which was accepted by a publisher during his first week at law school. He passed the bar exam and then did part-time legal work. He went on to practice law, continuing to write children's books in the evenings. Nearly ten years later, Sachar was making enough money from the sales of his books to leave the law profession and devote himself to writing full-time.

One of Sachar's most well-known works, *Holes*, won a Newbery Award in 1999. Sachar says when he started writing the book, it was more about the place than the characters. As he wrote, the characters became more developed. It took him a year and a half to write the book, the same length of time Stanley was sentenced to Camp Green Lake.

Text Questions

1. Where did Louis Sachar receive the inspiration for his stories?
   a. from the books he read
   b. from things that happened in his life
   c. from his job
   d. from his teachers

2. Based on the text, what can you infer about the author of *Holes*?
   a. He doesn't have a strong understanding of childhood behavior.
   b. He had an unhappy childhood.
   c. He finds inspiration for his books from real-life events.
   d. He enjoys writing books about law schools.

3. Which statement is not true?
   a. There is a real Wayside school building that is sideways.
   b. Sachar helped in classrooms and on the playground as a lunch supervisor.
   c. It took Sachar a year and a half to write *Holes*.
   d. One of Sachar's most well-known works, *Holes*, won a Newbery Award in 1999.

4. What does the word *inspiration* mean as it is used in the first paragraph?
   a. breathing
   b. something supernatural
   c. an action that prompts a reaction
   d. something that influences someone to do something creative

5. After reading this passage, what can you learn from Sachar about success?

   _____

   _____

Name_____

Woman of Justice

In an arena historically dominated by males, Sandra Day O'Connor had the honor of being the first woman nominated to serve on the Supreme Court. President Reagan nominated her in 1981, and she served until her retirement in 2006.

Justice O'Connor held a variety of positions as she gained legal and political experience. Early in her career, she served as Deputy Attorney General. O'Connor served as a civilian attorney in Germany and later as Assistant Attorney General for the state of Arizona. She served three terms as an Arizona state senator. From there, she continued to move up within the court system, serving as judge of a county Superior Court and then, a few years later, she was appointed to the Arizona Court of Appeals. Throughout her career, O'Connor remained active in civic and cultural organizations.

During her career, O'Connor earned a reputation as a moderate conservative. She often played an important role in key decisions affecting the justice system. She believes that justices are limited to the duties of the judicial branch, without their authority extending to executive or legislative roles. That is, justices do not create laws, nor do they implement or enforce laws. The role of the judicial branch is to interpret the law and apply it to cases of dispute. Although the Supreme Court spends much time determining whether or not laws are in fact constitutional, that power and authority is not granted in the Constitution. Many of the duties set forth in the Constitution refer to cases and rights between states or between the federal government and other parties.

In retirement, O'Connor has expressed her opinion that judges should not be elected. Rather, they should be appointed based on merit. She believes this would lead to better-qualified judges. O'Connor developed an interactive website program to teach middle-school students about the court system. Sandra Day O'Connor continues to make a positive impact in the lives of Americans.

Text Questions

1. Which is a synonym for the word *moderate* as it is used in the third paragraph?
   a. tolerant
   b. inexpensive
   c. radical
   d. average

2. Which position provided Sandra Day O'Connor with political experience?
   a. Deputy Attorney General
   b. civilian attorney
   c. Arizona State Senator
   d. Arizona Court of Appeals

3. Throughout her career, how did Justice O'Connor approach legal decisions?
   a. as a conservative
   b. as a moderate conservative
   c. as a moderate liberal
   d. as a liberal

4. Based on this passage, why might Sandra Day O'Connor have been nominated to the position of Supreme Court Justice?
   a. She knew the president.
   b. She had experience as a civilian attorney overseas.
   c. She was active in civic and cultural organizations.
   d. She had a wide range of experience, both political and legal, and had risen up within the court system.

5. Based on what you read and any background knowledge you have, do you agree or disagree with O'Connor's opinion regarding the role of a Supreme Court Justice? Give reasons to support your answer.

_____

_____

_____

Name_____

The Father of Public Libraries

Few "rags to riches" stories compare to that of Andrew Carnegie, a Scottish immigrant who later became one of the most famous and wealthy industrialists of his time. He was born in Scotland in 1835. The son of a weaver, his family expected him to follow in his father's steps. However, the Industrial Revolution changed their plans. Mechanized looms replaced weavers, and Andrew's father had to beg for work. Carnegie vowed that when he was older, he would rise up out of poverty. At the same time, Carnegie learned from relatives about equality in the workforce and the rights of common workers.

Carnegie's family fled to America to seek better opportunities. Carnegie began his career among the working class, taking jobs in factories and the telegraph industry. In each job he held, Carnegie did his best. He embraced new and greater responsibilities. In time, he followed a coworker from the telegraph office into the railroad business. He worked for the railroads throughout the Civil War. After the war, Carnegie realized the potential of iron and steel. He resigned from the railroad to work for a bridge company before investing in the steel industry. Carnegie was willing to take incredible risks for the ideas and technology in which he believed. He said workers should form unions to protect their rights. However, Carnegie pushed his employees to work long hours for low wages. After working in the steel business for several years, he sold his company to J.P. Morgan.

Carnegie believed it was a disgrace to die rich. He turned his efforts to giving away his millions. Acting on his opinions that people should help themselves, he supported institutions of higher learning. Carnegie also established over two thousand libraries. He valued peace and built a "palace of peace" in the Netherlands that would later become an international court. Before he died, Carnegie gave away over 350 million dollars, a fortune even by today's standards.

Text Questions

1. What is one thing that might be said of Andrew Carnegie?
   a. He wasn't willing to put forth the effort.
   b. Sometimes his actions didn't match his words.
   c. He was too short-sighted and didn't make wise investments.
   d. He supported slavery during the Civil War.

2. From the passage, you can infer that . . .
   a. Carnegie's investment in the steel industry was a risk.
   b. Carnegie didn't support unions.
   c. Carnegie made most of his money working in a factory as a laborer.
   d. Carnegie supported charities.

3. What is the main idea of the third paragraph?
   a. It introduces Carnegie's background and family life.
   b. It explains why Carnegie was a successful businessman.
   c. It describes Carnegie's business career.
   d. It describes the ways in which Carnegie invested his money in helping people.

4. What do you think Carnegie meant when he said it was a *disgrace* to die rich?
   a. A person loses the respect of others if he has wealth and doesn't help others with it.
   b. People who are rich often behave poorly.
   c. People who die rich are typically dishonest.
   d. Their family would be unworthy of receiving the inheritance.

5. What can you apply to your own life from reading biographies about people such as Andrew Carnegie?

_____

_____

Name_____

Margaret Thatcher, Prime Minister

Our younger years often help form our beliefs, and our experiences affect how we choose to live. Such is the case with Margaret Thatcher. She became the first woman to lead a western democracy. Thatcher grew up in a close community that had strong values. She learned self-reliance, honesty, and the value of charitable work. Thatcher took chemistry classes in college, but she had a greater interest in politics. While growing up, her father served as a counselor in their community and discussed current events and issues with her. Thatcher went to college at Oxford, where she was elected president of a student association. This was the beginning of her political experience.

Thatcher ran for the Labor seat at Dartford. She lost both times she ran but enjoyed the campaign and displayed strong public-speaking skills. She went on to train as a lawyer and was later elected to Parliament.

Thatcher held a variety of political offices. She gained further experience as Education Minister. Five years later, she was elected as the leader of the Conservative party. The Conservatives won the majority in Parliament in 1979, and the next day, Margaret Thatcher became the Prime Minister of the United Kingdom.

During her terms of political leadership, Margaret Thatcher helped revive the economy. She spoke out against the mindset of decline that had prevailed since World War II, and she helped reshape the nation's foreign policy. Her reforms and policies contributed to the spread of democracy and the growth of free markets during the period following the Cold War. Even though Thatcher's leadership role was controversial, today she is viewed as an influential and respected world leader.

Text Questions ···

1. Which of the following is <u>not</u> an area in which Margaret Thatcher was influential?
   a. economic reforms
   b. foreign policy
   c. democratic ideals
   d. space exploration

2. Based on the passage, what can you conclude about Margaret Thatcher?
   a. She didn't understand economics.
   b. She was concerned about the welfare of her country.
   c. She wanted to become famous.
   d. She struggled to maintain her grades in college.

3. What does the word *decline* mean as it is used in the third paragraph?
   a. deterioration
   b. rejection
   c. acceptance
   d. descending

4. What background and experience did Thatcher bring to her role as prime minister?
   a. daughter of a counselor
   b. elected to Parliament
   c. lawyer
   d. all of the above

5. As a female political leader, what are some ways Margaret Thatcher might have a lasting influence?

   _____

   _____

   _____

Name_____

Author of Adventure

A brief review of Gary Paulsen's life shows why he is such a prolific writer. When he was young, a librarian handed him a book and showed him how to obtain a library card. From that point on, Gary became an avid reader. He spent hours reading alone, which may have fueled his taste for adventure. Paulsen ran away from home at age 14 and traveled with a carnival. Add to that a summer of farm chores and two runs in an Alaskan dogsled race. Throw into the mix various jobs including engineer, construction worker, truck driver, and sailor. With his diverse history, Paulsen has a wealth of experiences from which to draw on to write his stories.

Taking a big risk, Paulsen left a job as a satellite technician to pursue the field of writing. He worked as a magazine proofreader while working on his own writing at night. Later, he moved from California to Minnesota, renting a cabin by a lake. There, he wrote his first novel. During this time living in the woods, Paulsen tried his hand at dog racing. When forced to give up his dogs due to his health, Paulsen began to put the same energy he had devoted to dog training into his writing. According to Paulsen, he stays focused when he works, not doing anything else, which explains the number of books he has published.

Paulsen observes closely and cares about the world around him. He encourages his readers to do the same. These characteristics, along with his belief in young people, make him a popular author. Three of his books—*Hatchet*, *Dogsong*, and *The Winter Room*—have won Newbery Awards. With over 175 books published, Paulsen leaves readers with a lasting legacy.

Text Questions

1. What likely inspired Paulsen to write stories about survival in the wilderness?
   a. He worked as an engineer.
   b. He lived in the north Minnesota woods.
   c. He liked to read.
   d. He won awards for his writing.

2. Which is a synonym for the word *legacy* as it is used in the last paragraph?
   a. gift
   b. money
   c. property
   d. bequest

3. Which characteristics make Gary Paulsen a popular young-adult author?
   a. He carefully observes the world in which he lives.
   b. He has had a wide variety of experiences.
   c. He believes in young people.
   d. all of the above

4. Which of the following is <u>not</u> true about Paulsen's early life?
   a. He was an avid reader.
   b. He did chores on a farm.
   c. He sailed on the ocean with his father.
   d. He ran away from home to work with a circus.

5. Based on what you read in the passage, what might inspire you to read a book written by Gary Paulsen?

   _____

   _____

   _____

Name_____

Pelé

Edson Arantes do Nascimento is known to the world as Pelé. He is considered by many experts to be the greatest soccer player in history. Pelé was named the Co-Player of the Century in 1999 by FIFA.

Pelé was born in Brazil and played professionally there for two decades. His performance in the 1958 World Cup made him a soccer legend. The national team won three World Cups during the time he played with them. Later in his career, Pelé joined a team in the North American Soccer League.

His father struggled to earn a living as a soccer player. That didn't stop Pelé from trying the game, even after growing up in poverty. No one knows for sure how he got the nickname "Pelé," but he had the name from the time he kicked a sock filled with rags in the streets.

While playing on a youth team in Brazil, his coach suggested he try out for the Santos professional soccer club. Pelé was 15 and scored his first goal within the year. He went on to score many more goals for his team. Based on his performance, he was recruited to play for the national team. Pelé was a key player in Brazil's World Cup win in 1958, and he also helped the team win even more championships.

After Pelé joined the New York Cosmos, he helped make soccer more popular in the United States. His final game was an exhibition game between New York and Santos. In that game, he competed for both sides. Over the course of Pelé's career, he scored 1,283 goals!

Since retiring from soccer in 1977, he has continued to stay busy. Pelé has served as Brazil's Minister for Sport, and he has been a United Nations ambassador for ecology and the environment. In 1975, Pelé also won the International Peace Award for his work with UNICEF.

It's easy to see why at one point in his career, Pelé was named Brazil's "national treasure."

Text Questions

1. In what year did Pelé help the Brazilian team win the World Cup?
   a. 1940
   b. 1958
   c. 1974
   d. 1977

2. Which factor has probably not contributed to Pelé's popularity?
   a. He used to kick a sock filled with rags in the streets.
   b. Pelé joined the New York Cosmos, which helped make soccer more popular in the United States.
   c. In his final exhibition game between New York and Santos, Pelé competed for both sides.
   d. Over the course of Pelé's career, he scored over 1,200 goals.

3. How much time does two decades represent?
   a. two years
   b. ten years
   c. twenty years
   d. forty years

4. In which paragraph can you read about Pelé's contributions to humanity?
   a. in the first paragraph
   b. in the second paragraph
   c. in the fourth paragraph
   d. in the sixth paragraph

5. What can you learn from this inspirational sports figure?

_____

_____

Name_____

Harland David Sanders

Harland David Sanders is better known to most as Colonel Sanders, the founder of Kentucky Fried Chicken.

Harland Sanders was born in a small shack in September of 1890. Six years later his father died, leaving Harland to watch over his siblings while his mother entered the workforce. His duties at home included cooking, and within a year, he had begun to develop quite an aptitude as a cook. Following his mother's remarriage, he left home and subsequently dropped out of school in his early teens.

Throughout his life, he worked a wide variety of odd jobs. He was a farmer, insurance salesman, mule tender, and among other things, a political candidate. While working at one of his jobs as a service-station operator, he began cooking chicken. He sold it as part of a boxed meal for hungry travelers who stopped in for gas.

His food became so popular that he was listed in the popular restaurant guide *Adventures to Good Eating*.

In 1935, the governor made him a Kentucky Colonel for his contributions to regional cooking. Less than five years later, he purchased a motel and restaurant. Within a year, he had perfected his "secret recipe" for pressure-cooked chicken, but when World War II broke out, he lost most of his business and was forced to close.

After the war, he franchised his Kentucky Fried Chicken for the first time. Sanders spent the next several years developing his business. After one of his restaurants failed due to low traffic flow, Sanders began franchising in earnest.

He became the first fast-food owner to expand internationally. At one point, there were 600 restaurants. He eventually sold the chain of restaurants and traveled thousands of miles each year as a goodwill ambassador for the franchise.

Success came late in life for Colonel Sanders, and he gave heavily back to charities. Even today, over thirty years after his death, his trusts continue to provide money for charities and scholarships.

Text Questions

1. What inspired Harland Sanders to develop a chicken recipe?
   a. His siblings' favorite food was chicken.
   b. He learned to cook chicken while working on a farm.
   c. While working at a service station, he sold cooked chicken as part of a boxed meal.
   d. He knew he would be able to franchise his recipe and sell it to many people.

2. Which word best characterizes Harland Sanders?
   a. lazy   b. procrastinator   c. persistent   d. greedy

3. Which of the following is true about Harland Sanders' life?
   a. He watched over his siblings and helped at home with the cooking while his mother entered the workforce.
   b. His recipe for cooking chicken failed miserably.
   c. After one of his restaurants failed due to low traffic flow, Sanders gave up on his dream of franchising.
   d. Success came early in life for Colonel Sanders.

4. What does the word *franchise* mean as it is used in the text?
   a. freedom from restriction
   b. a special right or exemption granted by the government
   c. the right to vote
   d. the right to market a product in a specific area

5. What can we learn from reading about Harland Sanders and his life?

_____

_____

Name_____

Walt Disney's Greatest Storyman

Sometimes we think more about how animation is created than the people behind the scenes. Bill Peet has written and illustrated over thirty books for children, and he is one of the major storytellers behind well-known animated movies.

Bill Peet began to develop his creative abilities at a young age. Peet grew up in Indianapolis, near the edge of the city, with access to the countryside. He also had the opportunity to visit his grandfather's farm, which bordered wilderness. Those experiences, combined with trips to the zoo, provided the foundation for future drawings of animals. When Peet entered school, his constant drawing sometimes became a problem, although one teacher encouraged his drawing. He dared to dream of a career in which he could put his drawing habit to use. He won a scholarship to an art school after high school and studied there for three years.

After art school, Peet needed to figure out a way to earn a living. He heard that Walt Disney was looking for artists, so he moved to California. There, Peet sketched and planned screen stories. He eventually became a storyman. Animated movies are made up of many individual drawings. Peet did the complete storyboards for two movies, *The Sword in the Stone* and *101 Dalmatians*. He also worked on *Peter Pan*, *Dumbo*, and *The Jungle Book*.

Peet's children's stories began as bedtime stories for his sons. He illustrated his stories with many animals and some people, too. Peet claims the reason for this is he loves to draw animals.

Bill Peet used different media for his drawings. He drew in pastels, pencils, and ballpoint pen. He dabbled in oil painting for a brief time. Many of his book illustrations are done in colored pencils and ink.

Two of Peet's animated works won awards. He's more well-known, though, as "Walt Disney's Greatest Storyman."

Text Questions

1. Based on the passage, which of the following movies did Bill Peet not work on?
   a. *A Bug's Life*
   b. *Dumbo*
   c. *101 Dalmatians*
   d. *The Jungle Book*

2. What does the word *access* mean as it is used in the second paragraph?
   a. able to approach
   b. a way of using something
   c. the ability to get to a place
   d. to retrieve data from a computer

3. What inspired Bill Peet's drawings of animals?
   a. the countryside near his home
   b. his grandfather's farm and wilderness
   c. visits to the zoo
   d. all of the above

4. What characteristic might have contributed to Disney's acceptance of Peet as a main storyman?
   a. his high-school drawings
   b. his ability to write and illustrate stories
   c. his growing up in the city
   d. his oil paintings

5. How can your passions and abilities relate to possible careers in the real world? Give examples to support your answer.

   _____

   _____

   _____

Name_____

Barbara McClintock, Nobel Prize Winner

Our current understanding of genetics is rooted in the study of plants. While a student at Cornell University, Barbara McClintock took biology classes and the only genetics course available. She expressed a great interest in her learning. The professor then invited her to attend his second course, offered only to graduate students. She studied the behavior of chromosomes and decided to pursue an advanced degree. She would study chromosomes and their genetic content for the remainder of her career.

During her career, McClintock taught botany at Cornell and went on to become a research associate. She later taught at other universities and worked with an agricultural science program as a consultant. After earning her Ph.D., McClintock received fellowships from various schools. This enabled her to continue her studies and research. She received honorary degrees and awards of achievement from several institutions. Perhaps her most prestigious award was when she was awarded the Nobel Prize in Medicine in 1983.

Barbara McClintock worked with chromosomes and genes in maize. She focused on the relationship between plant reproduction and how some plants mutated. She discovered that chromosomes could jump during plant breeding. This means that genes can change positions on the chromosome. After more research, McClintock proved that certain genes could turn physical characteristics—such as the color of leaves—on or off. Scientists later discovered a relationship between McClintock's research on genetic mutations and bacteria that develop resistance to antibiotics. Such research helps us better understand how viruses and bacteria act.

Although her early work gained recognition in the scientific community, her later research on genetics was not initially well received. Only later, when her discoveries were confirmed by molecular biologists, did she receive additional honors. Described by a friend as a solitary person, Barbara McClintock focused her life on her research, which was her passion.

Text Questions ·····································

1. You can tell from the context of the passage that the word *chromosome* means . . .
   a. the colored part of a plant.
   b. the part of the cell nucleus that carries the genes responsible for hereditary characteristics.
   c. something that makes bacteria resistant to antibiotics.
   d. something that causes a virus.

2. Which was Barbara McClintock's most notable award?
   a. The Merit Award
   b. MacArthur Foundation Grant
   c. National Medal of Science
   d. Nobel Prize

3. Which statement from the text best describes McClintock's research?
   a. She discovered that genes can change positions on the chromosome.
   b. She received honorary degrees and awards of achievement from several institutions.
   c. She studied the behavior of chromosomes and decided to pursue an advanced degree.
   d. Barbara McClintock was a solitary person.

4. What is the main idea of the third paragraph?
   a. It describes McClintock's educational background.
   b. It provides details about her scientific career.
   c. It explains her research and its implications for science and medicine.
   d. It describes the honors and awards she received.

5. Based on what you read, what contributions did Barbara McClintock make to science and medicine?

_____

_____

Name_____

Washington's Crossing of the Delaware

Many people are aware of the historical event when General George Washington crossed the Delaware River, but few understand the difficulties involved before and after the attack.

The Continental Army soldiers were signed up for very limited amounts of time. Many of their enlistments were expiring, and many had deserted. Washington sent some men out into the area to recruit new soldiers. Normally that would have been hard to accomplish, but due to the harsh treatment of the people by British soldiers, many people wanted to fight against them.

Another concern was ice floating in the river, as well as the river itself freezing. Washington's spies had told him that when the Delaware froze over, the British were considering walking across and attacking him. Washington had to move both men and artillery across at night.

On Christmas night, 1776, Washington split his forces into three units, called columns, to cross the Delaware at three different places. Each column had to move men as well as artillery. Only Washington was able to get both across in heavy sleet and snow. One other general managed to get his men across, but when unable to successfully transport his artillery, he returned with his men to the bank.

With fewer men and less artillery than he had hoped for, Washington still decided to attack. On December 26th, he divided his troops into two units and defeated the British. There were only nine American casualties. The British sustained 120 casualties and 1,000 men were captured. Washington ordered the British supplies to be plundered and their rum destroyed prior to the return trip across the Delaware.

This victory over the British raised the spirits of the American colonists and helped turn the tide in the Revolutionary War.

Text Questions

1. Which of the following did <u>not</u> contribute to the difficulty of the crossing?
   a. Washington had to move both men and artillery across at night.
   b. There was ice floating in the river.
   c. They crossed in heavy sleet and snow.
   d. It was hard to recruit new soldiers.

2. What does the word *casualties* mean as it is used in the text?
   a. people who are hurt or killed in an accident
   b. people in the military who are wounded or killed in active service
   c. anything lost or destroyed by an unfortunate event
   d. anyone who is a victim of a natural disaster

3. What was the author's purpose in writing this passage?
   a. to help readers understand the challenges Washington faced
   b. to teach readers about river ice
   c. to explain how an army plans an attack
   d. to describe what happens after an attack

4. Why did Washington have to move his forces at night?
   a. The British treated their people harshly.
   b. Washington wanted his men to cross the river at three different places.
   c. Spies reported the British planned to walk across the frozen river to attack.
   d. After the attack, the forces had to make the return crossing.

5. Based on what you read in the text and your background knowledge, how did this historical event contribute to the development of the United States?

   _____

   _____

Name_____

Animated Cartoons

Cartoons have been around longer than you might think. In 1640, Athanasius Kircher was the first man who attempted to put drawings into motion. He drew images on layers of glass slides and had them move within a lantern, giving the appearance of movement.

In the early 1800s, it was determined that movement can also be accomplished by placing fixed images on paper. This was called "the persistence of vision." To illustrate this, John Paris invented the Thaumatrope. It was a two-sided plate with a different image on each side. Paris took an image of a bird on one side and an empty cage on the other. He used two strings and wound it so that when pulled tight, it spun and the two images "moved," creating the illusion of the bird in the cage.

Mathematician William Horner invented the Zoetrope in 1867. It was a roll of paper with drawings on it, placed inside a turning drum with slots. As it turned and one looked through the slots, the images appeared to move. It was actually first called The Wheel of the Devil but was later renamed the Zoetrope.

Later, in the 1800s, Thomas Edison invented the Kinetoscope, the first cinema machine. One looked into a slot where a reel of photos or pictures passed, and the images moved seamlessly.

Based on Edison's invention, images were eventually placed on film that moved at a high rate of speed. The cartoons were all hand drawn and carefully filmed to show natural movement.

Today, cartoons are made via computer technology, and the old-fashioned method of hand drawing every image is uncommon. Cartoons have expanded from being intended primarily for children to providing entertainment for all ages. After over three hundred years, they still have not lost their appeal.

Text Questions

1. Which device was invented first?
   a. the Zoetrope
   b. the Kinetoscope
   c. the Thaumatrope
   d. the cinema machine

2. What is the best way to describe animation?
   a. Still images appear to move.
   b. It brings objects to life.
   c. It is used to make movies more exciting.
   d. It can only be accomplished with computers.

3. What does the word *persistence* mean as it is used in the second paragraph?
   a. refusing to give up
   b. remaining
   c. continuing an effect
   d. repeating a question

4. Which statement best describes the first animated cinema movies?
   a. He drew images on layers of glass slides and had them move within a lantern, giving the appearance of movement.
   b. The cartoons were all hand drawn and carefully filmed to show natural movement.
   c. Today, cartoons are made via computer technology, and the old-fashioned method of hand drawing every image is uncommon.
   d. By spinning the two images, Paris created the illusion of movement.

5. What makes the techniques of animation so fascinating to people?

   _____

   _____

Name_____

Handheld Calculators

People today have access to "handheld" calculators in many different mediums: computers; smartphones; and small, individual calculators. Push a button here or a button there, and it computes complex calculations instantly. We think of this as "modern" technology.

One of the earliest handheld calculators first became available in the early 1960s. Personal computers came into widespread use twenty years later, and cellular phones with calculators sometime after that. Thousands of years ago, long before the invention of batteries or electricity, early versions of a calculator were already in use.

The first calculator was called an "abacus," also known as a "counting frame." An abacus looks like a wood rectangle with a series of wires stretched across. Small rocks or beads are slid along the wires. There are other types using small ropes or grooves made in hard sand along which small beads slide.

People would use an abacus to solve addition, subtraction, multiplication, division, square root, and cube root problems with amazing speed. These counting devices are so quick and portable that they are still used today in some countries among trade merchants.

Abaci were standard issue in most American grade schools until the mid 1900s. With the advent of handheld calculators, they quickly became obsolete.

Text Questions

1. Which phrase or statement best defines an abacus?
   a. a handheld calculator
   b. a wood rectangle with a series of wires stretched across; small rocks or beads are slid along the wires
   c. used for addition, subtraction, multiplication, division, square root and cube root with amazing speed
   d. quick and portable

2. Which is a synonym for the word *advent* as it is used in the fifth paragraph?
   a. coming
   b. arrival
   c. approach
   d. appearance

3. In which situation might an abacus not be used?
   a. by your ancestors
   b. by merchants in foreign countries
   c. by students in the 1950s
   d. by your parents at the store

4. What is the main idea of the text?
   a. A battery-operated calculator is the only way to solve arithmetic problems.
   b. Everyone should have a handheld calculator.
   c. An abacus is an effective counting device.
   d. An abacus is obsolete.

5. In what ways have handheld calculators made our lives easier?

   _____

   _____

   _____

Name_____

The Emancipation Proclamation

The Emancipation Proclamation was an executive order issued by President Abraham Lincoln on January 1, 1863. The power to issue an executive order is granted by the Constitution and is subject to judicial review—that is, a federal court may rule that something is constitutional or not.

It was issued during the Civil War and freed slaves in the ten states still in rebellion against the United States. The order did not make slavery illegal, make former slaves citizens, or compensate their ex-owners.

The purpose of the Emancipation Proclamation was to eliminate slavery and bring the country together.

Although issued January 1, 1863, President Lincoln never signed the order into law. A Constitutional Amendment supporting the Proclamation was ratified by the states in 1865.

When Lincoln first presented the proclamation to his cabinet in 1862, they were opposed to it. They felt it was too radical. Eventually, Lincoln overruled his cabinet and issued the order as he thought best to do.

One of the major non-slavery issues was that by issuing the order, it kept Europe from joining the war on the side of the Confederacy. Britain and France were interested in the cotton industry in the South and were prepared to become involved so as to have a part of that economy. However, the majority of Europe was against slavery. Because the Proclamation directed the attention of the war to slavery, it became an instrument in making the war an international issue.

Regardless of the particulars of issuing the Emancipation Order, it is one of the greatest documents in the history of the world.

Text Questions ....

1. What was the purpose of the Emancipation Proclamation?
   a. to end the war
   b. to free the slaves in the Confederate states
   c. to encourage Europe to join the war
   d. to proclaim that Lincoln was in charge of the war

2. Who proposed the Proclamation?
   a. Europe
   b. the slaves
   c. President Lincoln
   d. President Lincoln's cabinet

3. What does the word *radical* mean as it is used in the text?
   a. illegal
   b. extreme
   c. unfriendly
   d. advanced

4. Which of the following happened first?
   a. Lincoln issued the Emancipation Proclamation.
   b. Lincoln signed the Proclamation into law.
   c. Lincoln presented the Proclamation to his cabinet.
   d. The states ratified the Proclamation with a Constitutional Amendment.

5. What lasting effect did the Emancipation Proclamation have on the United States?

_____

_____

Name_____

Prohibition

From 1920 to 1933, there was a nationwide ban on the sale, production, and transportation of alcoholic beverages. It was called "Prohibition."

Prohibition was set in place by the ratification of the Eighteenth Amendment to the United States Constitution. The 18th Amendment was overturned in 1933 with the passage of the 21st Amendment.

The Prohibition movement started in earnest after the formation of the Anti-Saloon League in 1893. Together, with the support of similar organizations like The American Temperance Society and The Woman's Christian Temperance Union, these groups were able to get Prohibition laws passed locally, and from there, the national movement grew. In 1881, Kansas became the first state to outlaw alcohol.

During this time, breweries were very prosperous, and saloons were opening at an alarming rate. The consumption of alcohol grew to the point that it was considered by many to be an epidemic.

Prohibition began on January 17, 1920, when the Eighteenth Amendment went into effect. A total of 1,520 Federal Prohibition Agents (police) were given the task of enforcing the law.

During Prohibition, people were allowed to make limited amounts of certain beverages. Also, it is important to note that drinking alcohol was not illegal; only the selling of it was.

Many illegal establishments sprang up that served alcohol. Organized crime also got a major boost during this time. Bootlegging (delivering illegal alcohol) and other violent crimes grew enormously in many major cities.

Overall, the consumption of alcohol declined during Prohibition. One of the major reasons Prohibition failed was the inability of the government to regulate it. Too many people wanted to drink who had always been good citizens, and they refused to view drinking as breaking the law. As a result, the law was unpopular and ignored.

Text Questions

1. What was illegal under Prohibition?
   a. selling alcohol
   b. producing alcoholic beverages
   c. transporting alcohol
   d. all of the above

2. Which Constitutional amendment set Prohibition in place?
   a. the 18th Amendment
   b. the 20th Amendment
   c. the 21st Amendment
   d. the 23rd Amendment

3. Why did Prohibition fail at that time?
   a. People wanted to use alcohol for medicine.
   b. People used alcohol for religious reasons.
   c. The government was not able to effectively regulate it.
   d. Consuming alcohol became an epidemic.

4. What does *prosperous* mean as it is used in the fourth paragraph?
   a. ominous
   b. successful
   c. controversial
   d. lucky

5. Based on what you read, do you think Prohibition would succeed or fail today? Give evidence and reasons to support your answer.

_____

_____

Name_____

The Great American Dessert

Frozen desserts have been around much longer than you might imagine. Over two thousand years ago, Alexander the Great enjoyed snow and ice flavored with nectar. During the Roman Empire, runners were sent to the mountains for snow, which was then flavored with fruit or juice. Much later, the great explorer Marco Polo brought a recipe from the Far East that was similar to sherbet. Historians surmise this evolved into the ice cream we know today.

Frozen desserts incorporating cream appeared in France, England, and Italy during the same time period. At first, it was a dish for royalty. Ice cream was first served to the public at a café in Paris in the late 1600s. The dish had milk, cream, butter, and eggs.

Ice cream didn't arrive in America for another hundred years. Historical records indicate George Washington and other early presidents dined on ice cream. A merchant's advertisement from the time claims ice cream was available "almost every day." Even so, it was a dish reserved mostly for the elite.

In the early 1800s, insulated ice houses made the storage of ice cream much more practical. By the middle of the century, ice cream had become quite an industry in America. The Industrial Revolution resulted in an increase in ice-cream production. New freezing processes and equipment made it easier to make ice cream.

Ice cream evolved through the invention of various products such as "ice-cream sodas." Some people claimed such treats were too rich to eat on Sunday. On Sundays, the carbonation was left out, leading to the ice-cream sundae. During times of war, ice cream became a tangible way to boost the morale of the troops. During the rise of the supermarket and prepackaged foods, ice-cream parlors declined. Recently, however, specialty ice-cream shops have become popular once again.

Text Questions

1. Which of the following best describes early frozen desserts?
   a. cream poured over ice
   b. snow flavored with fruit or juice
   c. a concoction made with milk, cream, sugar, and eggs
   d. a mixture of salt and snow poured over syrup

2. Which is a synonym for the word *morale* as it is used in the text?
   a. assurance
   b. resolve
   c. confidence
   d. spirits

3. Who might be credited with a frozen dessert that led to ice cream as we know it today?
   a. Alexander the Great
   b. the Romans
   c. people in the Far East
   d. George Washington

4. According to the passage, how did technology influence the ice-cream industry?
   a. Insulated ice houses and improved freezing techniques made it easier to produce and store ice cream.
   b. Advances in communication and advertising made it possible for more people to know about ice cream.
   c. When presidents ate ice cream, that made it more well-known to the general population.
   d. Advances in transportation made it possible to bring ice cream to more people without having it melt.

5. What would you predict to be the next new development in the ice-cream industry? Give reasons for your answer.

_____

_____

Name_____

The History of Airships

Airships have been made famous by the Goodyear blimp at sporting events and the famous Hindenburg disaster. These unusual flight machines have quite a history.

In 1783, the Montgolfier brothers made history when they heated the air inside a balloon. The balloon was made of taffeta and was varnished with alum. They sent three animals on an eight-minute, two-mile flight across the royal palace of Versailles. This was the first flight to ever carry living creatures. Rewarded for their efforts, the brothers were recognized as nobility. To this day, standard hot-air balloons carry their name.

At the same time, others were experimenting with balloon flight. Some men in Paris used hydrogen instead of hot air for a two-hour manned flight. With the success of this and other flights, hydrogen gas became the preferred gas in airships until helium was produced on a larger scale after World War I. Steering was an ongoing problem that plagued airships. It became evident that a change in shape would be

necessary to solve the dilemma. The machines also needed forward propulsion. Engines proved heavy and cumbersome. In 1884, electricity was used to power the floating balloons, but they still hadn't solved the problem of reliable steering.

Count Zeppelin observed war maneuvers in balloons during the Civil War and the Siege of Paris. He petitioned for a commission to develop steering for airships. His first airship, Luftschiff Zeppelin 1, flew in 1900. This marked the beginning of the golden age of airships.

Airships weren't golden for long. In the next 40 years, there were over 45 accidents involving airships. Over ten people died. Some airships simply exploded in midair, and others drifted and hit objects. At least one accident was due to a lightning strike that ignited the hydrogen into a massive eruption.

Airships are now primarily used for advertising, sightseeing, surveillance, and research purposes.

Text Questions

1. Which gas was used before helium to lift airships?
   - a. oxygen
   - b. hydrogen
   - c. nitrogen
   - d. carbon dioxide

2. Which is a synonym for the word *dilemma* as it is used in the third paragraph?
   - a. argument
   - b. difficulty
   - c. danger
   - d. problem

3. What was one obstacle that needed to be overcome in airship technology for them to become truly successful?
   - a. lift
   - b. construction materials
   - c. fuel
   - d. steering

4. Which of the following is <u>not</u> a common use of airships today?
   - a. passenger transport
   - b. surveillance
   - c. research
   - d. advertising

5. In your opinion, how does the development of airship technology contribute to society as a whole?

   _____

   _____

Name_____

Pirates of the South China Sea

Cheng I led what may have been the largest pirating confederation in history. Chinese pirating peaked during the late 1700s. Cheng I organized six pirate fleets, each sailing under a different color flag: red, white, black, yellow, blue, and green. He commanded the red fleet and had over 200 sailing vessels, called junks. Shortly after the turn of the century, Cheng I had built his fleet to include 600 junks. Over 30,000 pirates sailed at his command, and his fighting force had over 150,000 men. To avoid conflict, Cheng I assigned each fleet its own territory. They were stationed over a massive area. His enterprise threatened the whole of southern China.

After Cheng I's death, his wife, Cheng I Sao, took over command. Cheng I Sao operated under strict rules. Pirates were required to buy, rather than steal, goods from coastal villages. In turn, villagers had to sell their goods to the pirates. Anyone who disobeyed was treated very harshly. All ships entering the South China Sea had to pay tribute to Cheng I Sao's command or suffer.

In some cases, Cheng I Sao took prisoners and sold them for ransom. British Chief mate John Turner was one of those taken prisoner. He returned to England alive with gory tales about how the Chinese pirates treated their prisoners.

The pirates were not particular about what they ate. It is said that, at times, pirates encouraged the rats on board ship to breed so they could eat them.

Cheng I Sao's rule, like most pirates, was short-lived. In 1809, the black flag fleet attacked Cheng I Sao's red fleet and won.

Text Questions

1. What does the word *confederation* mean as it is used in the text?
   a. independent nations with a common defense
   b. a group of associates in unlawful acts
   c. a group of soldiers
   d. organization of rogue vagabonds

2. What did Cheng I do to decrease the potential for conflict among his fleets?
   a. He assigned each to its own territory.
   b. He stationed them great distances from each other.
   c. He only sent out one fleet at a time.
   d. He had a fighting force to help keep the peace.

3. What is the main idea of the second paragraph?
   a. It gives details about Cheng I's pirate fleets.
   b. It describes the strict rules Cheng I's wife established when she took command.
   c. It tells about a British prisoner who escaped and returned to England.
   d. It summarizes the end of Cheng I's pirate command.

4. Which of the following is <u>not</u> true about Cheng I's pirate command?
   a. Over 30,000 pirates sailed with his fleets.
   b. He had 150,000 men in his fighting force.
   c. He commanded the black fleet.
   d. He led a large pirate confederation.

5. What might be some reasons for pirate leaders' commands to be short-lived?

   _____

   _____

   _____

Name_____

The Beginnings of Fountain Drinks

Soft drinks have been around for many years and have made a tremendous impact on society. Coca-Cola®, for example, was invented by Colonel John Pemberton in 1886. Some say he wanted to create a delicious new beverage. Others claim the invention happened by accident. What we do know is Pemberton created flavored syrup, and carbonated water was added to the syrup at a local pharmacy. As it had carbonated water in it, it was initially sold only at pharmacies for five cents a glass. During the first year of Coke, about nine servings per day were sold. Today, daily servings are estimated at 1.8 billion around the world.

Prior to Pemberton's death in 1888, the financial interests of the company were sold to various people. The majority went to an Atlanta businessman, Asa Candler. Four years later, Candler had acquired sole ownership. Today, the company is worth billions.

Candler expanded the distribution of the soft drink to soda fountains around the country. Meanwhile, Joseph Biedenharn installed bottling equipment in his Mississippi store in 1894 and began selling the first bottles of Coca-Cola to local farms and lumber camps. A few years later, a couple of businessmen from Tennessee proposed the large-scale bottling and distribution of Coca-Cola and were subsequently sold the worldwide rights to do so for one dollar. Over time, the drink became distributed throughout the country, and soon it was available around the world.

The popularity of soft drinks inspired many similar products. As Coca-Cola became more popular, the owners became more concerned with protecting their product from competitors. Consumers were reminded to settle for nothing less than the real Coca-Cola. This led to an advertising slogan still heard today, "It's the real thing."

Coca-Cola now has over 3,500 products, sold in over 200 countries. The company continues to thrive and seeks to inspire moments of fun and happiness while encouraging integrity and making a difference.

Text Questions

1. What is the main idea of the text?
   a. It provides an overview of the development of a particular product.
   b. It traces the story of one particular inventor.
   c. It describes the marketing strategy for a particular product.
   d. It focuses only on the invention of the product.

2. What role did the pharmacy play in the history of Coca-Cola?
   a. Its inventor worked for a pharmacy.
   b. One hundred years ago, we didn't have convenience stores or fast-food places.
   c. Carbonated water was available at pharmacies as a medicinal product.
   d. The inventor needed access to glass bottles.

3. What does the word *integrity* mean as it is used in the text?
   a. completeness
   b. perfection
   c. taste
   d. sincerity

4. What contributed to the growth and development of the product?
   a. The sale of the company by the original owner before his death.
   b. The ability to bottle and distribute it to a wider geographic area.
   c. The fact that it was first sold at pharmacies.
   d. The development of similar products by other companies.

5. How can we benefit from understanding the mission and values of popular products?

_____

_____

Name_____

The Louisiana Purchase

In the early 1800s, Americans were expanding westward. Pioneers such as Daniel Boone were navigating new trails and roads. Americans were moving into all areas of the continent.

At that time, the United States consisted of 17 states. The area of the Louisiana Purchase was comprised of what would eventually be 15 states and doubled the land size of the country.

Louisiana was a territory owned by the French. New Orleans may have been its biggest city, but many Americans lived in and around the city. As a result, American ships transported materials on the river. The federal government wanted to protect its citizens and settlements as well as expand the country.

France had recently been battling a revolt in Haiti that had been expensive, both financially and in loss of soldiers. Napoleon wanted to prepare for war in Europe and needed money. The Louisiana territory was far away, and France owed the United States

money. President Jefferson wanted to purchase land, so the deal seemed profitable for both sides.

Initially, Jefferson sent Robert Livingston to France to buy New Orleans and the surrounding area, but Napoleon turned him down. President Jefferson then sent James Monroe as an envoy to France to complete the deal. At first, all President Jefferson wanted was to buy New Orleans for three million dollars. Napoleon offered the entire Louisiana Territory. On April 30, 1803, the deal was made to purchase the Louisiana Territory for a total of fifteen million dollars.

Of the purchase price, about 40 percent was paid. The remaining amount consisted of French debts cancelled by the United States government.

Immediately upon buying the territory, Jefferson commissioned Meriwether Lewis and William Clark to explore the territory. The total land purchased was 828,800 square miles and remains the most extraordinary land purchase in our history.

Text Questions

1. Which of the following statements is an opinion?
   a. The area of the Louisiana Purchase was comprised of what would eventually be 15 states and doubled the land size of the country.
   b. President Jefferson wanted to purchase land, so the deal seemed profitable for both sides.
   c. On April 30, 1803, the deal was made to purchase the Louisiana Territory for a total of fifteen million dollars.
   d. At first, all President Jefferson wanted was to buy New Orleans for three million dollars.

2. What does the word *envoy* mean as it is used in the text?
   a. a diplomat
   b. an ambassador of goodwill
   c. an agent sent by a government to complete a transaction
   d. a representative

3. Which of the following is not a reason the United States wanted to purchase the Louisiana territory?
   a. The federal government wanted to protect its citizens.
   b. It was an opportunity to continue westward expansion.
   c. Many Americans lived in New Orleans, so President Jefferson initially focused on purchasing the city.
   d. France owed the United States money.

4. How much of the purchase price was paid in cash?
   a. less than half   b. half   c. more than half   d. all of it

5. Based on what you read and any background knowledge you have, how would you explain the significance of Lewis and Clark being commissioned to explore the new territory?

_____

_____

Name_____

Julius Caesar, Kidnapped

In the days of Julius Caesar, pirates roamed the Mediterranean. The Roman navy didn't bother attacking them as they were paid to provide servants for Roman senators. The slaves worked the plantations in Italy.

In 75 BC, Julius Caesar was sailing on the Aegean Sea when he was kidnapped by Cilician Pirates. Rather than acting like a captive, Caesar acted like their leader. He even demanded silence while he slept. He wrote and recited poetry, played games, and exercised with the pirates.

Eventually, the pirates demanded ransom for their prisoner. When they told Caesar they were demanding twenty silver talents, he laughed at them. Apparently, they still didn't understand who they had kidnapped. He demanded they ask for fifty talents, to which the pirates readily agreed. After all, that would be over one million dollars in today's money.

Caesar sent some of those with him home to collect the money. He was left with one friend and two servants to contend with his captors. It took thirty-eight days to collect the silver, which was promptly delivered to the pirates. The pirates then set Caesar free.

During his time in captivity, Caesar had promised the pirates that when freed, he would return and have them put to death. They never took this threat very seriously.

Caesar was unable to get official permission to return and carry out judgment against the pirates. So he decided to try and do so himself. Caesar gathered men, readied ships, and set sail for the harbor of Miletus where their ship had laid anchor.

He captured the pirates and placed them in a prison. Then he reclaimed not only the silver but also took the pirates' spoils for himself. True to his word, the pirates were all punished as promised.

Text Questions

1. Why was Caesar kidnapped?
   a. The pirates wanted to capture a famous person.
   b. Pirates demanded ransom for their prisoners.
   c. The pirates wanted Caesar to entertain them.
   d. The pirates knew Caesar wouldn't be able to get a judgment against them.

2. Which of the following statements best shows Caesar's leadership ability?
   a. Caesar was sailing on the Aegean Sea when he was kidnapped by Cilician Pirates.
   b. Caesar wrote and recited poetry, played games, and exercised with the pirates.
   c. Caesar gathered men, readied ships, and set sail for the harbor of Miletus where their ship had laid anchor.
   d. Caesar had promised the pirates that when freed, he would return and have them put to death.

3. What can you infer about Caesar from this passage?
   a. He was a persuasive speaker.   c. He was a natural leader.
   b. He was a shrewd planner.   d. all of the above

4. Which is a synonym for the word *reclaimed* as it is used in the last paragraph?
   a. rescued   c. recovered
   b. cultivated land   d. subdued

5. Why do people find stories like this interesting? Include evidence to support your answer.

_____

_____

_____

Name_____

That Phone in Your Pocket

A key concept behind cell-phone technology is the notion that space can conduct electricity. Within twenty years of the initial hypothesis and research, successful experiments led to the first telegraph. This may not seem related to cell phones today, but it was a major breakthrough in long-distance communication.

It was another fifty years before the technology expanded beyond the telegraph. In the 1920s, police cars began installing mobile radios. The government created the Federal Communication Commission (FCC) in 1934. One of their first tasks was to assign certain channels to specific uses, such as emergency and government use.

A mobile radio telephone service was developed in the mid-1940s, but heavy interference caused it to be impractical. During this same time period, the first radio car phones were built. Again, heavy interference doomed the effort to failure. By the end of the 1940s, the FCC authorized several channels to be used as Radio Common Carriers, which made it possible for corporations and private organizations to use mobile phones. These were the first link between mobile phones and telephones, instead of operating radio to radio.

Car phones became true mobile phones separate from radios. The early units were large and bulky and required an operator to make the connection between users. The next major development made use of a single channel operating at a higher frequency, eliminating the need for operators.

As early as 1970, the FCC assigned specific frequencies for cell phones. Within a year, AT&T proposed the first mobile telephone system to the FCC, based on dividing cities into "cells." Not long after, the first mobile handset was designed and demonstrated to the public. Early cell phones were bulky and expensive and not readily available to the public.

The rest, as they say, is history. The cell-phone industry has become an ever-growing empire, with the number of cell phones in use quickly approaching the number of people on the planet.

Text Questions

1. Which technology is most closely related to cell-phone development?
   a. electricity
   b. radio
   c. television
   d. computers

2. What does the word *frequency* mean as it is used in the text?
   a. something that occurs often
   b. the number of times something occurs in a given period of time
   c. a rate of repetition
   d. the number of vibrations or sound waves within a unit of time

3. Which of the following was a problem faced by early cell-phone technology?
   a. crowded channels
   b. interference
   c. size and expense
   d. all of the above

4. Which statement does <u>not</u> describe the benefits of the development of cell phones?
   a. The first telegraph was a major breakthrough in long-distance communication.
   b. The FCC assigned certain channels to specific uses, such as emergency and government use.
   c. The early units were large and bulky and required an operator to make the connection between users.
   d. By the end of the 1940s, the FCC authorized several channels to be used as Radio Common Carriers, which made it possible for corporations and private organizations to use mobile phones.

5. How do you envision cell-phone technology in the future? What features might be added?

_____

_____

Name_____

Livestock Reduction

Drastic times call for drastic measures, or so it would appear. At the end of the Great Depression, the government established a stock-reduction program. Over the course of time, over 200,000 sheep, goats, and horses were killed. The government claimed the arid land of the southwest would support only six head per acre. Stock reduction was intended to increase soil conservation and reduce overgrazing.

Unfortunately, these events coincided with years of depression and economic hardship. Those who relied on livestock for their existence, such as some Native Americans, were devastated by the orders.

Each family was permitted to claim a certain number of sheep or goats. In some cases, some stock could be given to other family members who did not yet meet the quota. This spared some animals, but not all, from certain death. The remaining livestock were shot. Not surprisingly, stock reduction also contributed to the near-extinction of Churro sheep.

The stock-reduction plans changed the way people lived. Families who had previously supported themselves by raising stock now had to find other ways of bringing in income. Men were forced to find wage-paying jobs, even if it meant leaving their communities. The Native Americans, in particular, had been sheepherders for generations. They believed the sheep gave strength to the people to survive. Herds represented status in the community.

Shortly after the beginning of the program, the Navajo chairman asked the government to reconsider. His request cited "economic loss of wages and war effort." In response, the government issued special grazing permits to reduce the impact of stock reduction during the war. In theory, this would prevent taking too much stock from people who had no other source of income. The war provided a temporary way out for some, but it took time to rebuild the herds and recover economically after the war.

Text Questions

1. Which of the following was <u>not</u> an impact of the stock-reduction plan on native people in the southwest?
   a. economic loss and hardship
   b. people leaving communities to find work
   c. loss of status in the community
   d. the increase of soil conservation

2. What does the word *coincided* mean as it is used in the text?
   a. was exactly alike in shape and position
   b. occurred at the same time
   c. was equivalent in importance to other events
   d. was related to

3. How does the fourth paragraph contribute to the development of the main idea?
   a. It gives details that explain how this event took place.
   b. It describes how this historical event affected people and the way they live.
   c. It describes the interaction between people and the government.
   d. It explains what caused this event.

4. Which of the following statements is <u>not</u> a provision of the stock-reduction plan?
   a. The arid land would support only a limited number of livestock.
   b. Each family was permitted to claim a certain number of sheep or goats.
   c. They could give some stock to other family members who did not yet meet the quota.
   d. The government issued special grazing permits to reduce the impact of stock reduction during the war.

5. How might this historical event have affected people in other parts of the country?

   _____

   _____

Name_____

Salt of the Earth

Salt is such a common element that we don't often think about its source. Historically, salt has been used for preservation. It preserves food so it doesn't spoil. We season our food with salt.

The many uses for salt have made it a valuable commodity over the centuries. Entire economies have been built on the production and trade of salt. In ancient Rome, salt was used as currency. In some countries, roads were built specifically for the transportation of salt from mines to seaports. At various times in history, exclusive rights and taxes on salt have led to wars and revolutions. China, Africa, and India are countries that have all experienced conflicts over salt. Our own history in America is not immune to the value of salt. The Massachusetts Bay Colony held rights to produce salt for many years. The Erie Canal was built, in part, to transport salt.

Salt plays other cultural roles as well. It is used in religious rites for purification or offerings. Its value is reflected in language. When salt was used as currency during times of slave trade, people might say someone was "not worth his salt." We say a dependable person is "the salt of the earth."

Long ago, people obtained salt by boiling seawater. The water evaporated as steam, leaving behind nearly pure salt. Salt can also be mined from underground deposits as a mineral. Often these deposits were formed by past evaporation and shifts in rock layers over time. Most of the salt produced this way is in the form of rock salt. A third way of producing salt is a little more complex. A dome is erected over a salt deposit. The salt is drilled out of the earth and water is added to the salt to dissolve it. The resulting brine is then boiled causing the water to evaporate, leaving just the salt once again. Much of this salt is what we know as table salt.

Text Questions

1. Which of the following is not a method for mining salt?
   a. trading with other countries to obtain salt
   b. boiling salt water to cause evaporation
   c. mining salt out of underground deposits
   d. drilling salt and adding water to make a brine, then boiling the brine to evaporate the water

2. Which is a synonym for the word *commodity* as it is used in the second paragraph?
   a. money
   b. belonging
   c. merchandise
   d. stock

3. Which statement explains one reason why salt is a valuable commodity?
   a. We season our food with salt.
   b. Salt is used for food preservation.
   c. Roads were built specifically for the transportation of salt from mines to seaports.
   d. Exclusive rights and taxes on salt have led to wars and revolutions at various times in history.

4. What does it mean to say someone is "the salt of the earth"?
   a. That person's language is seasoned with interesting words.
   b. That person knows how to save and preserve important things.
   c. That person is among the lower levels of society.
   d. That person is reliable, trustworthy, and dependable.

5. What are some other ways people use salt? Give examples to support your answer.

   _____

   _____

   _____

Name_____

Claiming the South Pole for Mankind

Roald Amundsen set out to claim the last uncharted place on Earth. He wanted to reach the South Pole. A few years earlier, he had sailed the Northwest Passage of the Arctic. While making plans to continue his exploration of the far north, he learned of others who also planned to explore the North Pole. Secretly, he began planning an expedition to the South Pole instead.

His journey was not without rival. Captain Scott of England was also headed for the South Pole. Amundsen knew about the competition, so he started out early before the weather was truly manageable. As a result, a few of his dogs died and members of his team suffered from frostbite. Amundsen retreated to his base and assessed the situation, deciding to wait until the spring before attempting the journey again.

Amundsen brought valuable experience to the expedition. He had sailed previously as part of a scientific voyage. The ship became stuck on the pack ice, and the crew was forced to stay in the Antarctic until winter was over. Amundsen used the experience to make observations that later led to improvements in polar equipment. He spent three years in the Arctic, which further prepared him for his conquest of the South Pole. He learned from the native people and applied their survival techniques to his own experience.

The winter layover gave Amundsen and his crew the opportunity to carefully scrutinize and test supplies and equipment. He went over every detail, keeping in mind the harsh environment they would face.

Finally, at the start of the Antarctic spring, Amundsen set out with four companions to make the eight-hundred-mile trek across the ice. He reached his goal in December of 1911. The crew set their country's flag on the geographical South Pole. Before they left their polar camp for home, Amundsen left a letter for Scott. Scott found and kept the letter, which later proved the success of Amundsen's expedition.

Text Questions

1. What organizational structure did the author use for this passage?
   a. compare and contrast
   b. problem and solution
   c. chronological
   d. cause and effect

2. Which statement describes one way in which Amundsen was experienced for such a polar expedition?
   a. He had been part of a crew that got stuck in a temperate zone during the winter.
   b. When stuck on pack ice, Amundsen ignored his situation.
   c. Amundsen had never spent any time in polar environments.
   d. He learned from native people in the Arctic and applied their survival techniques.

3. What is the purpose of the last paragraph?
   a. It summarizes the success of Amundsen's expedition.
   b. It gives details about the journey.
   c. It explains why Amundsen was successful.
   d. It describes the competition Amundsen faced.

4. What does it mean to say Amundsen *assessed* the situation?
   a. He set a value on what it would be worth to reach the South Pole.
   b. He set the amount of tax future explorers would have to pay.
   c. He determined how important it was to him to beat Captain Scott.
   d. He evaluated the significance of the factors that had caused them to turn back.

5. What might we learn today from comparing and contrasting Amundsen's and Scott's polar expeditions?

_____

_____

Name_____

Braces

Dental braces are also called orthodontic braces. They are used by dentists to realign and straighten teeth. In doing so, they can also improve dental health.

Braces have been used for thousands of years. Mummies have been found with braces. Ancient Greeks and Romans were found to have used braces. Over two hundred years ago, teeth were first extracted to help with overcrowding. Once teeth weren't as crowded, braces could straighten teeth. A century later, wires and mild pressure were used to move teeth. During the twentieth century, the application and use of braces continued to be perfected.

About forty years ago, dentists developed braces that can be worn on the inside of the teeth and, therefore, are not visible. These were called lingual braces. One example was iBracesTM, made with the aid of digital computer imaging. They were popular for over a decade. Then, tooth-colored ceramic braces were invented. Ceramic braces can be any color the patient chooses.

Years ago, dentists learned that plastic dental appliances could aid in making minor movement changes in teeth. Not too long ago, two people who had braces developed a system using clear plastic molds. They applied 3D computer-aided technology, and the "Invisalign®" method was developed. The dental community was skeptical. Neither of the two inventors were dentists, nor had they studied in the field of medicine. Regardless, over the last ten years or so, these clear plastic brace appliances have become very popular.

Where will orthodontics go from here? Imaging continues to improve. Creative, new methods allow various metals to be used, such as nickel titanium alloys. Braces will soon be worn for shorter periods of time. They will continue to be less visible and will obtain better results.

Text Questions

1. What is the primary purpose of braces?
   a. to make teeth white
   b. to extract extra teeth and prevent overcrowding
   c. to improve dental health
   d. to straighten teeth

2. What does the word *realign* mean as it is used in the text?
   a. to remove
   b. to make straight again
   c. to bring components of a machine into proper coordination with each other
   d. to come to agreement again

3. Which of the following is not specifically a development in medical technology?
   a. Tooth extraction helped with overcrowding.
   b. Wires and mild pressure were used to move teeth.
   c. Dentists developed braces that can be worn on the inside of the teeth and, therefore, are not visible.
   d. 3D computer-aided technology was used to develop a system using clear plastic molds.

4. What is the purpose of the first paragraph?
   a. It describes the history of early braces.
   b. It gives details about the development of orthodontic technology.
   c. It introduces the topic with a general statement of purpose.
   d. It summarizes the topic and considers future development.

5. In what ways might braces improve dental health? Give examples to support your answer.

_____

_____

Name_____

Microbursts

One of the least known weather phenomena is the microburst. It is a wind occurring beneath certain clouds that is strong enough to damage buildings, knock down trees, and crash airliners. Microbursts can produce wind speeds higher than 175 miles per hour, which is greater than many tornadoes and hurricanes.

Microbursts are fast-moving columns of air that develop beneath cumulonimbus clouds. These are the same clouds that produce thunderstorms and tornadoes. The air develops quickly and moves straight down from the cloud base. It then moves along the ground and curls back up and around in a circular manner. They are also called "cloud sneezes."

Since 1975, eight airline crashes have been directly attributed to microbursts. The crashes occur during either takeoff or landing. Let's consider an aircraft landing as an example. Flying low in its approach, the aircraft encounters the outer area of the microburst's curling wind. The pilot senses the updraft and forces the nose of the airplane down to compensate. As the airplane continues, it encounters the strong downdraft at the center. Because the nose of the plane is already lowered, the down-moving air forces the nose rapidly lower, and the pilot is unable to compensate. This forces the airplane down to the ground.

The most famous microburst airline crash was Delta Airlines Flight 191 at Dallas/Fort Worth International Airport on August 2, 1985. The airliner crashed on approach due to a microburst, and 137 passengers and crew members died.

As a result of that airliner crash, the government sought ways to detect microbursts with various types of weather radar. This and other precautionary measures have lessened the number of airline crashes due to microbursts.

Text Questions

1. What primary structure does the author use to organize the thoughts in the text?
   a. cause and effect
   b. compare and contrast
   c. problem and solution
   d. sequential or chronological approach

2. What is the main idea of the second paragraph?
   a. how people can avoid a microburst
   b. how a microburst is formed
   c. how a microburst affects airlines
   d. how the government has stopped microbursts from happening

3. Based on what you read in the text, what is the best way to describe the effect a microburst has on aircraft?
   a. A microburst limits a pilot's visibility during landings.
   b. The extreme shifts in wind direction make it difficult to navigate the plane safely.
   c. The force of wind in a microburst prevents a plane from taking off.
   d. The extreme wind speeds knock aircraft sideways, and they crash.

4. What does the word *compensate* mean as it is used in the third paragraph?
   a. to make equitable with financial return
   b. to make amends
   c. to counteract or make allowance for
   d. to navigate

5. According to the text, what is the most dangerous aspect of a microburst?

   _____

   _____

Name_____

Invasive Plant Species

Invasive species are plants that have an adverse effect on specific habitats and regional areas. They can either be plants nonnative to an area, plants brought in by various means, or plants that damage native plants. In the United States, the government lists at least 50 invasive plant species not native to this country.

Invasive plants have certain traits that enable them to take over native plant species. Some traits include fast growth, fast plant reproduction, and the ability to alter their growth to adapt to the local conditions. Invasive species compete with native plants, keeping them from thriving.

Kudzu is a plant species indigenous to Asia that was introduced to the United States in the late 1800s. This vine was introduced for ornamental purposes and erosion control. In the southern United States, it has been growing at a rate of 150,000 acres per year, faster than it can be sprayed with herbicides or mowed to prevent its spread. In China, the plant dies back every winter, but it thrives in the warmer southern United States climate. It impacts the economy in various ways, such as disrupting power lines.

Native to Europe, Scotch broom is a member of the pea family. It looks similar to a bush and has yellow flowers. In Europe, it is grown for ornamental reasons and livestock feed. The plants compete with seedlings in reforested areas of the Pacific Northwest and California, resulting in lost timber production.

There are several ways to curtail invasive species. They can be controlled by mechanical means, such as mowing. Other solutions rely on the use of chemicals. Herbicides, insects, competitive plants, and biological agents can all be used in the fight against invasive species.

Invasive plant species are a challenge for authorities, a drain on the economy, and a danger to habitats. The first step in managing this aspect of the environment is education and awareness.

Text Questions

1. Which of these is an example of an invasive plant species?
   a. sagebrush
   b. kudzu
   c. crabgrass
   d. juniper

2. What does the word *indigenous* mean as it is used in the third paragraph?
   a. needy
   b. existing naturally
   c. belonging
   d. original

3. Which of these is <u>not</u> a trait of an invasive plant species?
   a. grows quickly
   b. reproduces quickly
   c. allows native plants to grow
   d. alters growth to adapt to local environmental conditions

4. The author probably wrote this passage to . . .
   a. inform the reader about invasive plant species.
   b. explain the origins of Scotch broom.
   c. describe how herbicides are used in agriculture today.
   d. tell how to get rid of weeds in your garden.

5. Why are invasive plant species a concern?

_____

_____

Name_____

Twins

Twins run in families, right? Not necessarily. There is more than one type of twins, and various factors influence each. Generally speaking, identical twins occur at the same rate across the population, regardless of external factors such as age or race. Fraternal twins occur at different rates, depending on various factors. Scientists have found indications that fraternal twins are hereditary, and the age of the mother and number of previous births may also be factors. Some cultural groups have a higher rate of twinning than others.

Identical twins occur when one egg is fertilized and splits into two separate zygotes. A zygote is the cell that is formed when an egg is fertilized. These two entities may remain in one amniotic sac to receive nourishment during development, or they may split into two separate sacs.

The other type of twins is fraternal, which occurs when two separate eggs are fertilized at the same time. This type usually develops in two separate sacs.

Because identical twins begin as a single cell, they receive the same genes; they are genetically identical. Therefore, they will always be the same gender and share many physical characteristics and personality traits. However, approximately 20 percent of our genes manifest themselves differently, which accounts for slight variations that may be observed in identical twins. Scientists have also observed instances in which the right side of one twin will match the left side of the other. These are called mirror twins.

Fraternal twins begin as two individual cells, and therefore, each has a unique set of DNA. The resulting offspring will look no more alike than any other siblings. As such, they may be the same gender or different.

Research on twins continues, due in part to our fascination with identical DNA, as well as the information to be learned regarding the unique DNA code of every human.

Text Questions

1. Which title would be a good alternative for this text?
   a. "One Versus Two"
   b. "Seeing Double"
   c. "DNA Studies"
   d. "Across Cultures"

2. Which word or phrase best describes twins who may not be the same gender?
   a. identical twins
   b. mirror twins
   c. fraternal twins
   d. cloned twins

3. What causes identical twins to look alike?
   a. They are born at the same time.
   b. They share the same amniotic sac.
   c. They are the same gender.
   d. They share the same DNA.

4. Based on the context, what can you infer the word *hereditary* means?
   a. passed down genetically from one generation to the next
   b. sharing the same beliefs about what causes twins
   c. inherited as a legal heir
   d. something explained by one's ancestors

5. Based on what you read and your background knowledge, in what other ways might studies of twins benefit scientific research?

   _____

   _____

Name_____

"Beam Me Up"

"Beam me up, Scotty" is a famous line from a science-fiction television show. In the show, a "transporter" was used to move people from one place to another. Could this science fiction soon become a reality?

Recent technology has made it possible to transport small particles, known as photons, from one location to another. This is called quantum transport. Currently, its application is confined to electronics, but the theory has been proven possible.

The laws of physics may make it impossible to ever build a transporter that will send a human from one location to another. Such a machine would have to send atoms at the speed of light. It would also have to map and send trillions of atoms to include DNA mapping. Then, the molecules would have to be put back in place perfectly without so much as one being out of place.

Two other problems are dematerializing and materializing. The breaking apart of a human into subatomic particles seems highly unlikely. An even greater problem is putting the person back together in a different location.

In actuality, if such a "transportation" machine could be built, it would likely work more like a three-dimensional fax machine. In other words, the person would be scanned and a replica assembled elsewhere.

At this time, the quantum transportation of humans seems extremely unlikely. However, at least one physicist—science writer Michio Kaku—thinks further development of the technology could happen in the future. Although, he says, it will first take centuries of work.

Even in our lifetimes, technology has developed in unimaginable ways. Who knows what the future holds?

Text Questions

1. What is the closest meaning of the word *quantum* as it is used in the second paragraph?
   a. a quantity or amount
   b. a portion
   c. a complex math problem
   d. a fixed elemental unit of energy

2. According to the passage, what is one problem with the theory of quantum transport as applied to human transportation?
   a. Trillions of atoms would have to be reassembled precisely.
   b. The theory was first applied to electronics.
   c. Scientists don't have a good understanding of DNA.
   d. It would require a fax machine.

3. What question does the passage explore?
   a. How would one construct a transporter?
   b. Why do we need transportation technology?
   c. Is technology from science fiction really possible?
   d. What does the future hold for humans?

4. Which of the following statements is true?
   a. The laws of physics make it possible to build a transporter that will send a human from one location to another.
   b. Recent technology has made it possible to transport small particles, known as photons, from one location to another.
   c. It is possible to break apart a human into subatomic particles.
   d. It is easy to predict ways in which technology will develop.

5. Based on what you read, what would be the advantages and disadvantages of developing this kind of transportation technology?

   _____

   _____

59

Name_____

The Science of Color

For centuries, color has been used in the science of psychology. Psychology is defined as the scientific study of the human mind and its functions. Scientists have discovered that color can affect mood and perception. As a result, it can affect how people behave.

We often perceive red as a power color. In business negotiations, wearing a bit of red may give one party the edge over the other. On the other hand, blue indicates a willingness to collaborate. If reaching a compromise is important, wear a bit of blue when you meet with the other person.

Studies show that the color of the medicines we take affects what we think about how they will affect us. Studies indicate that blue-colored street lights lead to less crime in that area.

People who are often cold prefer warmer colors, as it makes them feel warmer. Those who are often warm more often select cooler colors to feel cooler.

Sports teams who wear black have a tendency to have more penalties called on them. And people who wear all black are sometimes viewed in a negative way.

Specific colors affect our moods in various ways. Red raises energy and creates excitement. Yellow reminds us of sunshine and creates joy and happiness. However, babies cry more in bright yellow rooms. Blue is calming and makes people relax. Green relieves stress and is the easiest for eyes to look at. Dark purple creates a feeling of luxury. Orange creates excitement and enthusiasm and is used in workout rooms.

As researchers learn more about color and how it affects us, they will also be able to dispel common myths about color. For example, pink may not have a calming effect on aggressive prisoners, and blue food may indeed suppress the appetite.

Color creates moods, emotions, and may even play a role in explaining our personalities.

Text Questions

1. Which paragraph gives information about how specific colors affect our moods?
   a. the first paragraph
   b. the third paragraph
   c. the fifth paragraph
   d. the sixth paragraph

2. Why do scientists study the effect of color on people's moods and behavior?
   a. People need to understand more about how the brain functions.
   b. Color doesn't make any difference in how people behave.
   c. We can use information from color research to orchestrate specific situations to achieve desired results.
   d. We can determine the difference between true and false statements about color.

3. According to the text, which color might make a person feel happy when studying?
   a. yellow
   b. purple
   c. black
   d. orange

4. What does the word *collaborate* mean as it is used in the second paragraph?
   a. to make someone upset
   b. to work together
   c. to cooperate with an enemy invader
   d. to be on the same sports team

5. Based on what you read, what do your favorite colors say about your personality? What evidence have you seen of this in your life? Give an example to support your answers.

   _____

   _____

Name_____

Audiology

Just as technology for audio devices (such as headphones) has advanced, medical tests and treatments for hearing impairments have also improved. Recent developments now make it easier to test a person's ability to hear. Audiology is the study of hearing.

When someone has his or her hearing evaluated, one or more tests may be done. Some tests check the physical health of the auditory system. The ability of the eardrum to withstand pressure is also measured. Other exams assess a person's ability to hear sounds at different frequencies. Finally, there are tests that measure the ability to hear and understand normal speech.

Sounds are measured in decibels, or loudness. They are also measured in frequency, which is the number of vibrations per second. The sounds of everyday life can be mapped on a grid based on these two levels. For example, a dog barking might register at 70 decibels but at a low frequency. Birds chirping are a higher-pitched tone, or higher frequency, but often low on the decibel scale.

People with normal hearing can hear whispers and other sounds at low decibel levels across all frequencies. Those with mild to moderate hearing loss may have trouble hearing high or low pitched sounds, or sounds quieter than 60 or 70 decibels. Hearing loss may be conductive, which relates to how the ear functions. Sensory loss has to do with the ear's ability to transmit sound waves through the inner ear. Neural loss happens when there is damage to the nerve that transmits sound messages from the ear to the brain.

The sounds of human speech are dispersed across the decibel and frequency grid in a shape referred to as the "speech banana." People may be able to hear sounds in this range but may have trouble understanding speech when there is a lot of background noise.

Medical advances in testing and treatment options make it possible for people to be less hindered in everyday life due to hearing loss.

Text Questions

1. What does the word *impairments* mean as it is used in the text?
   a. damages
   b. solutions
   c. spoils
   d. frequencies

2. What is the main idea of the fourth paragraph?
   a. It explains how hearing loss is measured.
   b. It describes different types of hearing tests.
   c. It describes the types of hearing loss.
   d. It summarizes how people hear speech.

3. What is one factor that can make it difficult for people to hear the sounds of speech?
   a. People normally speak too quietly for the human ear to hear.
   b. Some people wear earphones to listen to music.
   c. There is no medical treatment for hearing loss.
   d. Background noise can interfere with hearing.

4. Which of the following describes how sounds are measured?
   a. loudness, or decibels
   b. frequency, or pitch
   c. transmission of sound waves
   d. both a and b

5. How will advances in audiology benefit people?

_____

_____

Name_____

How Are Mountains Formed?

Many people enjoy the mountains for the recreational opportunities they offer, but have you ever wondered how all those mountains were formed? Not all mountains were made by the same process; each way produces different types of rock and other characteristics.

Some mountains are considered volcanic. This type of mountain occurs mostly around the Pacific Ocean. A tectonic plate along the rim of the ocean is forced under another plate. As it sinks down, it melts and is then pushed up through the crust and erupts as a volcano. A good example of this is the Cascade Range along the western coast of the United States. Another type of volcanic mountain is called a hotspot. As a plate of Earth's crust moves over molten material, the magma pushes to the surface through weak spots in the crust and forms into a mountain. One good example of this is the Hawaiian Islands.

Another type of mountain is a folded mountain. This occurs when two plates collide, and one rides on top of the other. The plate that goes over the other will fold and buckle and create mountains. The Rocky Mountains in the western United States are one example of this type of mountain range.

Mountains can also be formed when a plate of Earth's crust breaks. One side rises to create mountains, and the other drops and creates a valley. This process is called fault block and can be seen in the Sierra Nevada Range in the western United States.

Mountains are also formed by erosion. When a volcano erupts, large areas of volcanic magma can be created. Water and winds wear down the material to form mountains. Sometimes, these mountains are called plateau mountains. The Catskills in New York fall into this category.

Left in their natural state, mountains provide us with valuable natural resources as well as recreation.

Text Questions

1. Which of the following is <u>not</u> a term to describe a process by which mountains are formed?
   a. volcanic
   b. folded
   c. fault block
   d. glaciation

2. What do all types of mountains have in common?
   a. They are the result of shifting tectonic plates.
   b. They are formed by changes in Earth's crust.
   c. They are covered by forests.
   d. They are formed from magma beneath the surface of Earth.

3. What does the word *collide* mean as it is used in the third paragraph?
   a. attack one another
   b. come into contact with each other
   c. come into conflict
   d. have opposing views

4. Which of the following is an example of mountains formed by erosion?
   a. the Rocky Mountains
   b. the Hawaiian Islands
   c. the Catskills
   d. the Sierra Nevada Range

5. Why do people study the formation of mountains?

   _____

   _____

Name_____

Telling Time Without a Clock

Telling time without a clock may seem like an impossible task, but with a little bit of practice, you can use the sun, moon, and stars to gauge the approximate time of day (or night).

During the day, the sun appears to travel across the sky. If you are in the northern hemisphere, face the south. As you look south, the sun rises in the east (from your left) and sets in the west (to your right). If the sun is halfway between your left and right, it is noon. If it is before noon, you can approximate how far the sun is between the east and the center. If it is after noon, look for the position of the sun between the center and the right. Knowing the time of sunrise and sunset will help you to be more accurate.

At night, you can also tell time by using the stars. To do this, we use the North Star. Locate the two stars that are at the edge of the Big Dipper, farthest away from the end of the handle. Those two stars line up with the North Star. That line also acts as the hour hand on a 24-hour clock, where midnight (0) is straight up and noon (12) is straight down. Just to the left of 0 is sunset to midnight, and to the right is midnight to sunrise. If it is winter, deduct one hour for each month before March 7 to adjust. If it is after March 7, add one hour per month. The reason for this is that March 7 is the date on which the star clock points to exactly midnight.

It gets a little more complex during certain times of the year, especially if daylight saving time must be considered. Although using constellations and planets to tell time is an interesting and potentially useful skill, next time you need to know the time, it may be easier to just look at your watch!

Text Questions ···

1. What background knowledge would be helpful to better understand this passage?
   a. living in a place where the skies are clear
   b. understanding what causes day and night and how it is affected by the time of year
   c. knowing the names of the constellations
   d. having a precise watch

2. Based on what you read, how could you find east and west if you didn't have a compass?
   a. observe the position of the sun
   b. look at the Big Dipper
   c. wait until lunchtime, and look directly overhead
   d. look at a map of the constellations

3. What does the word *gauge* mean as it is used in the text?
   a. a standard scale of measurement
   b. the thickness or capacity of something
   c. a device for measuring something
   d. a way of estimating something

4. Which of the following affects our ability to tell time by looking at the sky?
   a. where we live
   b. the time of year
   c. the time of day
   d. the position of the north star

5. Why do you suppose we adjust the time when looking at the stars at different times of the year?

   _____

   _____

   _____

Name_____

Physics for Our Amusement

Amusement parks are full of science—the science of physics. The rides we enjoy are machines that operate under the laws of force and motion. A ride called Gravitron gives us a clue as to which principles of science are at work.

A vector describes distance as well as direction, such as two meters northeast or five miles northwest. For a vector quantity, the direction is measured in terms of an angle. In this case, the angle is between zero degrees (north) and 90 degrees (east). Velocity measures the distance per unit of time or how far an object travels in a specific amount of time. If something accelerates, it changes speed during that period of time, affecting the total distance traveled.

These principles apply to the Gravitron ride in terms of how force is applied and how it affects the riders. Newton's first law of motion states that if an object is moving with a constant velocity, the forces exerted on that object will add up to zero. During the ride, the machine moves in a circle, so that riders are constantly changing direction. As they change direction, the velocity constantly adjusts, resulting in acceleration, even though the machine maintains a constant speed.

The second law of motion states that if there is acceleration of an object, force will be exerted on that object. Therefore, when the ride speeds up, the riders experience force. In the spinning chamber, the net acceleration force is toward the center of the room.

At this point, Newton's third law of motion becomes a factor. It states that if one object exerts force on another object, that object will exert an equal and opposite force. The spinning chamber exerts the force of circular acceleration on the riders. However, their bodies exert an equal and opposite force on the wall in such a way that they don't move away from the wall.

Contrary to what some believe, physics can be fun!

Text Questions

1. In which direction is the force of acceleration on the ride?
   a. toward the center of the room
   b. away from the center of the room
   c. in the direction the room spins
   d. toward the floor of the room

2. What is the main idea of the second paragraph?
   a. It introduces how an amusement park operates on the laws of physics.
   b. It explains terms that are used to discuss force and motion.
   c. It defines the laws of motion.
   d. It explains the effect of the ride on the people who ride it.

3. Which law of motion explains why the riders are forced back against the wall of the spinning chamber?
   a. Newton's first law of motion
   b. Newton's second law of motion
   c. Newton's third law of motion
   d. the law of velocity

4. What does it mean to say the riders experience *acceleration*?
   a. They feel as if they are changing direction.
   b. They feel as if they are going faster.
   c. They feel as if they are going slower.
   d. They feel as if they are getting heavier.

5. In what other amusement park rides might one observe the laws of force and motion? Give examples to support your answer.

_____

_____

Name_____

Antarctic Ice Sheet

The South Pole is on the continent of Antarctica. On average, this land mass is windier, drier, and colder than any other place on Earth. It also has some of the highest elevations on Earth. The polar ice cap is larger than that of the North Pole. The ice cap covers almost the entire continent, stretching across millions of square miles. The permanent ice is thousands of feet deep.

Scientists believe the icing of Antarctica is ancient. The ice has glaciated, which means it has formed from snow. Snow falls onto the ice, which is compacted, and then becomes glacial ice. Ice streams flow downhill towards the ocean. Large amounts of glacial ice move out over the ocean creating ice shelves. The ice shelves can break off, creating icebergs that eventually melt. The glacial ice floating on the ocean surface is called sea ice. In contrast, land ice covers the continent.

Recently, researchers have been trying to determine if the ice of Antarctica is growing in size or shrinking.

They want to understand what factors might be causing any changes in the ice.

For several years, the amount of land ice has been decreasing. Scientists attribute part of this to recent record warm winter events. A section of the northern ice shelf recently collapsed, alarming scientists. The Antarctic sea ice has grown over that same time period. While both the growth and loss of ice is occurring at a very slow rate, the exact reasons for the changes are not fully known. Changes in temperature and winds play an important role. It is also possible this is a normal Earth weather cycle, and the loss of ice is typical. It's too early for scientists to be certain about long-term causes and effects.

Generally, scientific observations indicate lower temperatures in the Antarctic than in the Arctic. For now, climate changes appear to be affecting the South Pole more slowly than the North Pole.

Text Questions

1. What is the primary comprehension skill you need to understand this passage?
   a. compare and contrast
   b. making inferences
   c. making connections
   d. cause and effect

2. What does the word *collapsed* mean as it is used in the text?
   a. suddenly broken into pieces
   b. lost its defenses
   c. shrunk in size
   d. melted quickly

3. Which statement best summarizes the current state of land ice in Antarctica?
   a. The Antarctic sea ice has grown over that same time period.
   b. The exact reasons are not fully known, but changes in temperature and winds play an important role.
   c. Both the growth and loss of ice is occurring at a very slow rate.
   d. For several years, the amount of land ice has been decreasing.

4. Which of the following statements is an opinion?
   a. The polar ice cap is larger than that of the North Pole.
   b. It is also possible this is a normal Earth weather cycle, and the loss of ice is typical.
   c. Large amounts of glacial ice move out over the ocean creating ice shelves.
   d. The glacial ice floating on the ocean surface is called sea ice, as opposed to land ice, which covers the continent.

5. What do you predict will happen next in the study of climate changes in the Antarctic?

   _____

   _____

Name_____

Garbage to Good

According to the Environmental Protection Agency, Americans create millions of tons of garbage per year. Of this amount, one-third is either recycled or composted, and just over 10 percent is burned. Over half of all garbage goes to landfills. Landfills are costly to build and can be a source of pollution.

Efforts have been made to reduce the impact of solid waste on landfills. Many innovative uses for waste have been developed. One use for waste is to create energy.

When waste is used to create energy, it results in heat or combustible gases. The most common way to achieve this result is through burning, or incineration. But burning waste can have hazardous emissions, so strict guidelines must be followed. Before such guidelines were developed, gas emissions were heavily acidic. This created acid rain that was harmful to both people and structures. Now filters are used, which make emissions cleaner than most home fireplaces.

Aside from the emissions that are produced, the residue that remains can be highly toxic and must be handled very carefully.

The most common method of creating energy from incineration is by using the heat created from burning the waste to boil water. The boiling water powers steam generators, which make electricity for homes and businesses.

Today, new ways of using waste to create electricity or fuels are being developed. They are very complicated. One example is the thermal method, which uses extremely high temperatures without burning.

The goal is to transform waste into a benefit for us. Sweden has run out of waste to transform into energy. Now they purchase waste from other countries. Perhaps someday we will also be able to make total use of our waste.

Text Questions

1. According to the passage, how much of our garbage goes to landfills?
   a. one-third
   b. 10 percent
   c. 50 percent
   d. more than half

2. What is does the word *innovative* mean as it is used in the second paragraph?
   a. renewed
   b. new methods
   c. altered
   d. unimaginative

3. What is a positive result of burning waste?
   a. Burning waste results in heat or combustible gases.
   b. Without filters, burning creates acid rain that is harmful to both people and structures.
   c. The heat created from burning waste is used to boil water, which powers steam generators to make electricity.
   d. The residue that remains from burning waste can be highly toxic and must be handled very carefully.

4. Which title would be a good alternative for this text?
   a. "Waste Equals Energy"   c. "A New Way to Generate Heat"
   b. "A Model Country"   d. "Burning Our Garbage"

5. What do you think it will take for our country to implement effective uses of waste material? Give reasons to support your answer.

   _____

   _____

Name_____

The Exciting Field of Engineering

The field of engineering is growing right along with technology. Careers in engineering include designing, planning, and building new things. For example, architectural engineers design, plan, and construct buildings and other structures. Engineering can also be applied to mechanics, medicine, chemistry, and transportation. Another way to think of engineering is that it has to do with products, machines, systems, or structures. In other words, almost everything in our world relies on engineering at some level.

Engineers are curious about how and why things work. An engineer will receive special training in a specific aspect of engineering. Often, things have more than one type of system, or aspect of design. For example, designing and building a computer requires electrical engineers for the wiring and circuitry. Someone has to design and create the hardware. This includes the keyboard, screen, and case that hold the electronic components. Software engineers contribute an operating system and programs that make the computer perform the desired functions.

Regardless of the end product, engineers follow a process that is sometimes called research and development. People want something that will perform a certain way or complete a specific task. Often, when something new is being created or built, a problem will be identified. Engineers need to assess the problem and find a way to solve it. Once the end result has been identified, engineers think about a design that might meet the requirements. Then they consider the available resources. Brainstorming possible solutions is part of the process, with ideas sketched and developed. The feasibility of each idea must be considered, as well as the advantages and disadvantages. Which idea seems most likely to accomplish the end result?

Engineers then build a model or prototype. This helps them envision how the final product will perform. At this stage, it's easier to test the outcome and make changes as needed.

Every time you modify a bicycle, change a character in an interactive game, or build a ramp for a skateboard, you're using engineering principles!

Text Questions

1. Which of the following is <u>not</u> listed as an area of engineering?
   a. chemical
   b. electrical
   c. architectural
   d. resourceful

2. Which type of critical-thinking skills are mostly discussed in this passage?
   a. problem and solution
   b. cause and effect
   c. collaborating with others
   d. using reasons and evidence to convince others of a viewpoint

3. What does the word *feasibility* mean as it is used in the third paragraph?
   a. possibility
   b. ability to be carried out
   c. creativity
   d. practicality

4. What is the main idea of the third paragraph?
   a. It defines and introduces the field of engineering.
   b. It gives an example of a product that requires different types of engineering.
   c. It gives an overview of the process of product development.
   d. It suggests practical engineering applications.

5. Describe a time when you used principles of engineering and followed the process described in this passage, from identifying a problem to designing a proposed solution.

_____

_____

Name_____

How We Use Corn

We might not think of corn as an ancient grain, but it is. For centuries, it has been known and grown as maize in the Americas. Scientists believe the original wild form of corn has long been extinct. Through the years, corn has been cultivated to the point where it is truly a domesticated crop. In its present state, it does not grow and propagate without man's intervention.

Corn is prepared and eaten in a variety of ways. Cornmeal is made by grinding whole corn. It is used for making cornflakes, cornbread, pancakes, and tortillas. Cornstarch is made from the endosperm. It is used in baby powder, as a thickening agent, and in some plastics. Corn syrup is made from cornstarch. As a sweetener, it is cheaper to produce than sugar cane.

We produce a biofuel, or gas, from corn called ethanol. Cars can run on a mixture of gasoline and up to 10 percent ethanol. Oil is also produced from corn and is used for many things, including cooking. After oil is pressed from corn, the germ remains. It can be used for livestock feed or added to industrial glue for strength.

Plastic made from corn uses over 50 percent less fossil fuels than other plastics. These products also decompose more easily in landfills. A common use of such plastic is food containers and disposable silverware.

Other uses for corn and its products include snack foods, medicinal teas, cosmetics, and soap. Corn is used in agriculture for animal bedding, feed, and fertilizers. We use corn products to make matches and carpet. It's even in batteries and crayons! It's hard to imagine a crop worldwide that has as many uses as corn.

Text Questions

1. What does the word *domesticated* mean as it is used in the text?
   a. to adapt wild plants for human use
   b. a crop grown in home gardens
   c. tamed for human use
   d. to bring a crop from a foreign country and make it commonly grown in your own country

2. What might be a factor leading to the development of such a variety of uses for corn?
   a. It takes little effort to process.
   b. It has been a cultivated crop for hundreds of years.
   c. It grows in any climate.
   d. It only grows in certain areas.

3. According to the passage, which of the following is not a product made from corn?
   a. batteries
   b. crayons
   c. light bulbs
   d. matches

4. Which statement best illustrates how corn products are beneficial to the environment?
   a. In its present state, corn does not grow and propagate without man's intervention.
   b. As a sweetener, corn syrup is cheaper to produce than sugar cane.
   c. Corn can be used for livestock feed or added to industrial glue for strength.
   d. Plastic made from corn uses over fifty percent less fossil fuels than other plastics and decomposes more easily in landfills.

5. Based on what you read, how would you describe the economic impact of corn cultivation?

   _____

   _____

Name_____

International Space Station

Even before man first walked on the moon in 1969, people have long been fascinated with the idea of living in space. Some might argue that we have finally achieved that dream. The International Space Station has been orbiting Earth for more than a decade and has had over two hundred visitors. This orbiting laboratory conducts ongoing experiments and observations. It also serves as a spaceport for space shuttle launches. Astronauts conduct spacewalks from the station as well.

As an international laboratory, the space station helps foster goodwill and facilitates the sharing of information between countries. Since its launch in 1998, many countries have participated in the space station's mission. The United States, Russia, Canada, and Japan have all participated. Other countries from the European Space Agency have also been involved.

There have been several expeditions to the space station, with crew members staying in space for various lengths of time. Experiments and observations lead to the development of new technology and applications. For example, cell-phone cameras, water filtration and purification, and medical imaging are all related to space exploration. Crew members have had the opportunity to research principles of gravity that lead to advancements in the medical field, as well as making future space travel easier.

The current expedition is gathering data related to how long-term space missions affect the human body. They are undergoing vision, cardiac testing, and exercise in the gym. Experiments are also being conducted to help develop methods to use radiation in Earth's atmosphere to supplement the space station's power supply. Crew members inventory and investigate gear from the station and incoming shuttles.

Text Questions

1. According to the passage, which country is <u>not</u> involved in the space station's mission?
   a. United States
   b. Russia
   c. Egypt
   d. Japan

2. What is the purpose of the first paragraph?
   a. It describes the work of the current expedition.
   b. It explains the purpose of the space station.
   c. It describes the international scope of the space station.
   d. It explains how the space station contributes to our study of asteroids.

3. Which of the following space station research has benefitted people on Earth?
   a. using radiation from Earth's atmosphere as a power supply
   b. the development of cell-phone cameras, water filtration and purification, and medical imaging
   c. researching principles of gravity to simplify future space travel
   d. serving as a spaceport for space shuttle launches

4. What does the word *facilitates* mean as it is used in the text?
   a. makes it easier   c. discourages
   b. requires no effort   d. makes it faster

5. Do you think the benefits of space exploration outweigh the risks and costs? Give evidence to support your answer.

   _____

   _____

Name_____

Geothermal Energy

As we continue to rely on oil and natural gas for energy, our supply of these precious resources is constantly decreasing. Now, more than ever, it is critical that we find and utilize new and existing forms of alternate energy. Geothermal energy is one such alternative.

Geothermal energy is heat stored in Earth below the surface. It is both sustainable and clean, generating no pollution. It uses no fossil fuels.

Natural hot water at or just below Earth's surface has been used for thousands of years. Geothermal heat has been used to directly heat buildings for more than one hundred years. Water is pumped through pipes underground, and the heat is then pumped through a building.

In this country, most geothermal hot-water reservoirs are in the western states, Alaska, and Hawaii.

The earth is very hot beneath the surface. Deep inside Earth's core, it is hot enough to melt rock. Some magma rises towards the surface of the earth and heats large pots of water, also under the surface.

There are different ways to use geothermal energy. In direct thermal energy, hot water very near Earth's surface is piped directly into buildings providing heat. That same water is then pumped back down and reheated. A geothermal heat pump uses cooler water even closer to Earth's surface. Geothermal power plants use water or steam from deep under the ground. The heat source is brought to the surface, and water vapor is used to turn turbines to generate electricity.

As with most forms of alternative energy, the initial costs are very high. But once in place, it is very efficient to sustain. In fact, a geothermal heat pump in a house will pay for itself within ten years. Given the intensity of the heat within the earth, geothermal energy offers a largely untapped energy source.

Text Questions

1. What does the word *intensity* mean as it is used in the last paragraph?
   a. that there is more heat than the earth can hold
   b. extreme temperatures
   c. amount of energy within the earth
   d. the amount of force exerted

2. Which of the following is not a method of using geothermal energy?
   a. direct thermal energy
   b. geothermal heat pumps
   c. hydroelectric power plants
   d. geothermal power plants

3. Which statement best explains why geothermal energy is currently of interest?
   a. Our supply of precious resources is constantly decreasing.
   b. Geothermal energy is heat stored in the earth below the surface.
   c. Some of the magma rises towards the surface of Earth and heats water also under the surface forming large pools.
   d. The initial costs of geothermal energy are very high.

4. According to the text, how do geothermal sources provide us with energy?
   a. Water turns turbines, which generate electricity.
   b. Hot water or steam from under the surface of the earth provides water vapor, which turns turbines that generate electricity.
   c. Boiling water is kept in reservoirs to provide heat.
   d. Heat is used to start a fire, which sparks an engine to provide power.

5. Based on what you read, what are some reasons for and against further development of this alternate energy source?

_____

_____

70

Name_____

Football for Kids

Should children be allowed to play football, or is it just too dangerous? Recent studies and polls suggest a surprising shift in attitude. According to a recent online poll conducted by Robert Morris University, nearly half (40 percent) of the one thousand respondents believed tackle football should be banned below the high-school level. Additionally, a recent news report stated that Pop Warner football participation had declined by almost 10 percent over a two-year period.

The main issue for banning football relates to head injuries, specifically concussions. A concussion is a brain injury that usually has immediate symptoms. Often a player sits out a game until the concussion has healed. However, medical reports document that some concussions occur without any symptoms and thus go untreated. If left untreated, a concussion can lead to even more health issues. Research also suggests that players who sustain too many concussions are more

likely to acquire permanent brain injuries. Not all football players suffer from concussions, but some would argue that even one is too many.

Instead of a ban on football, many argue that better helmet technology could reduce the number of concussions. Routine physicals and better detection of concussions could further ward off long-term problems.

Another solution to combat concussions is to alter the way players can tackle. New rules redefine the ways a player can be tackled, by either pushing a ball carrier out of bounds without fully extending the arms, or by fully wrapping the player with both arms before bringing him or her to the ground.

Football is an American game that has been played for more than one hundred years. It has millions of fans and is played throughout the United States across nearly all age levels. Should it be banned?

Text Questions

1. What percentage of those polled believed football should be banned?
   a. 50 percent   c. 45 percent
   b. 40 percent   d. 51 percent

2. What is one reason the author gives for not banning football?
   a. Football is a new sport in the United States.
   b. Students do not know how to tackle correctly.
   c. Players could use flags instead of tackling.
   d. Better helmet technology could prevent head injuries.

3. Which is a synonym for the word *combat* as it is used in the text?
   a. fight
   b. agreement
   c. war
   d. oppose

4. Which of the following is the main issue leading people to suggest a ban on football for younger grades?
   a. Younger students don't understand the game.
   b. Fewer children are playing Pop Warner football now.
   c. There is concern that too many players receive head injuries.
   d. Players may get injured more than once.

5. How would you answer the question at the end of the article? Give reasons and evidence to support your answer.

   _____

   _____

Name_____

Men on Mars?

In our ongoing quest to explore the place in which we live, we have reached beyond Earth into outer space. First, people dreamed of traveling to the moon. That has been accomplished. Now, scientists at NASA are investigating what it would take to send people to Mars.

According to NASA, a primary concern with a Mars landing is astronaut safety. Mars lacks the ozone layer of Earth's atmosphere, increasing the amount of solar ultraviolet radiation that reaches the planet. Scientists also want to learn more about the chemical aspects of the Martian soil before exposing people to that environment. Also, more studies need to be conducted on the prolonged effects of low gravity on the human body. After spending several weeks in space on shuttles or the space station, some astronauts reported experiencing blurred vision. Finally, there is the question of the psychological effect of being so far from Earth for an extended period of time.

Currently, NASA plans to use robots to explore the Martian environment. Robots will analyze the radiation in the atmosphere and search for water resources. Before humans travel to the red planet, technology will need to be developed for descent and landing to keep the level and effect of g-forces safe for humans.

Why are agencies such as NASA putting time and money into research? In the past, the development of technology for the space program has had benefits here on Earth. Some areas include medicine, recycling, solar energy, and others.

News sources cite reports of people signing up to go to Mars, a multibillion-dollar venture. Why? Humans are, by nature, explorers, and the pull to the unknown is strong to the human spirit. Those who take a slightly more scientific approach would like to investigate possible life forms on Mars. They wonder what Mars can teach us about Earth.

Text Questions

1. Which of the following is <u>not</u> a concern for astronaut safety?
   a. ultraviolet radiation
   b. psychological effects
   c. low gravity
   d. improved vision

2. How would you describe the structure the author uses to organize the text?
   a. argumentative
   b. persuasive
   c. narrative
   d. informative

3. What is a synonym for the word *cite* as it is used in the last paragraph?
   a. commend
   b. mention
   c. summon
   d. rehearse

4. What is the main idea of the third paragraph?
   a. It explains the technology we will need to go to Mars.
   b. NASA will study Mars before sending a manned space flight.
   c. Space technology benefits people here on Earth.
   d. People like to explore the unknown.

5. What other issues can you think of that might be involved in sending manned space flights to Mars? Give reasons and examples to support your answer.

   _____

   _____

Name_____

The Philippines

The nation of the Philippines is an archipelago. That means the nation is a group of islands. More than 7,000 islands make up the nation, but only about 2,000 are occupied. The capitol of the nation is Manila, on the island of Luzon. Manila has over 1.6 million people in the city—the most people per square mile than any other major city in the world. Almost 100 million people live in the Philippines.

During the 16th century, the Spanish landed and made Manila the capital of the Spanish West Indies. Since then, the Filipino people have fought for independence from various nations including Spain, Japan, and the United States. Today, the Filipinos have their own democracy under President Benigno Aquino III.

The Philippines is on the Pacific Ring of Fire and has many natural disasters. Every year, the nation has an average of between six and nine typhoons that hit land. The last major typhoon was Typhoon Yolanda, which was the strongest typhoon ever recorded on land. Many were killed or injured, and hundreds of thousands more people were displaced after high winds and floodwaters destroyed their homes. An average of twenty earthquakes also occur daily, although most are not felt.

Because of their varied past, the Philippines is a mix of East, West, Spanish, and Asian cultures. The two official languages of the Philippines are Filipino and English. Their colorful culture makes the Philippines a popular tourist destination.

Text Questions

1. According to the text, what type of land form is an *archipelago*?
   a. a mountain range
   b. a chain of islands
   c. a series of canyons
   d. a large glacier

2. Which natural disaster does the Philippines not experience?
   a. typhoons
   b. earthquakes
   c. floods
   d. tornadoes

3. According to the text, what is one reason the Philippines is a popular tourist destination?
   a. There are millions of people in the Philippines.
   b. Many countries have influenced the culture of the Philippines.
   c. Some of the islands are uninhabited.
   d. It is exciting to witness a typhoon.

4. What is the best way to define a *typhoon*?
   a. a violent tropical cyclone
   b. a snow storm
   c. a large wall of water
   d. a meteorite

5. How might the current democracy have an effect on the people and culture of the Philippines?

_____
_____
_____
_____

Name_____

United States Spy Agencies

Many people have heard of the Federal Bureau of Investigation (FBI) and the Central Intelligence Agency (CIA). The United States actually has 16 different spy agencies. It is a very complicated and complex group, and they report to different departments within the government.

The National Geospatial Intelligence Agency analyzes geospatial information. People working for this group look at images such as missile-launching sites. They study geography and terrain. Their research provides combat support for the Department of Defense.

Another agency assesses foreign nuclear weapons programs. It is called the Office of Intelligence and Counterintelligence. Intelligence is information that agencies collect, analyze, and distribute in response to government leaders' questions and requirements. This agency serves an important role in the intelligence community. It also provides scientific expertise, analysis, and technology.

The National Reconnaissance Office designs spy satellites for the government. Then they build and operate the satellites. They also gather satellite information.

Along similar lines, the National Security Agency provides "signals intelligence." This means they intercept signals between people or countries. They have the ability to break codes. Who, why, and how they are signaling are of vital importance. They are also responsible for the safe transmission of our own secret signaling.

With so many different intelligence agencies, it is difficult yet important that they all cooperate and share information with each other. The work they do can win or lose wars or even prevent wars from happening. Even in peacetime, their efforts protect citizens all around the world. Four separate agencies have been created just to ensure our network of spy and intelligence information flows smoothly between the various groups.

Text Questions

1. Which agency designs and manages spy satellites?
   - a. National Geospatial Intelligence Agency
   - b. Office of Intelligence and Counterintelligence
   - c. National Reconnaissance Office
   - d. National Security Agency

2. In which paragraph will you find the definition of *intelligence* as it is used in the text?
   - a. the first paragraph
   - b. the second paragraph
   - c. the third paragraph
   - d. the fifth paragraph

3. In what way are the different agencies expected to interact with one another?
   - a. They need to cooperate and share information.
   - b. They need details about what each agency is doing all the time.
   - c. They need to compete to see which agency is doing the best job of protecting the United States.
   - d. They need to present a united front to other countries.

4. What is the best meaning of the word *intercept* as it is used in this passage?
   - a. to hinder
   - b. to see or overhear
   - c. to cut off between two points
   - d. to seize or take

5. What is one of the main roles of the United States Intelligence agencies? Why is this important? Give reasons and evidence to support your answer.

   _____

   _____

   _____

Name_____

Word of the Year

One of the most famous dictionaries in the world is the *Oxford Dictionary*. Its trust and reliability for the spelling and usage of words is without equal. But how does a word get into this dictionary?

Scholars and others use a variety of methods to investigate potential new words. One way is to collect them from the Internet. Words are also obtained through technical journals, song lyrics, and other sources.

When words begin to show up in various ways, with increasing frequency, they are then scrutinized more carefully. Formerly, words that might be useful to writers were considered as potential new entries. That has changed, and now the words have to appear first in oral language to then be considered.

In the past, words had to be used for several years before being included in a dictionary. In today's digital age, however, words are sent worldwide in minutes, and usage increases in scope much more quickly.

The *Oxford Dictionary* has an annual "Word of the Year." A word-of-the-year selection team, consisting of lexicographers, dictionary editors, and consultants, chooses the word. They use the *Oxford Dictionary's* New Monitor Corpus, a research program that collects around 150 million words of current English in use each month, using automated search criteria to scan new web content.

The Word of the Year for 2013 is *selfie*. It is the term used when a person takes his or her own photo using a phone, tablet, or other device. The word was first noticed in 2003. In 2013, the use of the word grew tremendously and was selected. Past Words of the Year include *sudoku, podcast, carbon footprint,* and *unfriend*.

Text Questions

1. If the prefix *lexico-* means "word or words" and the suffix *-graph* means "written," what can you conclude the word *lexicographer* means?
   a. a person who searches for words
   b. a dictionary
   c. a person who compiles a dictionary
   d. a person who creates words

2. Which of the following does <u>not</u> play a role in the selection process for Word of the Year?
   a. current usage
   b. increasing frequency
   c. use on the Internet
   d. words students need to know

3. Why are new words added to the dictionary?
   a. to expand the size of the dictionary
   b. to help people who are learning to speak English
   c. to keep current with the Internet
   d. to reflect current usage and growth of oral language

4. What does the word *technical* mean as it is used in the text?
   a. referring to a particular science or profession
   b. showing technique or skill
   c. according to principles or rules
   d. including specific or formal points

5. Based on the criteria described in the passage, what word would you suggest for Word of the Year? Why?

   _____

   _____

   _____

75

Name_____

Global Warming

A widely debated subject in the last decade is global warming. Have humans really caused our planet to become warmer?

Scientists agree that global temperatures have risen by about one degree Fahrenheit over the last 150 years. In parts of the Arctic, the temperature has risen about two degrees. However, temperatures have fluctuated over that time span as well.

Due to limited data, scientists use several strategies to approximate temperature changes. Tree rings and sediment layers from oceans and lakes provide us with clues. Drilling cores through Earth's polar ice sheets also gives us information regarding the past thousands of years.

However, some scientists question if such evidence is valid. Some argue the data and computer-enhanced climatic programs are too vague to make definite claims regarding global warming. They note major temperature fluctuations throughout history. These changes are unrelated to anything man-made and could be just another weather cycle.

As a result, the debate continues as to whether or not any global warming is caused by man and if anything can or should be done about it.

The term "greenhouse gases" refers to changes in the atmosphere caused by human activity. Regardless of such gases contributing to global warming or not, from an environmental perspective, reducing these gases is a wise course to follow. One way to do this is to find alternate sources of energy other than burning coal. Emissions from automobiles, industrial plants, and power facilities can be more strictly regulated. Individuals can help by recycling and using environmentally friendly methods of travel.

The potential threat and reality of global warming is being taken seriously by scientists worldwide.

Text Questions

1. Which evidence is stated in the passage to support the theory of global warming?
   a. melting polar ice
   b. changes in animal populations
   c. rising temperatures worldwide
   d. decreased ozone in the atmosphere

2. What would be a good resource to learn more about this topic?
   a. a scientific climate research site
   b. a book about the Arctic
   c. a talk show on television
   d. your friends at school

3. In the second paragraph, what does it mean to say that temperatures *fluctuated* over time?
   a. They vary in different parts of the world.
   b. They change frequently.
   c. They changed dramatically.
   d. They rose and fell with the tides.

4. Which of the following statements is an opinion?
   a. Global temperatures have risen by about one degree Fahrenheit over the last 150 years.
   b. Drilling cores through Earth's polar ice sheets gives us information regarding the past thousands of years.
   c. Computer-enhanced climatic programs are too vague to make definite claims regarding global warming.
   d. There have been major temperature fluctuations throughout history.

5. What do you think should be done, if anything, to combat global warming? Give reasons and evidence to support your answers.

   _____

   _____

   _____

Name_____

3D Printing

Imagine you want to make the perfect plastic storage container for your locker or a drawer at home. You could take the measurements and go shopping, but it would be more convenient to simply enter the measurements into your computer and print it out at home. One cell-phone manufacturer is using this technology and making custom phone cases for customers with three-dimensional (3D) printers.

Additive manufacturing makes 3D printing possible. This ability to manufacture small items and parts is now a reality and will become more prominent in the years to come.

Surprisingly, the technology is approximately 30 years old. Early 3D printing started with a solid object, and a model was made by removing thin layers of material. Today, printheads deposit thin layers of liquid plastic or other materials onto a platform. In this way, material is added to make the model.

Materials such as metal alloys, plastics, aluminum, and stainless steel are used in three-dimensional printing.

Paper and ceramic powders are also used. Printers have been set to create a wide variety of objects. There have even been experiments to create human organs.

Making a 3D item is a multistage process. First, a CAD (computer-aided design) model is made of the object. From there the program is transferred to a printer-friendly version. The printer is then set to make the object.

As you might imagine, 3D printing can be very expensive. Some printers initially cost $250,000 and liquid plastic can be $800 per gallon, but technology has drastically reduced the price. Today, 3D printers that make items with dimensions of eight inches square are less than $30,000. Some small home printers can cost less than $1,000.

3D printing is intricate and powerful. It is expected to dramatically change manufacturing and consumer purchasing as we now know it.

Text Questions

1. What is the meaning of *three-dimensional* as it is used in this passage?
   a. It appears to be real.
   b. An object has depth in addition to height and width.
   c. It lays flat and cannot be measured in height.
   d. It can only be viewed with special glasses.

2. What tools does 3D printing require?
   a. a screwdriver and screws
   b. a computer and a printer
   c. a camera and film
   d. models and clay

3. According to the passage, which of the following is not a material used in 3D printing?
   a. wood
   b. ceramic powders
   c. plastic
   d. metal alloys

4. What is the purpose of the first paragraph?
   a. It explains the process of 3D printing.
   b. It gives details about why 3D printing will not work.
   c. It gives examples to introduce the topic.
   d. It gives examples to explain the process of 3D printing.

5. For what applications might 3D printing be useful?

   _____

   _____

   _____

Name_____

Is Recycling Worth It?

Some people claim recycling is the best way to conserve our raw natural resources. They believe that reducing waste will, in turn, reduce the amount of landfill space required. We primarily recycle plastic, glass, paper, and metal. It is said that recycling saves money, landfill space, and helps the environment. On the other hand, many people wonder if recycling is worth the effort.

One factor to consider regarding recycling is the cost. Those who argue against it wonder if it is cheaper to create more landfill space and bury the recyclables. It takes a lot of energy to recycle. The energy used in recycling processes can be both expensive and damaging to the environment by producing harmful greenhouse gas emissions.

Another cost factor is curbside recycling. It costs money and requires transportation. Vehicles create pollution. However, over the past few decades, the process has been streamlined. Now, in many cities, the process is less expensive.

Others argue that it depends on how many recyclables make it to the recycle stations. If more recyclables are on hand, it is more cost-efficient to sort and recycle the items into reusable materials. For example, plastics are coded based on their type. Often different types of plastics cannot be recycled together. Until recently, separating them by hand was very time-consuming and expensive. Now, plastics are cleaned and used together to make new types of products.

Another issue is the demand for recycled items. If the demand is low, the recyclables sit and begin to decay. The good news is that through new technology and new products, the demand for recycled material and items is on the rise. This makes recyclables more valuable and cost-effective to produce.

Inefficiencies and legitimate questions regarding recycling remain, but the processes have improved to the point that the cost-effectiveness has become clear. Recycling is better for the environment than producing from new, raw materials.

Text Questions

1. Which of the following is <u>not</u> a factor to consider regarding recycling?
    a. cost of producing recycled products
    b. amount of recyclable material on hand
    c. demand for recycled products
    d. the effort to put scratch paper in the recycle bin

2. Based on the passage, what can you infer happens to items that are not recycled?
    a. They are burned.
    b. They go to a landfill.
    c. They are left at the curb.
    d. They sit and remain in their present form.

3. In the fourth paragraph, what does it mean to say something is *cost-efficient*?
    a. It produces an end result.   c. It uses a minimum of expense.
    b. It works well.   d. It produces the desired effect.

4. How would you summarize the author's opinion in this passage?
    a. There are costs associated with recycling, but improvements in the process make it worth the effort.
    b. Recycling is too inefficient and doesn't do any good.
    c. It is too expensive to recycle, and we should put things in existing landfills.
    d. Plastics should always be sorted carefully.

5. What are some of the benefits of recycling? Explain how you know.

_____

_____

78

Name_____

The Homework Debate

Groans arise from students everywhere at the mention of homework. Over the years, many studies have pondered the question of how much homework is necessary.

The primary argument against too much homework is that it pressures children to learn too much too soon. The concern is that homework only prepares them for tests and more homework, not current life experiences. As a result, learning ceases to become meaningful at an early age. In addition, some studies have shown that too much homework too soon makes a student feel negative about learning. As a result, children might be less inclined to do things that will enhance their education. Some children come from home environments that make it difficult to complete assignments. Homework might not be as helpful for these students. One proposed solution to this would be offering a longer school day, but people are concerned about the potential negative impacts on students' health and family life.

The arguments against homework are strong and make valid points. However, homework can supplement student learning. Appropriate homework allows students to interact more with academic content. One of the arguments for homework says students should spend extra time engaging in academic content. This is based on research that shows a relationship between higher academic scores and time spent in academic content.

Homework does have value. Some studies suggest the current trend of more in-depth homework is producing lower scores. But other research shows that appropriate homework increases student achievement. The proper amount of homework has long been subject to debate and changing trends. The goal is to keep students challenged, keep them learning, and keep them motivated. In this modern age, new trends will continue to take shape. The question is, what will these trends be, and how will they affect homework?

Text Questions

1. What does the word *enhance* mean as it is used in the second paragraph?
   a. to improve the quality of
   b. to increase in value
   c. to make more attractive
   d. to improve the clarity of a photograph

2. Which of the following is a valid argument <u>for</u> homework?
   a. It prepares students for tests and more homework.
   b. Studies show that spending more time in academic content increases student achievement.
   c. Homework may have a negative impact on students' health and family life.
   d. Some students are unable to complete homework assignments at home.

3. Based on what you read, what can you infer about appropriate homework?
   a. It should be relevant.
   b. It should contain practice questions for the test.
   c. It should never offer any new learning.
   d. It should repeat only what students read in textbooks.

4. Which statement seems least like an opinion?
   a. Learning should relate to current life experience.
   b. Children might be less inclined to do things that would enhance their education.
   c. Homework does have value.
   d. The proper amount of homework has long been subject to debate and changing trends.

5. In your opinion, how will computers affect what students should learn and the homework they should be assigned?

   _____

   _____

Name_____

Meteorites on Earth

On February 15, 2013, a meteorite exploded over the Ural Mountains of Russia. The Chelyabinsk Meteor was estimated to be 49 feet wide and weigh 10 tons. Before crashing into Earth, it was traveling at over 41,000 miles per hour. That is nearly 60 times the speed of sound. The meteorite entered Earth's atmosphere at a great speed and shallow entry. It exploded in the air at a height of 76,000 feet, which is over 14 miles. The blast was 20 to 30 times stronger than the atomic bomb used in World War II. It was brighter than the sun.

More than one thousand people were injured as a result of debris from sonic waves caused by the explosion. More than one million square feet of building glass shattered. Some meteorite fragments fell in a reservoir outside the town of Chebarkul, but no people were struck by the meteorite or fragments. The crash left a 26-foot-wide crater in the ice.

How many meteors strike the Earth? No one knows how many impacts have occurred over time, but more and more recordings are being made. The Meteoritical Society and other agencies track meteorites that strike Earth's surface. At least two impacts were recorded for 2012.

A major impact event is one that could cause the end of civilization. Some scientists believe that 65 million years ago, meteor strikes were the primary cause of the extinction of dinosaurs. This violent event is now known as the Late Heavy Bombardment.

Every year, NASA publishes dates when meteor showers are visible. Meteors become meteorites when they impact Earth, which happens rarely.

Text Questions

1. What made the meteorite impact in 2013 newsworthy?
   a. its size
   b. its speed
   c. its explosion
   d. all of the above

2. Which of the following describes how the impact affected people?
   a. The meteorite entered Earth's atmosphere at a great speed and shallow entry.
   b. More than one thousand people were injured as a result of debris from sonic waves.
   c. Some meteorite fragments fell in a reservoir outside the town of Chebarkul.
   d. The crash left a 26-foot-wide crater in the ice.

3. You can tell from the context of this passage that *impact* means . . .
   a. to hit with force.
   b. to have an effect on.
   c. to strike together.
   d. the power of an event to produce changes.

4. What is the main idea of the third paragraph?
   a. It describes the meteorite impact in Russia.
   b. It describes specific effects of the Russian meteorite.
   c. It discusses how we keep track of meteorites.
   d. It summarizes how meteorites affected the dinosaurs.

5. How does studying astronomical phenomena such as meteors and meteorites benefit people?

   _____

   _____

   _____

Name_____

Electric Cars

Electric cars seem to be everywhere in the news. They do not cause as much pollution as gasoline-powered vehicles. This means they are more environmentally friendly. However, the source of their electricity may not be.

Electric cars are powered by electric motors instead of gasoline engines. The electric engine derives its power from a controller. This controller gets its power from rechargeable batteries. If you look under the hood of a gas-powered car, it has hoses and valves. Conversely, the electric motor has wires and electric motors.

The first electric car was made in Germany in 1888 and was popular for many years. Electric cars started gaining popularity again toward the end of the twentieth century. Today, most major auto manufacturers have at least one electric car in their product line. Others, such as Tesla, produce nothing but electric cars.

Electric cars do not produce greenhouse gas emissions. They are also nearly silent. One drawback is that they are more expensive to design and produce. This cost gets passed along to consumers. Another negative aspect of these cars is the challenge of disposing the old batteries.

Some gas-powered vehicles can go about 350 miles before refueling, but many electric cars have a range of about 65 miles before needing to be recharged. Although, one electric car has a range of 300 miles. Maintenance for an electric car is generally more expensive. The battery packs are scheduled for replacement every seven years and can cost thousands of dollars.

At home, it takes over twelve hours to recharge the batteries on an electric car, although at a charging station, it takes only about 20 minutes.

Electric car technology continues to improve. If we find answers for cost and environmental factors, they may someday be the most prevalent cars on the road.

Text Questions

1. Which is a synonym for the word *prevalent* as it is used in the text?
   a. dominant
   b. accepted
   c. frequent
   d. common

2. What is one way in which electric cars differ from gasoline-powered cars?
   a. Electric cars are less expensive.
   b. Electric cars need refueling.
   c. Electric cars create less pollution.
   d. Electric cars have a longer driving range.

3. Which statement describes why electric cars might <u>not</u> be better for the environment?
   a. They are nearly silent.
   b. The electric motor has wires and electric motors.
   c. Electric cars do not produce greenhouse gas emissions.
   d. The battery packs are scheduled for replacement every seven years and must be disposed of.

4. What can you infer from the passage about what affects the popularity of electric cars?
   a. They became more popular as people started becoming concerned about the environment.
   b. They became more popular when people had more money to spend on vehicles.
   c. They became more popular when more companies started producing electric cars.
   d. They became more popular when public charging stations became available.

5. What are some ways in which the technology for electric cars might be improved to make them a better alternative to gasoline-powered cars?

   _____

   _____

Name_____

Tree Climbing: Not Just for Kids

Some people delight in the simple pleasures of life, such as climbing a tree. Tree climbing is now offered as a physical-education course at a college in New York.

Students at the school were previously learning climbing skills on indoor climbing walls. However, the program claimed to offer outdoor education. In an effort to solve the problem, instructors investigated their options. Suitable rock-climbing opportunities were over one hundred miles away—too far to travel for a college course. Additionally, inclement weather could make rock climbing hazardous. Their area had an abundance of trees, and climbing trees has practical career applications. The solution was simple—a course in tree climbing! A course was soon designed to focus primarily on recreational tree climbing, lacking the time and expertise to focus on career training.

Whether as part of a college course or independently, certain factors must be considered when participating in a sport. Risk factors and safety concerns must be addressed. Climbers should maintain respect for the environment, seeking little or no damage to trees during the climbing process. To prevent damage to the tree and potential personal injury, climbers are encouraged to consider the overall health of the tree before embarking on their adventure.

One career application of tree climbing is forest canopy research. As concern about the environment grows, the field of conservation and research has continued to expand. Scientists now recognize and study forest characteristics in temperate and urban forests as well as the rainforest. Another practical application that requires a good understanding of tree structure is that of arborists. These are the people who trim trees for utility companies and private citizens. They help people in urban and rural areas manage trees wisely.

More than one institution offers tree-climbing courses, including the United States Forest Service. For some reason, people seem to love being in trees.

Text Questions

1. Which of the following is <u>not</u> a career application related to climbing trees?
   a. research and study of forest canopies
   b. trimming for utility companies and private citizens
   c. choosing a tree that is healthy for climbing
   d. wise management of forests and trees

2. What does the word *temperate* mean as it is used in the text?
   a. moderate in indulging in appetites
   b. self-restrained in one's actions
   c. reasonable and fair
   d. mild, as in climate

3. What was the author's purpose in writing this passage?
   a. to explain reasons people climb trees
   b. to describe in detail the techniques used to climb trees
   c. to describe the dangers of rock climbing
   d. to give reasons why people should not climb trees

4. Which of the following is <u>not</u> something to consider when tree climbing?
   a. the overall health of the tree
   b. risk factors and safety concerns
   c. participating in a college course
   d. ways to climb without damaging a tree

5. What other applications can you think of for tree climbing that would benefit society?

   _____

   _____

   _____

Name_____

Weather Is a Current Event

Weather is a current event. People talk about the weather more than almost anything else. Some hurricanes make national news, due to the loss of lives and the amount of property damage they can cause. Tornadoes also leave devastation in their wakes. These types of severe storms often affect a specific geographic area. However, weather that affects people across large geographic areas becomes a national weather event.

The winter storm that swept across the country in December of 2013 may not hold the record for amount of snow, but it made the news for the number of states that were impacted. Within the same two-to-three-day period, severe weather affected much of the nation. This included snow, ice, sleet, wind, and record cold temperatures. The Pacific coast saw rare snow—up to two inches in some places. The western United States received blasts of Arctic air accompanied in some locations by gusty winds. This led to dangerous wind-chill factors. The icy path of the storm stretched across

two thousand miles, affecting at least nine states. Temperatures were expected to drop considerably below normal across the Midwest and across the nation. The National Weather Service posted alerts for winter storm activity in the western and eastern United States. The eastern United States had a forecast for heavy snowfall. At the same time, an alert for extreme wind chill was issued across the Pacific Northwest and the Midwest. One news report listed effects of the storm in 23 states. That's almost half of the United States!

This winter storm example is no longer current, but weather affects us every day. Scientists and climate researchers constantly monitor temperatures and weather trends. Their goal is to predict the weather. Their forecasts and observations affect more than our daily activities. Climate data gives us information on national and worldwide trends, such as global warming. This, in turn, informs the choices we make as a people and a society.

Text Questions

1. Why did this story include a weather event that has already happened?
   a. It was an example to show how weather can affect many people at the same time.
   b. It was an example of an event that caused great property damage.
   c. It illustrated a current trend in climate or climate change.
   d. It made the national news.

2. What is the main idea of the third paragraph?
   a. It describes major weather events.
   b. It describes an example of a national weather event.
   c. It summarizes how weather is a current event.
   d. It describes ways weather affects us.

3. Which statement does not explain how weather is a current event?
   a. People talk about the weather more than almost anything else.
   b. The winter storm of 2013 made news for a number of states.
   c. Weather affects us every day.
   d. Scientists and climate researchers constantly monitor temperatures and weather trends in their efforts to predict the weather.

4. What does the word *devastation* mean as it is used in the text?
   a. emptiness
   b. destruction
   c. helpless
   d. overwhelmed

5. In what ways could weather and how it affects us be considered a current event?

   _____

   _____

   _____

Name_____

Travel of the Future

Sometimes, invention is born out of frustration as much as necessity. Elon Musk has been playing with a new form of high-speed transportation. He sees it as an alternative to current high-speed rail projects. Musk works with an electric car company and a solar energy company. He calls his invention the Hyperloop.

Using the Hyperloop, people would travel in pods through low-pressure steel tubes. The capsules would reach speeds of about 760 mph. Existing high-speed rail systems in Asia reach speeds of 300 mph.

One way to think about how the Hyperloop would work is to think about a roller coaster. It's possible the capsules would receive an initial boost of power from spinning steel balls. The momentum would move the pod toward an electromagnet that would pull the unit forward. The magnet would then repel the pod, sending it toward the next magnet along the track.

The efficiency of the system comes from a couple of factors. Pods would be suspended on a cushion of compressed air, which would reduce friction. Musk also plans to use solar energy to power his system, making it environmentally friendly. The solar panels would be mounted on top of the tubes.

The Hyperloop would be efficient up to distances of about 900 miles. Beyond that, air travel would probably be more cost effective. Initially, he would propose transit between San Francisco and Los Angeles. The commute time between the two cities would be reduced to a little over 30 minutes. The trip would cost commuters about $20. Musk's plans include elevating the system on pylons in close proximity to a major freeway. He says this would reduce the need for land acquisition, thus cutting down on the overall cost of the project.

Whether or not the Hyperloop is feasible, one thing is certain—it adds new interest to the ongoing debate about efficient transportation.

Text Questions

1. What is one factor that would increase the efficiency of the proposed system?
   a. It will only travel short distances.
   b. It would rely on magnetic principles.
   c. The pods would be lightweight.
   d. The pods would travel on a layer of compressed air which would reduce friction.

2. What does the word *acquisition* mean as it is used in the text?
   a. something that is obtained
   b. something that is shared
   c. something that is added to the system
   d. something that is given away

3. Which current method of transportation is most like the Hyperloop?
   a. airplanes
   b. light rail
   c. high-speed rail
   d. automobiles

4. Which paragraph gives an overview of the principles that could make the Hyperloop work?
   a. the first paragraph
   b. the third paragraph
   c. the fourth paragraph
   d. the fifth paragraph

5. Based on what you read, what is your opinion of the feasibility of the Hyperloop? Give evidence to support your answer.

   _____

   _____

   _____

Name_____

The State of Hawaii

In 1959, Hawaii became the fiftieth state. In recent years, there has been a movement in Hawaii to secede from the United States and become a separate country.

Over a century ago, Hawaii was a separate country with its own monarchy. During that time, American missionaries and landowners brought about many changes with respect to politics, culture, economy, and religion. As a result, a constitution was adopted. Much of the power belonging to the ruler was taken away. At the end of the century, a group of Marines threw out the last monarch of Hawaii. A few years later, Hawaii became a trust territory of the United States. Fifty years after that, it became a state.

Today, there is a movement among several groups in Hawaii to secede from the United States and return to a sovereign nation. Hawaii has a population of over one million. About 200,000 are native Hawaiians. Many believe they were wronged throughout their history and would like such wrongs corrected.

Do they have a legal case? Some say they do. A professor of international law said he believes the Hawaiian Kingdom Government has a valid claim. He claims that international law provides for sovereign governments. Such law defines this as people living on their land and asserting their rights. He believes this is what the Native Hawaiians are doing.

The state has set up the Office of Hawaiian Affairs. They have petitioned the federal government to allow some form of self-government on ancestral lands. This would be similar to some Native-American reservations.

What the Hawaiians seek to do has widespread international and national implications. It will take a while to reach solutions. Resolving the issues could involve both the Supreme Court and the United Nations. For the moment, Hawaii retains valid statehood, enjoying the rights and duties of a member of the United States.

Text Questions

1. What is the main issue discussed in the passage?
   a. whether Hawaii is currently a state
   b. whether the Office of Hawaiian Affairs is a valid organization
   c. whether Hawaii should become a separate entity from the United States
   d. whether the monarchy should have been overthrown

2. Which of the following was the final event leading to the United States' control of the islands?
   a. The Marines overthrew the monarch.
   b. Some people from the United States acquired land in Hawaii.
   c. There were more non-native people living there than native Hawaiians.
   d. A constitution was adopted.

3. A good way to find the answer to the second question is to . . .
   a. search online for articles containing similar information.
   b. reread the entire passage and look for clues.
   c. identify the order in which each statement occurs in the passage.
   d. reread the second paragraph and identify the main idea.

4. Which is a synonym for the word *implications* as it is used in the last paragraph?
   a. assumptions
   b. inferences
   c. suggestions
   d. involvement

5. Based on what you read, what is your opinion on the issue? Give reasons and evidence to support your answer.

_____

Name_____

Virtual Learning

Technology has been an important part of education for years, but the prevalent use of the Internet is now allowing people a new way to learn. It's one thing to take an online class, but it's quite another to receive live feedback. Welcome to a new level of online distance learning.

For at least twenty-five years, distance education has been used in remote rural areas to provide students access to educational opportunities. A district may not have enough students or funding to hire teachers for all subjects. Video conferencing makes one-on-one interactions possible. Many students now prefer video content, further engaging them in the learning experience. Online distance learning also offers students classes in advanced subjects.

Distance learning methods are being used in other types of lessons as well. Teachers can now offer virtual field trips. Students use the Internet to view places of study. Through a videoconference, they can listen to guides at the destination, which enriches the learning experience. Even though there is a cost, it may be considerably less than transporting students to actual locations.

Finally, remote-access technology allows students to collaborate with those in other geographic areas. Students can work together on a variety of projects and topics of common interest. There is little if any cost in these endeavors. Students are enthusiastic as they work with peers.

Various organizations now offer videos on demand. This might be the same as having a guest speaker visit a classroom to talk about a specific topic. Streaming video can make the live presentation available to a broader audience. This technology is being used in flipped classrooms. When teachers use this teaching method, they record the lesson content for students to view prior to the lesson. Class time is then spent discussing and answering questions about the topic of study.

As you know, the standard classroom doesn't change overnight. It is hoped that education will combine the best of existing teaching methods with distance learning technology. The goal is for students to receive the best learning experience possible.

Text Questions

1. What does the word *endeavors* mean as it is used in the text?
   a. pastimes
   b. jobs
   c. efforts
   d. computers

2. According to the passage, which of the following is <u>not</u> an application of distance learning technology?
   a. video conferencing
   b. virtual field trips
   c. participating in a classroom lesson with a teacher
   d. collaborative learning experiences

3. Which statement best describes a virtual field trip?
   a. Students take a field trip to learn about the Internet.
   b. Students participate in a video conference to view a place of study and listen to a guide at the destination.
   c. Students work together on a variety of projects and topics of common interest.
   d. Students watch a video of another class going on a field trip.

4. What happens in a flipped classroom?
   a. Students take turns teaching and presenting the lesson material.
   b. Students use interactive whiteboards to create flip charts about the topic of study.
   c. Teachers use a video conference to teach students because there are not enough students in each class.
   d. Students watch a video of the lesson content before class, then discuss and ask questions during class about what they learned.

5. Based on what you read, write an argument describing the advantages and disadvantages of distance learning. Give evidence to support your arguments.

_____

_____

Fiction

Contemporary
Realism

Fairy Tales
Folklore

Historical

Fantasy

Mystery
Suspense
Adventure

Name_____

Bearskin

A soldier discharged from the war found himself in dire straits. As he bemoaned his fate, a stranger with a cloven foot appeared. He offered the warrior wealth if he demonstrated his courage. After the soldier shot a bear, another condition was required. "You must not bathe or groom yourself for seven years. If you die, you are mine. If you survive, you will be wealthy and free all your life long." They concurred, and the soldier acquired the bearskin as a cloak. From that moment forward, the soldier was known as Bearskin. Bearskin wandered the countryside, providing liberally for the poor and requesting their prayers for his life. Each year, his countenance became more monstrous so that people were terrified.

Alone one evening, Bearskin heard awful groaning. A decrepit man wept violently outside. Bearskin's compassion persuaded the man to tell his story. Impoverished, the man had lost all his property and now feared he and his daughters would starve. Bearskin satisfied the man's debts, and out of gratitude, the man offered one of his daughters in marriage.

The eldest daughter ran shrieking in fright at Bearskin's appearance. The next oldest insisted she would rather wed their recent visitor, a bear masquerading as a human. The youngest daughter said, "Father, this benevolent man assisted you in your trouble. If you promised him a bride, your word must be kept."

Bearskin removed a ring from his finger and separated it into two pieces, giving half to the bride. "Preserve it carefully," he instructed. "If I return in three years, we will marry. If not, you are released, for I will have perished."

At the end of the seven years, Bearskin gladly received his garment and a satchel of gold from the stranger. Bearskin and his bride joined their halves of the ring. Upon learning this was the same Bearskin and that their youngest sister would be his bride, the two older sisters ran from the house in rage and jealousy.

Text Questions

1. What did Bearskin ask of the poor people?
   a. that they repay him when their circumstances improved
   b. that they pray he would survive the seven years
   c. that they give generously to others
   d. that they wander the countryside with him

2. What role does the scene with the old man and his daughters play in the development of the story?
   a. It shows that Bearskin had courage and compassion regardless of what people thought of him.
   b. It shows another example of Bearskin giving money away.
   c. It surprises the reader to learn the man had daughters.
   d. It shows the stranger trying to catch Bearskin in a trap.

3. What does the word *decrepit* mean as it is used in the text?
   a. frightened
   b. ill
   c. wealthy
   d. elderly

4. What is the main idea of the text?
   a. You cannot trust strangers.
   b. Appearances can be deceiving.
   c. Make sure other people keep their promises to you.
   d. It is important to be wealthy.

5. How would you describe the character of the youngest daughter?

   _____

   _____

Name_____

Puss in Boots

Once, a young man inherited nothing except a cat named Puss from his father's estate. The cat heard his owner lamenting his fate and said, "Do not worry; I will help you. Have boots made for me and give me a bag." The master complied.

Puss used the bag and boots to snare game. Each time, he requested an audience with the king, saying, "I present you a gift from my master."

One day, the king and his daughter went to the countryside. Puss said to his master, "Follow my advice. Go bathe in the creek."

The king happened by, and Puss cried out, "My master, the marquis is drowning!" Recognizing the cat who had bestowed so many gifts, the king commanded assistance. Puss mentioned that thieves had taken his master's clothes, whereupon the king offered a suit.

Dressed in royal finery, the marquis was so handsome that the king's daughter secretly admired him. Puss

carried out his plan, traveling ahead of the king's carriage. Coming upon men mowing a meadow, Puss said, "When the king arrives, say this meadow belongs to the marquis or else!" And so the men followed the cat's instructions.

The cat repeated this scenario so that the king marveled at the marquis's estate. Finally, Puss arrived at an ogre's castle. All of the property Puss had attributed to his master belonged to this ogre. The ogre could transform himself into any creature. Puss said, "I heard that you can change into the smallest animal, but I believe this is impossible." Accepting the challenge, the ogre immediately became a mouse. Puss pounced on the mouse and ate him up.

When the king saw the castle, he asked if it also belonged to the marquis. Charmed by the marquis and his property, the king offered his daughter's hand in marriage. Puss became a great lord and never had to hunt for mice again.

Text Questions

1. What is one character trait Puss's master displayed?
   a. honesty
   b. obedience
   c. helpfulness
   d. perseverance

2. Why did Puss take gifts to the king at the beginning of the story?
   a. He was hoping for a good meal from the king.
   b. He caught more game than his master needed.
   c. He laid a foundation for the rest of his plan.
   d. He won an inheritance for himself.

3. What is the theme or moral of the text?
   a. It is easy to trick others into believing what they don't believe.
   b. One must be wealthy to win the hand of a princess.
   c. It is always wise to deceive others.
   d. Diligence and ingenuity can pay off greatly.

4. What does the word *bestowed* mean as it is used in the text?
   a. applied
   b. given
   c. devoted
   d. carried

5. How might this story have played out if the cat's master had spoken for himself?

_____

_____

Name_____

Felicia and the Carnations

Felicia, a young maiden, ventured into the forest to fetch water for her carnations. They, along with a silver pendant, were her only possessions. A stately queen approached the maiden and inquired, "What brings you here at this late hour?"

"I desire fresh water for my flowers."

Startled, Felicia realized her pitcher was now gold and full of fragrant water. "Take it," the queen assured her, "and remember I am your friend."

Felicia thanked her and begged the queen to stay while she retrieved the flowers as a gift. Discovering her brother Bruno had taken the carnations and left a cabbage in their place, Felicia ran back to the queen and offered her the pendant instead.

Returning home, Felicia threw the cabbage out the window. To her surprise, the cabbage spoke, requesting to be replanted in the garden. The cabbage then told her

the flowers were hidden under her brother's mattress. Dismayed, Felicia went in search of her carnations.

In her brother's room, a fierce army of rats guarded the straw mattress. She sprinkled water from the gold pitcher over the rats, which caused them to hastily retreat to their holes. At that moment, her brother entered and violently dragged her outside.

The queen appeared, desiring to punish the lad for his treatment of Felicia. "I am not angry with him," Felicia said.

A handsome nobleman suddenly arrived, knelt, and kissed the queen's hand. "Felicia, your care has restored my dear son!" she cried. The queen explained how fairies had left her son among the flower garden. "When you gave me the pendant, I knew the spell would soon be broken. Now you may marry him and live happily ever after."

Text Questions

1. What were the maiden's only possessions?
   a. a pitcher and a head of cabbage
   b. a pendant and a pitcher
   c. a pendant and flowers
   d. flowers and a head of cabbage

2. What does the word *dismayed* mean as it is used in the text?
   a. upset
   b. apprehensive
   c. fearful
   d. alarmed

3. Why does the queen want to punish Bruno?
   a. He left her son in the flower garden.
   b. He didn't take care of Felicia's carnations.
   c. He brought rats into the house.
   d. He treated Felicia cruelly.

4. Of these options, which happened third?
   a. A nobleman kisses the queen's hand.
   b. The cabbage speaks to Felicia.
   c. Felicia ventured into the forest.
   d. Felicia's pitcher was turned into gold.

5. How would this story be different if told from Bruno's point of view?

_____

_____

Name_____

The Firebird

The tsar had a great treasure, a tree that bore delicious pears. Every night a pear was stolen from the tree, so one night he had his son, Ivan, guard the tree. That night, the magnificent firebird came. Although Ivan tried to snare it, he managed to catch only a feather. The tsar scolded Ivan for letting the thief escape and sent Ivan away to catch the firebird.

Ivan met a wolf in the forest, who agreed to take him to the firebird. He told Ivan of a wizard who had as prisoner a princess of incomparable beauty. "Do not gaze on the princess," warned the wolf, "for her heart has been turned to wood. You will fall hopelessly in love with her, but she will not return your feelings." Venturing into the castle alone, Ivan forgot the wolf's warnings.

Ivan soon learned that Baba Yaga had stolen the firebird. If Ivan rescued the firebird, the wizard would grant him the choice between the firebird and the princess. Transporting him to Baba Yaga's cottage, the wolf warned him again, "The firebird is fastened to a raven by a golden cord. Bring the firebird, but leave the cord."

Paying no heed to the warning, Ivan departed with the firebird and the golden cord. Immediately, the raven woke up squawking, causing Ivan to be captured.

Meanwhile, the wolf fetched the princess. She disguised herself as a peddler and tricked Baba Yaga. Then she rescued Ivan and the firebird.

Uncertain, Ivan debated whether to choose the firebird or the princess. The wizard attempted to turn Ivan's heart to wood, but he was freed by the princess's tears. Ivan granted the firebird its freedom, and it chose to accompany him back to the tsar's castle.

Ivan's sister poisoned him and the princess. Owing Ivan a favor, the firebird flew to the Fountain of Life for magic water to revive them. The tsar banished Ivan's sister, and Ivan and the princess lived happily ever after.

Text Questions

1. Why did the firebird retrieve magic water from the Fountain of Life?
   a. The firebird wanted to live forever.
   b. The tsar asked the firebird to go to the fountain.
   c. The wizard forced the firebird to go to the fountain.
   d. The firebird was grateful to Ivan for rescuing it.

2. What does the word *debated* mean as it is used in the text?
   a. discussing opposing reasons
   b. considering in one's own mind
   c. disputing in a meeting
   d. quarreling

3. What role does the firebird play in this story?
   a. It brings good fortune to Ivan.
   b. It is the tsar's greatest treasure.
   c. It tricks Ivan when he doesn't heed the wolf's warnings.
   d. It captures the wizard and holds him prisoner.

4. How does the first paragraph contribute to the main idea?
   a. It sets up the circumstances of the quest for the firebird.
   b. It introduces Ivan and shows the reader his personality.
   c. It explains why Ivan receives warnings.
   d. It shows the reader the choice Ivan must make.

5. The firebird inspired the logo design for the 2014 Winter Olympic Games in Sochi, Russia. How might what you learn about the firebird in this story relate to an athletic event such as the Olympic Games?

_____

_____

Name_____

Prince Ricky

At his birth, Ricky was so hideous that it was uncertain if he was human. A fairy granted him intelligence and the ability to give the same good sense to his beloved.

In another kingdom, twin princesses were born. One was very attractive but lacked common sense. The second was ugly, but the fairy bestowed on her such cleverness that no one would notice her appearance. The fairy could not increase the first princess's intelligence but granted her the ability to bestow beauty on anyone who pleased her. As they grew, the elder princess became less intelligent and more socially awkward. Meanwhile, the younger grew more unpleasant in appearance, but people were attracted to her wit.

One day, Prince Ricky approached the beautiful princess and asked, "You are so attractive; how can you be distressed? Beauty is a great advantage."

"I would rather have good sense," replied the princess.

Ricky described his ability to grant intelligence to the one whom he loved the most. He offered her sensibility in exchange for her agreement to marry him within a year. In her feeble-mindedness, she consented and immediately found herself able to converse with ease. Many suitors sought her attention, but she could not decide. As she pondered one particular suitor, she wandered through the forest where she first met Ricky.

The ground opened up, revealing mysterious preparations for a great feast. Learning it was for Ricky's wedding the following day, she suddenly remembered her promise to marry him. Just then he appeared. "Alas," she declared. "You should not have given me such good sense; I find it so difficult to make a decision."

"Aside from my appearance, is there any reason we should not marry?" Ricky asked. The princess conceded that everything about him pleased her, save his ugliness.

"You have the power to make me handsome," he stated, and he explained that if she loved him and desired him to be handsome, it would happen. And it was so.

Text Questions

1. What does the word *decision* mean as it is used in the text?

   a. judgment   b. choice   c. conclusion   d. determination

2. Who or what transformed Ricky's appearance?

   a. the fairy's enchantment
   b. the princess's desire that he be handsome and possess the willingness to love him
   c. the end of the one-year waiting period
   d. the ugly but clever princess

3. What is the theme or moral of the text?

   a. Beauty and brains do not go together.
   b. Your life will be happy if you are beautiful.
   c. People consider wealthy people to be attractive.
   d. Beauty is in the eye of the beholder.

4. Which three traits are portrayed in the tale?

   a. power, wealth, and fame   c. beauty, cleverness, and ugliness
   b. honesty, laziness, and hard work   d. power, beauty, and charm

5. Would you trade attractiveness for intelligence? Give reasons to support your answer.

   _____

   _____

   _____

Name_____

The Old Woman and the Doctor

An old woman became almost totally blind from a disease of the eyes. After consulting a doctor, she made an agreement with him in the presence of witnesses that she would pay him a high fee if he cured her. However, if he failed, he would receive nothing. The doctor prescribed a course of treatment and visited her on a regular basis to apply ointment to her eyes. With each visit, he took away with him some article from the house, until at last, when he visited her for the last time and the cure was complete, there was nothing left. When the old woman saw that the house was empty, she refused to pay him his fee. After repeated refusals on her part, he sued her before the magistrates for payment of her debt. On being brought into court, she was ready with her defense. "The claimant," she said, "has stated the facts about our agreement correctly. I promised to pay him a fee if he cured me, and he, on his part, promised to charge nothing if he failed. Now, he says I am cured; but I say that I am blinder than ever, and I can prove what I say. When my eyes were bad, I could see well enough to know that my house contained a certain amount of furniture and other things. But now, when according to him I am cured, I am entirely unable to see anything there at all."

Text Questions

1. Why did the woman refuse to pay the doctor?
   a. She claimed he charged her nothing.
   b. She claimed he had received his payment.
   c. She claimed he did not cure her.
   d. She claimed he stated the agreement incorrectly.

2. What role does the magistrate play in this story?
   a. He will determine the best way to fix the woman's eyes.
   b. He will perform a marriage ceremony.
   c. He will judge if a crime has been committed.
   d. He will determine if payment is due.

3. What does the word *prescribed* mean as it is used in the text?
   a. wrote down ahead of time
   b. wrote directions
   c. advised a medical treatment
   d. imposed rules

4. What is the moral of the story?
   a. Through evildoing, one loses any reward for the good he has done.
   b. We would often be sorry if our wishes were gratified.
   c. Wealth unused might as well not exist.
   d. Things are not always as they seem.

5. How would you rule if you were the magistrate? Give reasons to support your answer.

_____

_____

_____

_____

Name_____

Mercury and the Woodman

A woodman was felling a tree on the bank of a river when his axe glanced off the trunk, flew out of his hands, and fell into the water. As he stood by the water's edge lamenting his loss, Mercury, the god, appeared and asked him the reason for his grief.

Learning what had happened, Mercury dove into the river and brought up a golden axe, asking if it was the one he had lost. The woodman replied that it was not, and Mercury then dove a second time. Bringing up a silver axe, he asked the woodman if it was his. "No, that is not mine either," said the woodman.

Once more, Mercury dove into the river and brought up the missing axe. The woodman was overjoyed at recovering his property and thanked his benefactor warmly. Mercury was so pleased with his honesty that he gave the woodman the other two axes.

When the woodman told the story to his companions, one friend was filled with envy of his good fortune and was determined to try his luck for himself. So he went and began to fell a tree at the edge of the river and soon let his axe drop into the water.

Mercury appeared as before, and upon learning that his axe had fallen in, he dove in and brought up a golden axe. Without waiting to be asked whether or not it was his, the fellow cried, "That's mine, that's mine!" He stretched out his hand eagerly for the prize. Disgusted at his dishonesty, Mercury declined to give the fellow the golden axe. Mercury also refused to recover the one that had fallen into the river.

Text Questions ....

1. Why did the woodman grieve?
   a. His companion was dishonest.
   b. His axe fell in the river.
   c. His fortune was gone.
   d. His axe failed to fell the tree.

2. What is the moral of the story?
   a. Slow and steady wins the race.
   b. Much wants more and loses all.
   c. Honesty is the best policy.
   d. Betray a friend, and you'll often find you have ruined yourself.

3. What does the word *benefactor* mean as it is used in the text?
   a. someone who supports someone else in their endeavors
   b. someone who gives another person protection
   c. someone who protects someone from danger
   d. someone who helps another person financially

4. How does a mythological character interact with the first woodman?
   a. He comes to his aid.
   b. He expresses disgust at his dishonesty.
   c. He rewards the human for his good deeds.
   d. He settles an argument between the woodman and his companion.

5. Describe a time when you practiced honesty in a situation similar to that described in the story.

   _____

   _____

   _____

Name_____

The Bear and the Travelers

Two travelers were making their way through the countryside, when a bear suddenly appeared on the scene. Before the bear noticed them, one rushed to an oak tree alongside the road and climbed into the branches to conceal himself.

The other was not as nimble as his companion and saw it would be impossible to escape. Fearing he would be attacked, he threw himself flat on the ground with his face in the dust and feigned the appearance of death. The bear came up and sniffed all around him with his muzzle close to the man's ear, but the man kept perfectly still and held his breath. He had heard that a bear will not touch a dead body, and indeed, the bear took him for a corpse and went away.

When the coast was clear, the traveler in the tree descended and inquired of his comrade what the bear had whispered to him when he put his mouth to his ear. "He gave me worthwhile advice," the other said. "Never travel again with someone who deserts you at the first sign of danger."

Text Questions

1. Which evidence best supports the moral?
   a. The first traveler climbed a tree without assisting his comrade.
   b. The second traveler remained to fend off the bear to save his comrade.
   c. The second traveler pretended to be dead.
   d. The bear gave the second traveler worthwhile advice.

2. What happens as a result of the man pretending to be dead?
   a. The bear attacks him.
   b. The man whispers advice to the bear.
   c. The companion quickly climbs a tree.
   d. The bear walks away from what appears to be a corpse.

3. What is another way to state the advice in the story?
   a. Do not trust a friend who talks to bears.
   b. Misfortune tests the sincerity of friends.
   c. Do not travel with a bear.
   d. Misfortune comes to those who are cowardly.

4. What does it mean to say the second traveler was not as *nimble* as his comrade?
   a. He was not as alert.
   b. He was not as quick-witted.
   c. He was not able to move as quickly.
   d. He was not as lightweight.

5. Which traveler chose the best course of action? Give reasons to support your answer.

   _____

   _____

   _____

   _____

Name_____

The Stag at the Pool

One warm summer day, a thirsty stag went down to a refreshing pond to drink. As he bent over the surface, he saw his own reflection in the water and was struck with admiration for his fine antlers. At the same time, he felt nothing but disgust for the weakness and slenderness of his legs.

While he stood there looking at himself, a lion advanced from the forest. The lion crouched to attack, but the stag leapt away across the meadow. In the chase which ensued, the stag easily maintained a distance from his pursuer. The stag kept his lead as long as the ground over which he ran was open and free of trees. But as he approached a wooded area, his antlers became entangled in the branches. The lion quickly caught up with him, and the stag fell victim to the teeth and claws of his enemy. "Woe is me!" the stag cried with his last breath. "I despised my legs, which might have saved my life, but I reveled in my horns, and they have proved my ruin."

Text Questions

1. What does the word *ensued* mean as it is used in the text?
   a. made sure something happened
   b. succeeded at a task
   c. followed at a distance
   d. happened as a result

2. What is the moral of the story?
   a. Do not let danger sneak up on you.
   b. Those who are proud often meet with ruin.
   c. What is worth most is often valued least.
   d. Stay away from that which may easily entangle you.

3. What did the stag view as his most valuable asset?
   a. his agility
   b. his magnificent antlers
   c. his delicate feet and legs
   d. his ability to outwit pursuers

4. How does the setting affect the outcome of the story?
   a. The stag is vulnerable to the lion when crossing the meadow.
   b. The forest provides a place for the stag to conceal himself from the lion.
   c. The stag's antlers become entangled in the branches of the forest.
   d. The pond attracts the lion to prey on the stag.

5. Give an example of a time when you have observed the moral of this story in real life.

   _____

   _____

   _____

   _____

Name_____

Two Fables

The Donkey and His Purchaser

A man who wanted to buy a donkey set out across the countryside. Upon arriving at the market, he began to peruse the animals offered for sale. When he found one that pleased him, he made an arrangement with the owner to take the donkey home on trial to see what he was like. The man brought the donkey home and put him into his stable along with the other donkeys. The newcomer took a look around and immediately went and chose a place next to the laziest and greediest beast in the stable. When the master saw this, he put a halter on him at once and led him back to his previous owner. The man was surprised to see him back so soon and said, "What, do you mean to say you have tested him already?"

"I don't want to put him through any more tests," replied the master. "I could evaluate what sort of beast he is from the companion he chose for himself."

The Farmer and the Stork

A farmer set some traps in a field, which he had recently sown with corn, in order to catch the crows that came to pick up the seed. When he returned to look at his traps, he found several crows caught. Among them was a stork, which begged to be let go. It said, "You shouldn't harm me, for I am not a crow but a stork, as you can easily see by my feathers. I am the most honest and harmless of birds." But the farmer replied, "It's nothing to me what you are. I find you among these crows, who ruin my crops, and like them, you shall suffer."

Text Questions

1. Why did the stork suffer?
   - a. He flew with the crows.
   - b. He was caught in a trap with the crows.
   - c. He was eating the farmer's crops.
   - d. He was different from the crows.

2. What choice did the donkey make?
   - a. to associate with a lazy, greedy donkey
   - b. to obey his new master
   - c. to betray his owner at the market
   - d. to remain by himself in the stall

3. What does the word *peruse* mean as it is used in the first fable?
   - a. to read thoroughly
   - b. to examine in detail
   - c. to review
   - d. to analyze

4. What is the common theme, or moral, of the two fables?
   - a. Those who seek to please everybody please nobody.
   - b. Every man should be content to mind his own business.
   - c. Pride goes before destruction.
   - d. A man is known by the company he keeps.

5. What is your opinion of the master's test of the donkey? Did it enable him to judge the donkey's potential usefulness fairly and accurately? Give reasons to support your answer.

   _____

   _____

   _____

Name_____

Samar and the Tigers

One day, Samar's mama and papa presented him with a fine suit of clothes. Meandering through the jungle, Samar encountered a tiger, who declared its intention to eat him. "No, accept my scarlet coat instead." The tiger was quite taken with such a splendid coat and agreed.

A second tiger approached, licking its chops. "Breakfast time!"

"I don't think so," Samar said. "How about these exquisite shoes instead?"

"Of what use are they?" the tiger scoffed. "You have two feet, I have four."

"But these are ear-shoes. You'll be the finest tiger around." The tiger put them on and strutted off.

The next tiger announced that Samar would make a tasty morning meal. "Not so fast. Here, take my umbrella instead."

The tiger protested, saying he had no way to hold it.

"Grasp it with your tail. You'll be the envy of the jungle." Samar held out the emerald umbrella.

Another tiger confronted him, and Samar sighed. "I suppose you're as hungry as your comrades." He pondered what he could offer as all he wore were his plum-colored pants. Finally, he held out the trousers to the tiger. "You'll be oh-so elegant," he said. The tiger looked at him suspiciously, then reluctantly agreed.

Samar sauntered along, uninterrupted, when suddenly he heard ferocious growling. Creeping through the undergrowth, he peered out to see the tigers chasing one another around a date palm with a vengeance. They had quarreled over whose garments were the finest and left all of Samar's clothing piled in a heap. The tigers chased each other, jaws snapping at tails, until they became a blur and melted into a pool of golden tiger butter. Samar put his clothes on and scooped up the tiger butter to carry home to his mama. She made pancakes piled high with melted butter and warm syrup, which Samar devoured.

Text Questions

1. What does the word *vengeance* mean as it is used in the text?
   a. with great force or fury
   b. in retribution for an injury
   c. in punishment
   d. excessively

2. What happened to the tigers?
   a. They attacked Samar and devoured him.
   b. They quarreled and then resolved their differences.
   c. They chased each other and became a pool of melted butter.
   d. They were turned into tiger butter by Samar's mama.

3. Which article of clothing did Samar surrender first?
   a. his gloves
   b. his shoes
   c. his coat
   d. his pants

4. What is the main idea of the text?
   a. Samar's parents were proud of him.
   b. Samar's quick and clever responses in the face of danger saved his life.
   c. Samar's journey into the jungle was foolish.
   d. Tigers will fight over anything.

5. Describe the strategy Samar used to survive his encounters with the tigers.

_____

_____

Name_____

The Turtle and the Lizard

A turtle and a lizard went to a field to steal ginger. When they arrived at the field, the turtle said to the lizard, "We must be very still, or we will be caught."

The lizard tasted the ginger and, very pleased, said, "This ginger is delicious."

"Hush," said the turtle, but the lizard did not heed the warning. He spoke even louder, alerting the man and causing him to rush out to catch the robbers.

The turtle could not escape quickly, and so he lay perfectly still, escaping the man's notice. The lizard dashed away, and the man pursued him. When they were gone, the turtle went in and concealed himself under the man's coconut shell.

After chasing the lizard quite a distance, the man gave up trying to catch him and returned to his bamboo house. He entered and sat down on the shell.

The turtle clucked loudly, and the man jumped up to survey his surroundings. Unable to tell where the noise came from, he sat down again. The turtle called a second time, and the man again could not identify the source of the noise. The turtle continued, and the man grew so agitated at his unsuccessful attempts to isolate the sound that he died.

The turtle escaped and soon met up with the lizard again. They walked along until, observing some honey in a tree, the turtle said, "I will go first and get some of the honey."

The lizard couldn't wait and bolted ahead. When he seized the honey, the bees stung him. Continuing on, the turtle and the lizard found a bird snare, and the turtle said, "That is the silver wire that my grandfather wore about his neck."

The lizard rushed to get it first, but he was caught in the snare and captured until the trapper came and carried him off. Then the wise turtle went on alone.

Text Questions

1. Why did the turtle conceal himself under a coconut shell?
   a. He wanted to hide from the lizard.
   b. He wanted to wait until the lizard was gone to go get the ginger.
   c. He wanted to trick the man and escape.
   d. He wanted to use the coconut shell as a disguise.

2. How would you compare the approach of the lizard and the turtle to the events in the story?
   a. The lizard was hasty and selfish, while the turtle was patient and wise.
   b. The turtle stood up to danger, but the lizard ran away.
   c. They both exercised caution.
   d. The lizard hid from danger while the turtle escaped.

3. This tale is reminiscent of which fable?
   a. "The Fox and the Crow"   c. "The Hare and the Tortoise"
   b. "The Tortoise and the Birds"   d. "The Boy Who Cried Wolf"

4. What does the word *agitated* mean as it is used in the text?
   a. violent   c. interested
   b. disturbed   d. excited

5. Why does the author say the turtle is wise? Give evidence to support your answer.

   _____

   _____

   _____

100

Name_____

The Perfect Princess

In a lost kingdom, in a castle that is now crumbled ruins, a young monarch sat on his throne. Since his father's death not too many weeks prior, he now had full responsibility for his people. The king's thoughts were consumed with only the needs of his peasants, and daily he grew more weary. His mother noticed the pallor in his cheeks and how his once sparkling eyes were dim.

"I must find him a wife," she said to herself. "Someone who can help shoulder his burdens."

She secretly sent her most trusted knights out to comb the lands for the perfect princess. A year passed, and her men returned with dismal reports of the fair maidens.

With the coming of winter, the queen set out on a journey of her own, revealing her true intentions to her son. Disguising herself as an old gypsy woman, she traveled to a kingdom across the sea. Enduring bitter wind and snow, the ship finally made it to port, and the queen slowly found her way to the gates of the castle. However, after hearing her foreign accent, the guard sent her away. Day after day, the old woman returned to the castle until finally the princess insisted on allowing her to pass.

During this time, the queen caught a horrible cold. The princess took pity on her and patiently nursed the woman back to health. When the old woman's health was restored, the princess presented the queen with enough money to return to her homeland, sending her on her way with an escort on the fastest vessel. Upon her arrival home, the queen sent a messenger to the king of the kingdom across the sea, declaring her intentions: she wished her son to marry the princess who had treated her with such compassion. And so they were married, and together they ruled with a patience and kindness that had never been seen before.

Text Questions

1. What was the quality that convinced the queen that this princess should marry her son?
   a. cleverness
   b. compassion
   c. impatience
   d. wealth

2. When did the queen become ill?
   a. when she had to assume responsibility for the peasants in the land
   b. when she grew concerned about her son's health
   c. when she was waiting to gain entrance into the foreign castle
   d. when her son married the princess

3. What does the word *pallor* mean as it is used in the text?
   a. paleness
   b. illness
   c. fearfulness
   d. darkness

4. What happened when the queen decided to set out on a journey?
   a. She revealed her intentions to her son.
   b. She took several of her hand maidens along on the voyage.
   c. She disguised herself as an old woman.
   d. both a and c

5. Which fairy tale does this remind you of? Give reasons to support your answer.

   _____

   _____

Name_____

The Lynx and the Hare: A Chippewa Fable

One winter, a lynx, who was famished, met a hare in the woods. As food was very scarce in the barren woods, the lynx licked its chops as it eyed the hare. The hare, however, stood up on a rock and was safe from its enemy.

"Sweet hare," said the lynx kindly. "Come here, my little white one. I wish to talk to you."

"Oh, no," replied the hare. "I am afraid of you, and my mother told me never to talk to strangers."

"You are very pretty," answered the lynx, "and a very obedient child to your parents, but you must know that I am a relative of yours. I wish to send some word to your lodge. Come down and see me."

The hare was pleased to be called pretty, and when she heard that it was a relative, she jumped down from the place where she stood, and was immediately attacked by the lynx.

Text Questions

1. What does it mean to say the lynx was *famished*?
   a. It was going to be well-known.
   b. It was going to die soon.
   c. It was very hungry.
   d. It was no longer strong.

2. What convinced the hare to talk with the lynx?
   a. The lynx claimed to be a relative.
   b. The lynx was very handsome.
   c. The hare's parents said it was okay to talk with the lynx.
   d. The hare wanted to obey the lynx.

3. What is the moral of the story?
   a. All that glitters is not gold.
   b. Flattery will get you nowhere.
   c. Barking dogs seldom bite.
   d. Pride goes before a fall.

4. In which paragraph does the lynx give the hare reasons to trust?
   a. the first paragraph
   b. the second paragraph
   c. the fourth paragraph
   d. the fifth paragraph

5. What stories have you read or heard that are similar? Explain the similarities and differences.

   _____

   _____

   _____

   _____

Name_____

The Miserly Farmer

As a farmer carted pears to the market, a monk with a torn cap and tattered robe happened along and asked for one. The farmer repulsed him, but the monk did not leave, at which the farmer began to insult him. The monk said: "You have pears by the hundred in your cart. Giving away one will not injure you. Why are you so angry?"

The bystanders told the farmer that he ought to give the monk a pear, but the farmer refused. An artisan saw the whole affair, and since the noise annoyed him, he bought a pear and offered it to the monk.

The monk thanked him and said, "I do not have much, but I will not be miserly. I have beautiful pears, and I invite you all to eat them with me, but first I must have a seed to plant."

He ate the pear, then used his pick-ax to dig a hole and plant a seed. The seed sprouted and grew. In a moment, it had turned into a tree, which blossomed and soon bore large, fragrant pears. The monk climbed into the tree and handed down the pears to the bystanders. Then the monk cut down the tree, shouldered the trunk, and walked away.

At first, the farmer gaped and stared, entirely forgetting the business he hoped to do with his pears. When the monk had wandered off, the farmer turned around and discovered the pears in his cart had all disappeared; the pears the monk had divided had been his own. He looked more closely and noticed the handle of his cart had been recently chopped off. Enraged, the farmer ran after the monk. Turning the corner, he spied the missing piece from the handle tossed along the side of the road. He then realized the pear tree, which the monk had chopped down, had been his handle. The monk was nowhere to be found.

Text Questions

1. Why was the farmer enraged?
   a. The bystanders made fun of him.
   b. The monk asked for a pear.
   c. The monk gave his pears to the people in the market.
   d. The monk chopped down the pear tree.

2. What does the word *repulsed* mean as it is used in the text?
   a. disgusted
   b. forced back
   c. resisted
   d. offended

3. What role does the artisan play in the story?
   a. He helps the monk plant the seed.
   b. He calms the bystanders.
   c. He is annoyed at the farmer.
   d. He buys a pear to give to the monk.

4. Which statement shows the monk's intentions?
   a. "I do not have much, but I will not be miserly."
   b. "First I must have a seed to plant."
   c. "Giving away one will not injure you. Why are you so angry?"
   d. Then the monk cut down the tree, shouldered the trunk, and walked away.

5. What is the moral of the story?

   _____

   _____

Name_____

Storms of Life

"Are you ready?" Walter nodded as he clambered up into his pa's truck. Finally, he had permission to accompany his father on his daily milk-delivery route. Walter had noticed that even in the midst of dust, failed crops, and hard times, life went on. He'd heard the grownups discussing how they'd stick it out no matter what, but he also heard their wishful thinking: *If only it would rain.*

The truck sputtered to life, with the rattling of chains in the rear. Walter's mother scurried off the front porch, waving to catch their attention. "George! Your lunch!" Walter reached out the window to accept the paper bag. He knew even without looking what the bag would contain. Cold biscuits left from breakfast, dried jerky, and maybe some peas she'd managed to salvage from the garden near the house. He didn't mind working in the garden; they were all grateful for it, but having a few hours today away from the farm felt like a vacation.

"Why are there chains attached to the rear bumper?" Walter hollered over the noise as they made their way down the lane rutted with potholes.

"If a dust storm comes up, I don't want the engine to short out from the static electricity in the air," his pa replied. "Can't afford the repairs or the time it would take away from the delivery route."

Walter quit trying to converse over the racket and, instead, idly gazed out the window. He watched as the bare wheat fields passed before his eyes. The fields, plowed and planted before the market fell, were now dried up and left exposed to the prairie winds. For entertainment, Walter decided to count how many rabbits he saw. He'd probably have better luck counting grasshoppers, as they seemed to be everywhere, ravaging the few remaining crops.

Pa jerked the steering wheel, and Walter was pulled from his thoughts. Walter stared, wishing he could shut his eyes and forget about the ominous black cloud that swirled their way.

Text Questions •••

1. Given the clues in the story, during what period of history is this story most likely set?
   a. the Civil War
   b. the Dust Bowl
   c. the Great Depression
   d. World War II

2. What is most likely the meaning of the word *salvage* as it is used in the text?
   a. Walter's mother was able to rescue the peas from peril.
   b. The peas were saved from someone else's garden.
   c. Walter's mother was able to sell the peas for money.
   d. Walter's mother was able to rescue the peas from being damaged by insects.

3. Given the setting, what does the ominous black cloud probably indicate?
   a. a heavy rainstorm
   b. a tornado
   c. a dust storm
   d. a steam locomotive

4. What is the main idea of the text?
   a. People get through hard times the best they can.
   b. Walter's family decided to give up.
   c. People can't get their work done when it rains.
   d. Chains keep engines from being affected by static electricity.

5. How do Walter's feelings change throughout the story?

   _____

   _____

Name_____

Held for Ransom

Sean stumbled on the uneven boardwalk as he made his way over to rest against the rough-hewn planks of the hotel. If only someone would have pity on him and take him in for a night, he could make himself presentable. If he cleaned up well enough, maybe he could convince someone of his prior bank clerk experience, and he could get a job to support himself.

"Hey you," voices mocked him as they passed by. "The port is that way, if you want to board a ship and go back to where you came from."

Running a hand through his unkempt auburn hair, Sean ignored the rude remarks and limped toward the hotel entrance, hoping for a drink of water. His body bore the trauma of the recent eight-week voyage in the ship's hold across the Atlantic. He'd boldly proclaimed his political views back in Ireland, which resulted in his transport against his will, but he'd learned his lesson.

No one would hear a peep out of him in Boston, not that any would listen with so many politicians here.

"Bank clerk, eh?" The manager peered over his spectacles, studying Sean. "Care to elaborate on your story?"

With effort, Sean kept his temper in check. He'd get this job on his own merits, or he'd go elsewhere. It hadn't taken him long to learn no one wanted to hear his tales of woe. His kidnappers claimed they'd taken him prisoner for treason, when in reality he had been held for ransom. A sentinel on board the ship had let it slip that a merchant had ordered his capture, hoping any ransom paid would satisfy the master's unpaid debts. When it was discovered Sean's family had no money, his captors threw him overboard. Fortunately, by the time this happened, the vessel had already entered the Boston harbor.

Text Questions

1. Why didn't Sean's family pay the ransom?
   a. The master's debts were paid.
   b. The ship had arrived in the Boston harbor.
   c. Sean's family didn't have any money.
   d. Sean was taken prisoner for treason.

2. Which of the following is the most recent event to happen in Sean's life?
   a. Sean stumbled on the uneven boardwalk.
   b. Sean ignored the rude remarks and limped toward the hotel entrance.
   c. One of the sentinels on board the ship had let it slip that a merchant had ordered his capture.
   d. He boldly proclaimed his political views back in Ireland.

3. What does it mean to say Sean had *prior* bank experience?
   a. He worked in a bank previously.
   b. His bank job was not very important.
   c. He kept the books for a religious institution.
   d. He was the first person in line to apply for the bank job.

4. What is the best summary of the story's problem?
   a. Sean must find a way to pay the ransom money.
   b. Sean is starting over in a new country and needs to find a job.
   c. Sean was held as a political prisoner.
   d. Sean endured a rough voyage across the Atlantic.

5. What might have happened if the truth about Sean's family had been discovered out at sea?

   _____

   _____

Name_____

Friend or Foe

Sunlight poured in the windows on that crisp autumn day in 1950, creating a glare that made the writing assignment on the chalkboard difficult to read. The door opened, and a short, dark-haired boy entered.

"Mrs. Lorenzo?" he asked.

Smiling, Mrs. Lorenzo announced his arrival. "Class, Raymond is joining us from Chicago." She directed him to a desk across the aisle from Marlene.

Whispering spread throughout the room as students watched Raymond limp to his desk. His school uniform, consisting of a button-up, long-sleeve shirt and tan shorts, did nothing to conceal the metal braces strapped to his legs with strips of leather.

"Polio," Patricia, Marlene's best friend, whispered. Marlene shivered. She was terrified of that disease. Every summer, newspapers reported the latest victims of the deadly virus. No one knew how it spread. Even if the virus didn't kill you, it could still leave you paralyzed. Doctors and scientists struggled to find a cure or way to prevent polio but with no success.

Patricia went pale as if she had seen a ghost. Some students averted their gaze, while others pointed and whispered with neighbors. Raymond kept his head down as he made his way to his seat.

Sighs of relief sounded around the room when the lunch bell rang. Scanning the lunchroom, Patricia noticed Raymond, sitting by himself. "No one wants to be around him," she observed as she stood. "Well, I'm going to invite him to eat with us."

"No, Patricia, you can't do that."

Raymond didn't notice her until she had reached his table and stood next to him. "What do you want? Another opportunity to tease?"

"No, just wondered if you wanted some friends." Patricia smiled.

"Why?" he challenged her.

Patricia lowered her head and whispered, "You look lonely . . . and, my brother died of polio two years ago, so I know what it's like."

"I guess that would be all right." For the first time that day, Raymond smiled.

Text Questions

1. What caused Raymond to limp?
   a. He had sprained his ankle.
   b. He wanted to get attention.
   c. He had previously had polio.
   d. He had been in an accident.

2. Based on what you read, which is <u>not</u> a medical effect of polio?
   a. People could die.
   b. It could paralyze people.
   c. Some people had to have braces to walk.
   d. It made it difficult for people to do schoolwork.

3. What does the word *paralyzed* mean as it is used in the text?
   a. make it so people could not help themselves
   b. make it so people didn't have any power over others
   c. make it so people couldn't move normally
   d. make a person die

4. In which way did Patricia react to Raymond?
   a. She offered to be a friend.
   b. She pointed at him.
   c. She teased him at lunch.
   d. She refused to eat with him.

5. What disease or condition might cause similar reactions in people today?

_____

_____

Name_____

Salvage, Anyone?

Gerald whistled in admiration. "Hey, with those swell slats in your wagon, we can carry more salvage in one load." They'd agreed to meet at the bus stop near Gerald's house to canvas the neighborhood for newspaper and aluminum to aid the war effort.

Henry's momentary silence goaded Gerald on even more. "You seem a little distracted. What'cha thinking about? Anna, the new girl? She does have some excellent qualities."

"I'm not thinking about her. Too many other things going on."

"Really? There's another girl?" Gerald couldn't help teasing.

"No, I haven't started to study for the history exam yet." Henry sighed as he turned up a walkway to knock on a neighbor's door, while Gerald went to the adjacent house.

"Thank you very much, ma'am." Henry balanced the cans he'd just received in his arms and staggered to the wagon.

"So what are you going to do?" Gerald continued the conversation where they left off. "The exam is tomorrow, and it covers three or four chapters."

"I know that, and you know that, but fortunately, Dad doesn't realize that. He'd have a fit if he knew I was gathering salvage instead of studying."

Gerald listened sympathetically, depositing the contents of a bulky sack into the wagon. "So why are you out here on a Sunday, taking time away from your studies to collect newspapers and tin cans?"

"I'm not sure. Hearing reports of all those guys enlisting to serve our country, and there isn't anything I can do . . ." His voice trailed off as they parted ways once again to solicit more donations.

"Hey, Henry, do you know anyone in the neighborhood who has a truck? This guy's got some old tires in his garage that he says we can get tomorrow." Gerald gestured over his shoulder.

Text Questions

1. Which statement gives the best clue as to the time period of this story?
   a. "We can carry more salvage in one load."
   b. Henry turned up a walkway to knock on a neighbor's door, while Gerald went to the adjacent house.
   c. "The exam is tomorrow, and it covers three or four chapters."
   d. They'd agreed to meet at the bus stop near Gerald's house to canvas the neighborhood for newspaper and aluminum for the war effort.

2. What does the word *adjacent* mean as it is used in the text?
   a. near or close to
   b. in the same neighborhood
   c. touching
   d. with a fence between

3. Why is Henry distracted from the task at hand?
   a. He'd rather think about the new girl.
   b. He hasn't started studying for the history exam.
   c. He keeps thinking about how to fix up the wagon, so they can carry more things.
   d. He's trying to keep track of which houses they've visited.

4. What prompted Henry to take time away from his studies?
   a. He wanted to impress his friend.
   b. He didn't want his dad to find out about the history exam.
   c. He wanted to help the war effort.
   d. He wants to get out of studying for the test.

5. How would you describe the story's problem and a possible resolution?

_____

_____

Name_____

Space Wars

Theresa entered homeroom and started toward her desk before pausing, a bit puzzled. Nearly all the students were gathered around Stephen's desk, which was unusual. Everyone liked Stephen just fine; he was the smartest guy in class and friendly enough, but he didn't quite fit in. Intrigued, she wandered over to see for herself what was happening.

"What's this all about?" Theresa asked Rebecca.

Motioning toward Stephen's desk, Rebecca said, "Steven's got a magazine. Do you remember the headlines from last summer?"

Not surprised that Stephen would not only have a magazine, but also have already read it, Theresa shook her head no. She hadn't paid any special attention to newspaper headlines, although she did remember someone saying something about sending a man to the moon.

"It's about the space program," Rebecca said, stepping to one side so Theresa could get a closer look at the glossy photograph in the magazine.

Overhearing their conversation, Stephen spoke up. "Specifically, this article's about the next steps we might take in space exploration. An administrator from NASA predicts a manned space station, as well as expeditions to Mars."

"Well, I don't see how launching people into space is going to do anything to help us with wars and rumors of wars here on Earth." Theresa fussed at nobody in particular.

Rebecca tugged her friend away from the gathering. "Don't sweat it; let the government worry about it." She turned her notebook to a clean page and began to doodle. "What are you going to wear to the all-skate Friday night?"

Ignoring Rebecca, Theresa stared absently out the window. She'd taken her friend's advice to heart and, leaving the cares of the world behind, was lost in a daydream about what it might be like to voyage into space and see the surface of the moon for herself.

Text Questions

1. What role does Stephen play in the story?
   a. He attracts attention because he is the smartest kid in class.
   b. He disagrees with Theresa about what is important.
   c. He brings a news magazine to class, which generates a discussion about current events.
   d. He provides comic relief for the tension in the story.

2. Which historical event does the story refer to?
   a. World War II
   b. the Civil Rights movement
   c. the first man on the moon
   d. a space shuttle accident

3. What does the word *predicts* mean as it is used in the text?
   a. describes plans NASA has already in place
   b. states facts about the space program
   c. tells exactly what will happen in the future
   d. says what he thinks will happen

4. How did Theresa respond to the discussion?
   a. She began to dream about what it would be like to travel to the moon.
   b. She debated the pros and cons of the space-exploration program with Stephen.
   c. She ignored the discussion and planned a Friday-night outing with Rebecca.
   d. She borrowed the magazine from Stephen to read the article for herself.

5. How would you describe the story problem, or conflict, for the main character?

_____

_____

Name_____

Leap from the Sky

"He'll surely break himself into bits on the cobblestones," a bystander muttered, shaking his head.

Craning his head to look at the strange contraption above, Antonio watched, spellbound. Everyone had gathered in the public square to watch this breathtaking event. For weeks, townspeople had talked of Faust's latest invention—a half-moon shaped piece of linen held open by a few light pieces of wood. This device, in theory, would allow Faust to float gently to the ground.

A gasp echoed through the crowd. "He's jumping off the ledge of the tower!"

Antonio's mouth dropped open in amazement as Faust descended from the sky, falling slowly enough that he might actually escape with his life. Local tales claimed the inventor had constructed his device based on a drawing Leonardo Da Vinci had made over a century

earlier. Antonio had heard how Faust dared to deviate from the original plans, changing the shape of the canopy from a pyramid-shaped chute because he wanted to create more drag.

"Call the doctor!" Antonio found himself swept along with the throng of people who rushed from the square toward the meadow outside of town, chasing the drifting form in the sky above. Would Faust ever land? It was unbelievable that the weight of the frame hadn't already pulled him to the ground in a heap of rubble.

The mob of people prevented Antonio from observing the actual event, but the cheers alerted him to Faust's successful landing. "What will this lead to next?" Antonio couldn't help contemplating the potential uses for this marvelous machine.

Text Questions ···

1. Why did Faust land in the meadow?
   a. He didn't want to land on the people.
   b. The parachute had faulty steering.
   c. He didn't want to injure himself on the cobblestones.
   d. He drifted in the breeze.

2. What does the word *bystander* mean as it is used in the text?
   a. someone who was observing but not participating
   b. someone who helped Faust ascend to the tower
   c. someone who stood by ready to catch Faust when he fell
   d. someone who watched and recorded the occasion for history

3. What kept Faust from crashing to the ground?
   a. the wood frame
   b. the grass in the meadow
   c. the billowing cloth canopy
   d. the ability Faust had to fly a machine

4. What is the main idea of the fourth paragraph?
   a. to show that Faust was the first person who had this idea
   b. to show the development of the invention of the parachute
   c. to show Antonio's amazement
   d. to show that Faust survived the experiment

5. How has the structure of parachutes changed, and what are they used for today?

   _____

   _____

   _____

Name_____

Maria Isabella Boyd

The soldiers surrounded our house, taking livestock for food and stealing our horses. Then, those Union soldiers broke into our house! They demanded to raise their flag in our house against our wishes. They were rude and insulted my mother. When I couldn't take any more abuse, I reacted and did something foolish.

I was placed on trial and should have been hanged, but due to my young age, I was acquitted by a board of inquiry. Even so, they placed me under surveillance at my father's hotel. "What a fantastic opportunity to spy on the Union army," I thought.

The Union officers and generals visited the hotel on a regular basis. Two guards were assigned to watch me, but nobody bothered to try to keep their talk secret from me, perhaps because I am a girl. I would always be so polite and charming, but I also listened very carefully.

Later, I would write down what I heard, give it to my maid, Eliza Hopewell, and she would carry it to the Confederate generals. After a while, when my notes proved to be correct, I was accepted as a true spy!

One evening in 1862, I overheard some Union generals making elaborate plans to attack a fort. This was such critical information that I went to see the general at the fort myself. I even had to dodge bullets to get there! For this endeavor, I was awarded the Southern Cross of Honor. I was later arrested and thrown into a Union prison.

After a month in prison, I was freed, arrested again, imprisoned, freed, and then finally sent to England for the duration of the war. The one thought that helped me through it all was that I had done all a woman could for her country's cause.

Text Questions

1. Which statement does <u>not</u> give a clue as to the time period of this story?
   a. They demanded to raise their flag in our house against our wishes.
   b. The Union officers and generals visited the hotel on a regular basis.
   c. I would always be so polite and charming, but I also listened very carefully.
   d. I overheard some Union generals making elaborate plans to attack a fort.

2. What is the main conflict in the story?
   a. The narrator was tried and hanged for treason.
   b. A young girl becomes a spy for the Confederate army while being held under surveillance.
   c. The narrator has to dodge bullets on her way to the fort.
   d. The maid was caught while delivering messages to Confederate officers.

3. What does the word *acquitted* mean as it is used in the text?
   a. she was released from a duty or obligation
   b. she paid a debt
   c. she conducted herself honorably
   d. she was cleared from a charge

4. Which title would be a good alternative for this text?
   a. "Escaping Imprisonment"
   b. "A True Spy"
   c. "A Confederate Spy"
   d. "Confederate Courier"

5. What role did spies play in the Civil War?

   _____

   _____

   _____

Name_____

The Raft

Marc shut the book with a satisfied sigh and leaned back against the headboard with his hands locked behind his head. Imagine, he thought, what it would be like to sail across the ocean like the men who had sailed a raft from South America to the Polynesian islands. Growing up in Hawaii, he'd logged hours in and on the ocean—surfing, kayaking, and snorkeling. Through his experiences, he had cultivated a healthy respect and love for the ocean. His favorite stories were about the people of the islands who had arrived in crude boats centuries earlier.

Jumping up, Marc struck his fist in his hand, exclaiming, "I'll do it! I'll build my own raft and sail to the Pacific coast to visit my cousins in California."

"Plan carefully, son," his dad said when Marc presented the idea to him. "There are many obstacles confronting you that you'll have to overcome. Consider the best wood to use, how you'll keep food fresh, how long your voyage will take, how you will navigate, and how you will steer."

Marc grinned, pleased his dad hadn't rejected the idea or teased him. "I realize survival out on the ocean is a challenge. I'll start small with a raft I can test in a local bay."

Eventually, Marc managed to tie some small, straight logs together. He constructed a mast and, with his mom's assistance, fashioned a sail out of a sheet. No navigational tools would be needed as he was just sailing from one side of the bay to the other.

He and his father placed the raft, which had been christened "Leaky," onto a trailer and they unloaded it at the dock. Marc jumped on the raft, hoisted the sail, and set forth for the other side of the bay. However, he'd forgotten one of the things his father had mentioned. He also failed to account for waves close to the beach. Sadly, Marc never made it to the other side.

Text Questions

1. What did Marc likely forget that his dad had mentioned?
   a. food for the journey
   b. a rudder for steering
   c. a mast for the sail
   d. navigational tools

2. Why did Marc decide to sail across the bay?
   a. He wanted to test his raft before going out on the ocean.
   b. He had never been out on the ocean before.
   c. He wanted to get to the other side of the bay.
   d. His raft was too small to sail on the ocean.

3. What historical event forms the basis for this story?
   a. men sailing a raft from South America to the Polynesian islands
   b. early explorers who sailed in crude boats and populated the islands
   c. the invention of rafting
   d. a hurricane in the Hawaiian Islands

4. What does it mean to say people sailed in *crude* boats?
   a. The boats were made out of natural materials.
   b. The men who sailed them used rough language.
   c. The boats were rough and not carefully made.
   d. There weren't any decorations on the boats.

5. What inspired Marc to build a raft?

_____

_____

Name_____

The Midnight Ride

Mom woke me before dawn, just as the roosters were starting to crow, so I could feed the chickens and do my other chores. For days, folks in town had been speculating about the British. Would there be fighting? From when and where would they come?

After a breakfast of oats, Pa and I went out to chop wood for the day. After Pa left for the silversmith shop, Mom and I worked on reading, ciphering, and writing. When that was done, I left to help the local minister of the Old North Church.

When I arrived at the church, I spotted several men whom I recognized as local leaders. These men, the "mechanics," as they were known, spied on the British and gathered to share information among them. The talk of the British was getting serious. I did my best to listen and tried to understand.

The minister gave me two lanterns and a task. "Clean the glass as shiny as possible, and make sure they have good wicks and plenty of oil." Afterwards I carried them up, one by one, to the top of the church tower. I left some flint and papers to start a fire in case I needed to light them. But why? This made no sense to me.

Pa came by in a rush, leapt off his horse before it stopped, and gathered the men for a hurried meeting. "Stay here at the church tonight," he said, then left.

After dark, I was reading by the fire when the minister scurried in. "Make haste to climb the ladder and stairs of the tower and light both lanterns." I didn't ask why but made my way to the top and lit both as bright as possible.

Soon after, I heard the pounding hooves of a horse as Pa raced through the countryside, letting his comrades along the way know that "the Regulars are on the move."

Text Questions

1. Which words relate specifically to the historical setting?
   a. shiny, bright, light
   b. church, tower, countryside
   c. folks, minister, leaders
   d. lantern, flint, wicks

2. What did the mechanics do?
   a. They worked in the silversmith shop.
   b. They mended wagon wheels.
   c. They spied on the British and shared information.
   d. They worked on the British ships.

3. What does it mean to say the townspeople were *speculating* about the British?
   a. They were guessing what the British might do next.
   b. They were pondering whether or not to join with the British.
   c. They were taking part in the risky venture of spying on the British.
   d. They were reflecting on the past history of the British.

4. What significant event in history does this story retell?
   a. The Boston Tea Party
   b. The Midnight Ride of Paul Revere
   c. The Boston Massacre
   d. The Stamp Act

5. Based on what you read, what is the role of the narrator of the story?

   _____

   _____

Name_____

Bombs Away

High-pitched air-raid alarms sounded as Mother gathered us, and we made our way into the cellar. German bombers were approaching the shores and would arrive at any moment.

We lit candles, and Mother worked on her sewing. "Can I please go back upstairs to watch the bombs fall?" my brother begged. I played with my dolls, and soon the distant booms began, rattling our house like a kettle drum.

The booming sounds grew increasingly louder as the ground trembled, and bits of dust fell from the ceiling. From time to time, Mom would glance upwards with a worried look.

After a while, the alarms whirled again, and the noise and ground shaking finally ceased. Mom cautiously led us upstairs. Broken dishes littered the kitchen, and the cupboard doors stood askew.

"We don't have any electricity, and the water isn't running," Mother informed us. "It's a good thing you helped fill the five-gallon drums with water so we'll be able to cook and drink. But most importantly, the house is still standing." She breathed a small sigh of relief.

I walked out into the front yard to discover that ours was not the only house with shattered windows. Several large fires were burning around London, including the house two doors down, which was now demolished and ablaze. People scurried with hoses to attempt to extinguish the fires.

Down the street, officials worked to secure ropes and stakes around an unexploded bomb. I'd heard that the bombs could get buried in debris and explode before being found.

Despite all the chaos, everyone pitched in to help each other and remained as positive as possible. So many people had been killed or lost their houses. Food was rationed, and we had little gas for our cars, but we held out hope that this was only temporary, and the end of the war would come soon.

Text Questions

1. What is accomplished in the first paragraph of the story?
   a. It introduces the characters.
   b. It explains the theme of the story.
   c. It sets up the story and introduces the problem.
   d. It foreshadows how the story problem might be resolved.

2. What does the word *demolished* mean as it is used in the text?
   a. overturned
   b. torn down
   c. constructed
   d. destroyed

3. Which statement gives the best clue as to the historical setting?
   a. Several large fires were burning.
   b. From time to time, Mom would glance upwards with a worried look.
   c. High-pitched air-raid alarms sounded.
   d. Broken dishes littered the kitchen, and the cupboard doors stood askew.

4. Based on clues in the story, in which country does this story most likely take place?
   a. Japan
   b. England
   c. China
   d. Russia

5. How did the events portrayed in the story shape the characters?

_____

_____

Name_____

Texas Quilts

"Hand me the scissors, please," Bessie said, as she reached for the black thread and prepared to cut a length. Threading her needle, she held the calico print circle in place on the muslin with her thumb.

Julia tilted her head to one side. "Do you plan to go around the petals like that in black also? I can't imagine how that would look. Wouldn't it detract from the fabric?" She watched Bessie make generous stitches with the ebony thread, one-quarter inch in from the edge of the circle.

Pausing, Bessie considered. "Well, I might. Guess I'll have to see how it looks when I get to that point." She resumed her stitching, working quickly to get as much done as possible before the sun got too high in the sky. Bright Texas sunshine poured through the window, the natural light ideal for the intricate detail work of quilting.

In the corner, Helen sat quietly sorting swatches of fabric, pieces from clothing no longer usable. She set blues in a pile and oranges and reds in another. "I reckon these would make a fine wagon-wheel pattern, don't you think?"

"Sounds like a lot of work to me," Julia stated. "Good thing you don't have too much of the orange and red; you can make it a smaller quilt." She idly sifted through the blues, adding some pieces of pink to the pile.

Bessie glanced out the window and started suddenly. "Dust storm coming!" She frantically began gathering quilt pieces, along with the paper pattern template, and stuffed them in pillowcases.

"Wait," Helen said. "Try to keep the colors sorted." Holding out a pillowcase to Julia, she pointed to the stack of blues and pinks and said, "Here, those can be used for a hexagon pattern."

Just as the girls finished stowing the fabric safely, Pa sauntered through the door. "Pack up, girls. Once we survive this, we're moving west."

Text Questions

1. Which title would be a good alternative for this text?
   a. "Three Sisters"
   b. "Dust Storm"
   c. "Fabric of Life"
   d. "Sunny Sewing"

2. What is a synonym for the word *idly* as it is used in the text?
   a. uselessly
   b. slowly
   c. lazily
   d. unprofitably

3. Which statement best describes the story problem?
   a. Bessie worked quickly to get as much done as possible before the sun got too high in the sky.
   b. "Dust storm coming!"
   c. Helen sat quietly sorting swatches of fabric, pieces from clothing no longer usable.
   d. "Pack up, girls. Once we survive this, we're moving west."

4. What is the purpose of the last paragraph?
   a. It offers resolution for the conflict between characters.
   b. It introduces a new character.
   c. It shows why the girls put the fabric pieces in pillowcases.
   d. It creates additional tension in the story.

5. What do you suppose happened to the quilts next?

   _____

   _____

Name_____

Farewell at Independence, Missouri

Independence, Missouri was bustling with people. Samuel pressed his nose against the general store's window and moaned, "Whenever will we get to see them?" Suddenly, he spotted the billowing canvas top of a covered wagon being pulled by four brown oxen. "They've arrived!" In his haste to greet the pioneers, he slammed the door, causing the bell to ring wildly.

The Abrams family extracted themselves from the wagon as Daniel, Samuel's best friend, dismounted from a gray gelding he'd been riding alongside. Daniel tied the horse to a hitching post as Samuel peered into the back of the wagon. He was dumbstruck by the sight of all of Abrams's belongings stuffed into the four-foot-by-twelve-foot wagon. Sacks of flour and sugar, boxes of medicine, and rolls of bedding crowded the interior. "We hung the guns from hooks last night," exclaimed Daniel, pointing to the hoops that stretched the canvas tight. "We'll have to rely on hunting and fishing out on the trail."

"Great job," Samuel slapped his comrade on the back. "Just imagine all the adventures you'll have—crossing rivers, meeting mountain men, encounters with Indians." He couldn't keep the jealousy from tinging his voice.

Daniel nodded. "Dad is anxious to start farming once we arrive in Oregon. It's supposed to be the best soil around, and it's all free!"

A bleak horn sounded mournfully. "We best get going," Daniel's dad said as he started towards the lead ox. "The ferry will be leaving soon."

"I guess this is farewell." Samuel lightly stroked the gelding's nose. "You are so fortunate. I'm stuck here, doing farm chores and attending school, while you're off to Oregon territory!"

"At least you don't have to leave all your friends and family." Daniel quickly gave Samuel a heartfelt handshake and mounted his horse. "Take care of yourself, Samuel." Daniel didn't look back as he trotted down to the river after the wagon.

Text Questions

1. What statement does <u>not</u> give a clue about how Samuel feels in the story?
    a. In his haste to greet the pioneers, he slammed the door, causing the bell to ring wildly.
    b. He couldn't keep the jealousy from tinging his voice.
    c. Samuel lightly stroked the gelding's nose.
    d. "You are so fortunate. I'm stuck here, doing farm chores and attending school, while you're off to Oregon territory!"

2. What is the main idea of the last paragraph?
    a. Daniel is excited for his new adventure.
    b. Daniel is sad to leave his friends.
    c. Daniel has to obey his parents.
    d. Daniel thinks their move is a good idea.

3. What does the word *extracted* mean as it is used in the text?
    a. to pull out with effort   c. to obtain something by pressing
    b. to separate   d. to concentrate a substance

4. What is one theme of the text?
    a. honesty   b. independence   c. acceptance   d. friendship

5. What would be your greatest anticipation in traveling to new territory by covered wagon? Your greatest hesitation?

    _____

    _____

Name_____

Penicillium

The Great War was over. Alexander could finally return to his research laboratory. The war, awful though it had been, renewed his motivation to find an answer for bacterial infections. His experience on the battlefront helped him realize that bacteria were just as deadly as bullets.

"Where did I leave those notes?" he muttered, as he sorted through the jumble in the lab. "I know that one enzyme from tears has an antibacterial effect, but it's just not strong enough. There must be a better solution. If I can only discover it."

After rummaging around a bit more, he gave up and tried to organize his lab. Since the war, the lab seemed in a constant state of disorder; piles of notes and books lay everywhere, and empty test tubes showed where experiments had taken place. He decided to start cleaning the pile of petri dishes out of the sink. He had used them to grow staph bacteria, but now he was ready to start some new experiments. As was his habit, Alexander opened each one, examining it before placing it in a cleaning solution. "That's funny," he said, as he opened one containing the characteristic mold. Strangely, around this particular mold sample, the bacteria had died.

"Look at this." Alexander handed the specimen to a lab assistant. "See if you can extract a sample of this mold, so we can identify it."

A little while later, the assistant identified the mold as *Penicillium notatum*. Alexander grew more of the mold and then tested it, over and over again. Each time, the mold killed the deadly bacteria in the petri dish. "This is the antibacterial effect I was looking for! Think of how many lives can be saved!"

Text Questions

1. What is the main character's goal in this passage?
   a. He wanted to clean his laboratory.
   b. He wanted to find a treatment for bacterial infections.
   c. He wanted his lab assistant to help extract the mold.
   d. He wanted to start some new experiments.

2. Which sentence gives you a clue as to the time period of the story?
   a. The Great War was over.
   b. The war, awful though it had been, renewed his motivation to find an answer for bacterial infections.
   c. Alexander handed the specimen to a lab assistant.
   d. Alexander grew more of the mold and then tested it, over and over again.

3. What does the word *specimen* mean as it is used in the text?
   a. a particular type of person
   b. one part of a group
   c. an example
   d. a sample taken for analysis

4. Which of the following could <u>not</u> be said about Alexander?
   a. He has a routine of checking petri dishes.
   b. He is motivated to find a solution.
   c. He is organized.
   d. He is persistent.

5. How does this historical discovery affect our lives today?

   _____

   _____

   _____

Name_____

Kit

"Payday!" The cry rang through the camp, and we all hustled to secure a place in line. The first opportunity I have to go into town, I've decided to take a bit of money to celebrate my recent 17th birthday. I clearly remember the day when I enlisted, lying about my age as I signed up to fight the Southerners, alongside other concerned citizens from Pennsylvania.

As a private, we're supposed to get paid $11 per month, but that doesn't always happen. Often the money arrives so late, I can't remember what month it's supposed to be for.

They rouse us early and sometimes feed us a morsel or two, but usually we have to do without food. We mostly eat hardtack, which are crackers made from flour, water, and salt. There might occasionally be a bit of dried pork, but if not, we forage for berries and hunt small game. I've seen fellow soldiers starve in these harsh conditions.

We drill each morning and afternoon, so we'll know our place on the battlefield and work together as a team.

They bark at us to listen and obey orders from the officers. Without it, they fear we would panic, and all order would break down.

Between drills we clean, fix our tattered uniforms, and mend socks (if we have any). We sometimes play a few games, such as checkers or dominoes, or we write letters to loved ones back home. But most of our time is spent being bored. I miss my parents, brothers, and sisters beyond belief.

When aren't we bored? When we fight. Imagine total madness. Shouting, cursing, and fear so bad you're certain you will die from it rather than being shot. The sight is horrific; men and boys are wounded, dying, and dead.

Eventually, this will all be over, and I shall once again go home and reunite with my family. I hope that in time we can all forget this horrible event.

Text Questions ....

1. What do you learn about Kit from reading this passage?
   a. He is an officer in the army.
   b. He has joined the Confederate forces.
   c. He thinks fighting is boring.
   d. He learns to drill and obey orders.

2. What is the main idea of the first paragraph?
   a. It introduces the main character, setting, and time period of the story.
   b. It gives the reader a clear idea of the conflict the main character will face.
   c. It explains the details of a confederate soldier's daily experience.
   d. It shows how the main character responds to his experiences.

3. Which title would be a good alternative for this text?
   a. "The Life of a Confederate Soldier"   c. "Behind the Front Lines"
   b. "Union Diary"   d. "A Letter Home"

4. What is the best synonym for the word *horrific* as it is used in the text?
   a. nerve wracking   c. dreadful
   b. scary   d. frustrating

5. Based on what you read, how would you describe Kit's view of the war?

   _____

   _____

Name_____

Labor for Grain

"Quit daydreaming and let's get chores done before Papa catches us idle," Regenard's brother, Marellus, urged. Caught in a daydream, Regenard jumped slightly and then shifted his attention back to his duties. The sight of the huge blades turning lazily in the breeze never failed to mesmerize him.

Regenard supposed the windmills eased their labor, but he could never completely agree with the theory. He recalled a day not long ago when a visitor had arrived on horseback, carrying a scroll with drawings, which he displayed to all the men at a town meeting. The stranger had described how the drawings had been meticulously copied and passed around, having been brought from the east by crusaders. Upon careful perusal of the sketches, they had reached a consensus to build such a contraption, called a "windmill," in their village.

"Garçon," the elder called, "gather the other boys to turn the blades!" Regenard and his brother dropped their milk pails and raced to the windmill. It was true, since they had built the monstrosity, they no longer needed as many horses to turn the mills and grind grain. It seemed, however, that there was no end of other work created by this labor-saving device. Occasionally, a shaft would need replacing. Or a mill stone would slip, which required every able-bodied man in the village, it seemed, to shove it back in place.

Grunting, Regenard worked alongside the others to turn the windmill so the massive wood sails could catch the wind. "Mind your head!" His brother nimbly ducked under the swinging blade, but Regenard didn't move quickly enough, and he was knocked senseless.

"Oh," he moaned, holding the lump on his forehead. Marellus produced a damp cloth, pressing it to the tender area. Strong arms then lifted him and carried him home. "Well," Marellus teased, as Regenard was laid on his cot, "that's one way to get out of carrying grain sacks today."

Text Questions

1. What can you infer about the time period from the setting of the story?
   a. The story takes place in modern-day times.
   b. The story takes place in pre-industrial times.
   c. The story takes place during the Industrial Revolution.
   d. The story takes place during the Westward Expansion.

2. What obstacle or problem does the main character face in the story?
   a. He is daydreaming and doesn't get his chores done on time.
   b. He has to do more work because of the windmill.
   c. He is injured while working at the windmill.
   d. He doesn't want to haul sacks of grain.

3. What does it mean to say the villagers reached a *consensus*?
   a. They took a survey to see who agreed to the plan.
   b. They gave the stranger permission to construct a windmill.
   c. They had a debate about whether or not to use the plans.
   d. They all agreed to build a windmill.

4. What role does the windmill play in the story?
   a. It provides tension and conflict in the story.
   b. It is an obstacle the main character must overcome to reach a goal.
   c. It sets the mood and tone of the story.
   d. It helps the reader understand the main character better.

5. How does windmill technology today differ from that described in the story? How is it the same?

_____

_____

Golf for Everyone

"Hey, Willie, I've gathered more balls this morning." Frank set the bucket down on the torn-up lawn and went to fetch their old clubs. Their proximity to the neighborhood golf course gave the friends ample opportunity to watch the masters from outside the fence, and Frank in particular was determined to learn the game. They had even devised a three-hole course in the backyard for practice.

Frank took his stance and swung the club a few times. He aimed his sights on the hole, trying to emulate the great players he'd observed. His family had no money for lessons, so he taught himself, trying to remember every nuance of the game. "I'm going to play on that course someday," he gestured vaguely across town with his club, "and I'm going to have my own caddy."

"How do you know about caddies?" Willie's gaze challenged Frank.

"I've been working over at the club to earn some extra income to help out; they pay me two bits per round."

Trotting dutifully to fetch wayward balls, Willie waited patiently for his turn. The game didn't hold nearly the fascination for him that it did for Frank, but he admired his comrade and was willing to help out, just for the enjoyment. It was also a great excuse not to do schoolwork, although Frank often got in trouble for neglecting his studies.

The next day, they walked a mile to catch the streetcar headed across town. After transferring twice to connecting streetcar lines, they walked over half a mile more to a public course, talking golf the entire time. "When I grow up, I'm not going to forget people like us. I'll have some young fellow caddy for me just like you're helping me now."

Text Questions

1. What is the theme or moral of the text?
   a. honesty
   b. courage
   c. perseverance
   d. sacrifice

2. Which statement will <u>not</u> help you answer the previous question?
   a. Frank in particular was determined to learn the game.
   b. His family had no money for lessons, so he taught himself, trying to remember every nuance of the game.
   c. "I'm going to play on that course someday."
   d. Frank often got in trouble for neglecting his studies.

3. What does the word *emulate* mean as it is used in the text?
   a. to rival
   b. to imitate
   c. to compete against
   d. to follow

4. What is the purpose of first paragraph?
   a. It introduces the conflict in the story.
   b. It introduces the characters and setting in the story.
   c. It sets the mood for the story.
   d. It shows the resolution of conflict.

5. What is the connection between Frank's situation and his dreams?

_____

_____

Name_____

Meeting of Two Worlds

Reagan glanced up from his browsing as the bell rang over the entrance to the bookstore. Puzzled, he watched for a minute as Darya advanced toward the counter as if to ask a question. It didn't make sense that Darya, one of the school's top athletes, was in a bookstore. Not wanting to be noticed, Reagan quickly found another volume to peruse. He wouldn't know what to say if she tried to start a conversation. Reagan let his thoughts wander a bit, thinking it would be nice to have someone to talk to or hang out with. Then he wouldn't be so lonely.

"Hey, Reagan." Her greeting startled him, and his breath caught in his throat as it became apparent he hadn't escaped after all. "Maybe you can help me."

He doubted it, but he managed to choke out a reply. "Me?"

"I'm trying to locate a book on soccer skills. I won't be able to go to camp over spring break, and I need to improve my game before the next season begins."

Reagan swallowed, then motioned randomly with his hands before he found his voice. "Sure. Over here." He figured it would save hassle and confusion if he just led the way, rather than try to point her in the right direction. As she followed him through the stacks, he dared to imagine they might not be so different after all. He felt a brief glimmer of hope, the sun shining suddenly where all had been gray. Immediately, one of Darya's teammates seemed to materialize, urging her to finish any purchases or they would be late for practice. Sighing, Reagan realized nothing had really changed; society would never let them break down those barriers, even if they so chose.

Text Questions

1. What might have happened if Darya's teammate hadn't come along?
   a. Darya would have found a book to read.
   b. Darya would have decided not to buy the soccer book.
   c. Darya and Reagan would have had a conversation.
   d. Reagan would have left Darya alone and gone back to reading.

2. Based on what you read, what can you infer about Reagan?
   a. He is not a very good student.
   b. He is not a very good athlete.
   c. He does not like to talk to people.
   d. He was in the bookstore with his friends.

3. What is one theme, or moral, of the text?
   a. Often we stereotype people and place them in groups.
   b. Darya showed compassion for Reagan by talking to him.
   c. Playing sports is an admirable pastime.
   d. It takes perseverance to find a book on soccer skills.

4. What happened when one of Darya's teammates *materialized*?
   a. She developed into a real friend.
   b. She took on the appearance of an athlete.
   c. She emerged from the shadows.
   d. She appeared suddenly and unexpectedly.

5. How might the story change if told from Darya's perspective?

_____

_____

_____

Name_____

Change of Plans

A pair of studded boots sat side by side waiting. Their owner wore dark socks with markings, and the boots were shrouded by studded pants—quiet, for he had removed the chains. He was not tall by any means but of medium stature with a slight build. His black ops jacket could easily be mistaken for a gang jacket. Warren Black stood out from the other passengers on the flight, which included tourists and natives bound for Ireland. He had no camera, and he did not look Irish.

Warren sat contentedly gazing at the small, curious medallion around his neck, with an imprint of a dying rose on one side and on the opposite, the sun. He stared at the edges, worn smooth, and the ebony finish, which was flaking in places to reveal a brilliant blue sheen. As the captain put on the seat belt warning, the plane jolted suddenly as if experiencing heavy turbulence.

Without warning, the left engine stopped spinning entirely, and the plane began to vault and buck as the pilot instructed everyone to remain calm. The plane continued its violent descent as Warren clutched the armrests on either side of him. The left wing hit the ground first, causing the cabin to shudder from the impact. The wing dug a deep trench into the grassland and was stopped short by a boulder. People screamed as the plane slowly tipped downward and came to a halt on its belly, all the landing gear torn up. As the passengers dismounted on the slides, a head count was taken. No fatalities and no severe injuries were reported. A young girl struggled to catch her breath, and Warren himself was experiencing some chest pains. In shock, the group moved slowly to the nearby village, but Warren opted to wander off to a nearby lake with his luggage to set up a tent. He made himself a fire and began cooking a small dinner.

Text Questions

1. Which phrase or sentence shows that no one was seriously injured?
   a. As the passengers dismounted on the slides, a head count was taken.
   b. No fatalities and no severe injuries were reported.
   c. A young girl struggled to catch her breath, and Warren himself was experiencing some chest pains.
   d. In shock, the group moved slowly to the nearby village.

2. What might be the reason for Warren's journey?
   a. He wants to tour Ireland and go sightseeing.
   b. He is Irish, and he wants to visit his homeland.
   c. He is on a special assignment for the government.
   d. He knows what to do in a crisis.

3. What does the word *violent* mean as it is used in the text?
   a. forceful
   b. mean
   c. unjust
   d. furious

4. What caused the accident?
   a. The left engine failed.
   b. The right engine failed.
   c. The pilot fell asleep.
   d. The landing gear malfunctioned.

5. How might this incident affect Warren's travel plans?

_____

_____

Name_____

Climb a Mountain

"Hey, Jordan, over here!" Jordan's best friend, Mahir, waved his hand, pointing to a fissure in the side of the cliff. "We could climb this!"

Jordan clipped his harness on and checked his rope and carabiners. He weighed one of them in his hand, calculating. Then he eyeballed potential placement locations, considering the difficulty of the task. "That crack is unbelievably small. I don't think we'd get up very high."

"At the time of a test, a person rises or falls," said Ghanim, Mahir's dad. Shaking his head in confusion over the foreign proverb, Jordan examined the crack. It was nothing more than a sliver in the solid face of the cliff. He shifted in his harness as Mahir gave the proverb his own interpretation: "If you're not falling, you're not trying hard enough." Jordan recognized the bit of advice from a previous climbing lesson.

His own father's voice echoed in his thoughts, as if in a half-forgotten dream. "Climb a mountain, son, and you climb the insecurity in your own life. You climb over your shadow, climb over your doubt." That was five years ago, before the automobile accident that took his dad's life. Jordan couldn't help replaying the story in his mind, how the other driver had veered out of control around a corner. Jordan's dad swerved across the lane of oncoming traffic, effectively blocking the other car from a cliff. But his father's car careened over the edge. The sudden move had saved the lives of three people in that car.

Jordan's dad had never hesitated. And now Jordan wouldn't either. Concentrating on his balance, he took a deep breath and began to climb.

Text Questions

1. What did Mahir do when he gave the proverb his own *interpretation*?
   a. He paraphrased it in different words.
   b. He restated it to say what he thought it meant.
   c. He argued with his dad about what it meant.
   d. He read it aloud to Jordan.

2. What must Jordan overcome to start the climb?
   a. his hesitation
   b. his memories
   c. his failures
   d. his father

3. What does the word *fissure* mean as it is used in the text?
   a. a long, narrow, deep crack
   b. something that is divided into parts
   c. a groove between parts of an organ
   d. a space between two rock walls

4. What is the theme or moral of the text?
   a. Practice makes perfect.
   b. People's real worth is known only through trial.
   c. Easier said than done.
   d. People who have a weakness show it.

5. How do the words of his father affect what Jordan decides to do?

   _____

   _____

Name_____

Friendly Ferns

Stooping, Mara glanced under the deck to reassure herself that the minute fern was still alive only to discover it had doubled in size. Today, finally, she had time to carefully transplant it to a different location. If asked, Mara wasn't sure she could explain the importance of these tiny plants that she had moved and tended, one each year, to develop her fern garden. Best to transplant when they were young; within a few years, they grew to half her height.

"Brandon, what are you doing?" Mara shuffled cautiously across the brick slippery with moss. Perhaps her brother would consider this an endeavor reminiscent of hobbits and agree to join her.

Mumbling came from the general direction of the computer room, a dead giveaway as to his whereabouts. Mara couldn't see the sense in perusing the idea any further; she'd never get him to surface if he was engrossed in a computer game. Wanting to get the project completed before it got too dark, Mara stuffed her phone in her pocket, swigged down half a glass of water, and headed back to the shed.

She had just finished rummaging around for digging tools and a bit of compost when her phone rang. Balancing the tools in the container that held the compost, she answered the call. "Sorry, Casey, not at this moment. I'm working with the fern garden, but I have an idea. Come visit until I finish this, then I'll help you practice." Casey was forever looking for someone to kick her a few balls so she could practice her dribbling and goal kicks for the girls' soccer team. They both laughed at Mara's soccer abilities, but Casey agreed it was better than nothing.

"Sounds like a good deal to me." Casey ended the call, and Mara sighed with relief. She hadn't mentioned this particular task to her friend, but Casey always sympathized even if she didn't fully understand.

Text Questions

1. What is the theme or moral of the text?
   a. The best way to move ferns is one at a time.
   b. If you don't have sports skills, you don't have to help a friend.
   c. It's good to accept people as they are.
   d. If you help a friend, he or she will help you.

2. Which statement is an opinion?
   a. Tiny ferns are beautiful.
   b. Plants are easier to transplant when they are small.
   c. You should use potting soil when transplanting a fern.
   d. Moss on brick can be slippery.

3. What does the word *minute* mean as it is used in the text?
   a. unimportant
   b. very small
   c. one part of an hour
   d. a specific point

4. Why didn't Brandon want to keep Mara company?
   a. He didn't like ferns.
   b. He didn't like to read about hobbits.
   c. He was engrossed in a computer game.
   d. He didn't hear Mara call him.

5. In what ways did Mara and Casey accept each other? Why is this important?

_____

_____

Name_____

Fast Pitch

Adar finished arranging her science-fair project just as Mr. Delaney entered the arena.

"Looks like you're ready for the judges," he greeted her. "Refresh my memory—what exactly are you trying to do with a Popsicle baseball diamond?"

Adjusting a notecard for better visibility, Adar said, "My project demonstrates the answer to my inquiry question." She went on to explain how she had written a major-league hitter asking for his tips on the best way to bat when the wind blew.

Not only had he sent some valuable information, but she'd also received a signed baseball card to add to her collection. She pointed out the handwritten letter that was part of the display.

Mr. Delaney leaned over to peruse the letter. "Hmm, says here one thing he incorporates is shifting his weight in the batter box to accommodate the wind. I'll be watching to see you try that at our next practice." Mr. Delaney smiled and moved over to the area where his students had their displays.

Sure enough, at practice a few days later, Mr. Delaney noticed Adar observing the wind speed and direction and adjusting her stance accordingly. Between drills, he sauntered over. "How did your project do at the science fair?"

Adar beamed. "I did the math, wrote my observations and analysis, and the judges thought the Popsicle model was great! I won an award, with an invitation to advance to the regional competition."

"Good for you! Hey, what flavor Popsicle did you use?" Mr. Delaney teased as he patted Adar on the shoulder and announced the next drill.

Text Questions

1. What does the word *diamond* refer to as it is used in the text?
   a. a mineral made of carbon
   b. a gem used in jewelry
   c. a closed plane figure with four sides
   d. the infield of a baseball playing field

2. What is an important fact in the story?
   a. A prominent sports figure took the time to respond.
   b. Popsicle sticks make interesting science fair displays.
   c. What students learn from a science project might not be applied to real life.
   d. Most science-fair projects require math.

3. How would you describe the relationship between Adar and Mr. Delaney?
   a. They are friends.
   b. Mr. Delaney is Adar's teacher.
   c. Mr. Delaney is Adar's coach.
   d. Mr. Delaney wrote a letter to Adar to help her with her project.

4. What will happen now that Adar has won an award?
   a. She will take her science-fair project home.
   b. She will compete in a regional science fair.
   c. She will write to the major-league player and tell him about her award.
   d. She will show her friends how to build a Popsicle model.

5. Why might the major-league player have been willing to respond to Adar's letter?

   _____

   _____

Name_____

Rescue Companion

Surf pounded as Roberto meandered down the beach, his companion Sam by his side. Suddenly, Roberto collapsed, gasping for breath, in a heap on the sand. Sam circled, anxious, then hurried off to fetch Roberto's uncle Tomás, a little ways up the beach. At first, his uncle assumed Roberto had just fallen and would rally to his feet. When that didn't happen, Tomás darted back to check.

"Hey, Berto, what happened?" When his nephew only groaned in response, Tomás hastened to reassure him. "I'll get the car and meet you in the parking lot."

Roberto moaned again, while Sam continued to pace around his master, licking his face. As Roberto struggled to lift his weight in the soft sand, Sam nudged him, then grasped his shirt and began to drag his comrade up the slope. With Sam's help, Tomás managed to get Roberto situated in the passenger seat and later, into the beach cottage where their family was vacationing.

His mother and aunt fussed over Roberto, asking about his symptoms and the cause of his mysterious ailment. "Sweat was pouring off me," he recalled. "I felt dizzy and shaky." Tomás affirmed that his nephew's skin was cold and clammy when he maneuvered him into the car. After further questioning, they determined Roberto had experienced a sudden drop in blood sugar due to his diabetes.

For the following two days, Roberto rarely left the couch, as his body recuperated and he regained his strength. During that time, Sam lingered close, more subdued than Roberto had ever seen him. Roberto wondered if Sam would become a more loyal companion in days to come or if he would revert to his previously independent ways.

Text Questions

1. How does the setting impact the story?
   a. The sound of ocean waves soothes Roberto.
   b. The ocean distracts Sam from helping Roberto.
   c. The sand gave Sam good traction as he dragged Roberto up the slope.
   d. The soft sand made it more difficult for Roberto to get up.

2. What was the second incorrect assumption Tomás made?
   a. He assumed Roberto had fallen and would get up on his own.
   b. He assumed Roberto would be able to get into the beach cottage without assistance.
   c. He assumed Roberto would be able to get to the car without assistance.
   d. He assumed Roberto would be fine once he took a nap.

3. When Sam circled, *anxious*, what did he display?
   a. worry
   b. doubt
   c. eagerness
   d. fear

4. Which sentence continues the development of an idea from the early part of the story?
   a. Tomás managed to get Roberto into the beach cottage.
   b. His mother and aunt fussed over Roberto.
   c. He regained his strength.
   d. Sam lingered close.

5. Describe a time when a pet (belonging to you or someone else) showed loyalty or gave assistance to a person.

   _____

   _____

Name_____

Perfect Planets

Kyle and Brennan lounged around after school, discussing their upcoming social-studies project. "Create a perfect society?" Kyle asked. "We'll have a great time dreaming, I suppose, but this doesn't seem like a very practical assignment. How will this help us prepare for exams?"

"Ah, come on, humor me, let's have some fun with this." Brennan encouraged Kyle to indulge in one of their favorite pastimes, *what if*. "What if you could make a perfect planet?" he asked. "How would you describe it?"

Not waiting for an answer, Brennan rubbed his hands together in glee. "That's easy. It would have the same appearance as Earth, with a few modifications."

Kyle dropped the straw from a juice drink onto the floor, wrapper and all, and poured the beverage into a glass. He hunched forward, holding the drink in both hands. "Such as?"

"More oceans, gigantic mountains, and a few grass-covered hills would be a nice touch, don't you think? Let's include rippling creeks, mossy trees, huge ferns,

massive redwoods." Brennan resisted the urge to grab colored pencils to sketch the wonders of his world.

"People?" Kyle quirked his eyebrows characteristically, in a way Brennan had never quite been able to imitate, even though they were identical twins.

"Of course. Now let's talk about the special properties of this planet. Snow feels warm to the touch, yet doesn't melt too quickly."

"Awesome." One of Kyle's favorite activities was inner-tubing in the snow; the more snow and the longer he could keep warm and dry, the better.

Brennan grinned. "It gets better—people on the planet don't have accidents or get hurt, and there aren't any diseases." At Kyle's skeptical glance, he continued. "No germs, no pollution."

Kyle nodded. "Maybe our assignment should have been to make *this* a perfect planet."

"Exactly!" Grabbing Kyle's juice drink straw, Brennan aimed it toward the wastebasket. "You could start by throwing away your garbage. No pollution, remember?"

Text Questions

1. What does it mean to say Kyle and Brennan were *identical* twins?
   a. They agree on many things.
   b. They look very similar.
   c. They dress very differently.
   d. They enjoy the same activities.

2. Based on what you read, what can you infer about Kyle's personality?
   a. He enjoys drawing pictures.
   b. He is practical when it comes to schoolwork.
   c. He thinks people should care about pollution.
   d. He doesn't want to do well in school.

3. Which sentence shows one of Brennan's values?
   a. People don't have accidents or get hurt.
   b. Snow feels warm to the touch.
   c. Let's have some fun.
   d. It would have the same appearance as Earth.

4. What overall conflict or problem can be identified in the story?
   a. Kyle and Brennan think that people should not try to change Earth.
   b. Kyle and Brennan disagree on what to do after school.
   c. Kyle and Brennan disagree on the best approach to a social-studies assignment.
   d. Brennan wishes Kyle would throw away his garbage.

5. What change do you think would help make Earth a more perfect planet?

   _____

   _____

Name_____

Restart

"Hey, new guy! Over here." Pike turned slowly, full circle, to discover three teens waving him toward the ditch that ran alongside the vacant field. Even though he had enrolled just yesterday, he instantly pegged these guys as belonging to a particular group. He knew, too, from past experience, the activities they engaged in that set them apart.

Raised in Africa by his aunt and uncle, Pike was now stateside, attending a different school every year as his relatives shuffled him about, agreeing on only one thing: Pike should finish his education in the United States. Everywhere he went, he heard the same thing, "You're Pike? Aren't you the one who lived in Africa?" He had determined this time around would be a new start and he'd even saved some money to purchase a new outfit for school.

Hesitantly, Pike walked toward the ditch, wondering if he even wanted to go there.

The one he'd identified as the leader spoke again. "My dad owns the local market. I'm sure he wouldn't mind if we helped ourselves to an after-school snack. Some soda, a bag of chips, what do you say?" Sounded harmless enough to Pike; he knew how to pull off something that simple without getting caught. Just as he took another step to follow them, he heard a slight rustle.

Turning, a glorious sight met his eyes—the prettiest girl he'd seen yet. Her long, blond hair caught the light, and she had shiny gloss on her lips. "Hi, I'm Melody. Have you had a tour of the school yet?"

His adviser had shown him around the day before, giving him a brief "here's what you need to know" introduction. However, he'd be a fool not to take this opportunity to begin to implement his new image. He trailed after her like a puppy, leaving the group of mischievous guys behind.

Text Questions

1. What was the leader of the boys inviting Pike to do?
   a. Have a snack at his house.
   b. Go to his dad's store to buy some snacks.
   c. Take a tour of the school.
   d. Shoplift some items from his dad's store.

2. What does the word *implement* mean as it is used in the text?
   a. a device used for a particular activity
   b. to fulfill or put into effect
   c. to give an instruction
   d. a tool used for scientific purposes

3. What is Melody's role in the story?
   a. She wants to help Pike decide what to do.
   b. She provides an alternative option for Pike.
   c. She makes fun of Pike because he's new to the school.
   d. She tells him he shouldn't go with the guys.

4. How would you characterize the guys who waved at Pike?
   a. They are athletes.
   b. They are part of the popular crowd.
   c. They often get in trouble.
   d. They are studious and get good grades.

5. Why do you suppose Pike wanted a new image?

_____

_____

Name_____

Tunnel Tour

"Come on, boys, this is our stop." Kenneth and Brian stood up quickly, following Mom to the passageway where they would exit the train after it rumbled to a halt. The doors opened, and the three of them shouldered their way out with the crowd, stepping away from the edge of the platform to assess their surroundings.

Brian pointed to a broad staircase fifty feet away. "Looks like we need to head that direction along with everyone else."

Once they reached street level, Mom asked Kenneth to consult his invitation. "What time is the reception? We want to allow plenty of time to locate the building and find your photograph hanging in the tunnel."

Kenneth had enjoyed sharing his photography with his teacher, including his shots from an earlier family vacation. Without his awareness, the instructor had entered one particular photo in a congressional art contest. One winner in each category, from each district, would have their entry displayed in the tunnel on Capitol Hill.

"I still can't believe you won," Brian congratulated his brother. "Thanks for inviting me to use one of your free tickets."

They made their way through the crowds of people hastening up Capitol Hill. Mom kept them moving right along so they would be able to check in with their senator, view the exhibit, and find the reception hall on time.

Fidgeting with his sleeves, Brian fussed about the humidity. "Why did we have to dress up so much? This is Kenneth's reception, not ours."

At last, they entered the tunnel with their escort. "Wow." Both boys stood mesmerized, turning slowly to take in the sight. They didn't stall long, though, quickening their steps to catch up with Mom and the senator.

There it was, just before the tunnel rounded a corner. Brian skidded to a stop to avoid missing it entirely on their brisk walk down the corridor: a seagull, soaring over a radiant white mountain.

Text Questions

1. Which is a synonym for the word *radiant* as it is used in the text?
   a. beaming   b. energetic   c. brilliant   d. bright

2. Which statement best describes the story problem?
   a. Kenneth's family couldn't find their way to the reception.
   b. The photograph wasn't displayed properly.
   c. Mom was concerned about making it to the reception on time.
   d. Kenneth's photograph didn't win the competition.

3. What role does the photograph play in the story?
   a. It is what caused the story to happen.
   b. It is a symbol for something that happens in the story.
   c. It is an obstacle for the main character.
   d. It sets the tone and mood for the story.

4. Why was it an honor for Kenneth's photograph to be displayed in the tunnel?
   a. His photograph was of a famous person.
   b. Only a few entries from each region were chosen.
   c. The senator had promised his photograph would be displayed.
   d. Kenneth's teacher wanted everyone to know about the photograph.

5. How would you imagine Kenneth's experience at the reception?

   _____

   _____

Name_____

Mountains and Mushrooms

"Fine! I'm going, I'm going!" Alyssa stomped out of the house, taking the bag of trash with her. It wasn't fair, she thought, that she had to do all the chores while her younger brother got to play video games. Snarling to herself, she continued to stew over the discrepancies. As the oldest, she didn't have fun watching Brent get away with things, as if their parents thought he was a perfect angel. In her opinion, Brent was a stuck-up, selfish brat.

Alyssa opened the lid of the trash can and dumped the bag in. Imagining it was Brent's face, she grinned and headed to the backyard before returning to complete the chores. She pulled the crumpled list out of her pocket and muttered to herself, "Scrub the kitchen, finish the laundry, vacuum the stairs." Alyssa closed her eyes briefly, savoring the moment. Nobody would bother her out here behind their cabin near the base of Mount Jabus. Beyond their fence, miles and miles of trails traversed the mountain.

Hiking was one of Alyssa's passions, while her brother hated outdoor activities. This gave her free reign of the trails, and what better time to go exploring? Hopping the fence, Alyssa set out on her trek, contemplating whether or not to return in time for dinner. Her parents might yell at her, but what did it matter? They wouldn't ground her because they knew she would return with renewed patience for her tasks. As she wandered along, Alyssa began to search for mushrooms. She had studied and learned the characteristics of over ten varieties and could tell which were poisonous and which were not. Poking around, Alyssa found a few Yellow Chanterelles. Then she spied a Matsutake, her favorite, which was difficult to find and known for its spicy aroma. She decided to continue her hunt a little longer before heading home.

Text Questions

1. What is the story problem?
   a. Alyssa needs to find mushrooms for dinner.
   b. Alyssa is frustrated with her brother.
   c. Alyssa finds poisonous mushrooms.
   d. Alyssa's brother follows her on the trail.

2. What does the word *discrepancies* mean as it is used in the text?
   a. differences
   b. lack of agreement
   c. complaints
   d. alternatives

3. How does Alyssa react to the perceived unfairness in how she and her brother are treated by their parents?
   a. She confronts them with her opinion.
   b. She forces her brother to help her with the chores.
   c. She takes some time away from the situation to cool down.
   d. She tells her parents to ground her brother.

4. What does it mean to say a mushroom has a *spicy aroma*?
   a. It has an exciting atmosphere.
   b. It has unusual characteristics.
   c. It smells awful.
   d. It has a pleasant fragrance.

5. What is one lesson readers can learn from the story? Give evidence from the story to support your answer.

   _____

   _____

   _____

Name_____

Runaway

Keyona crouched in the gravel next to the fence, willing herself invisible lest any family members should wander nearby. This was much more serious than an established game of hide and seek, in her opinion. She wanted a break from all of them, for an indefinite period of time, although she hadn't considered what she might do later, say, at dinnertime or when it got dark. It's not that she was afraid of the dark; she spent hours outside and was well acquainted with the neighborhood.

She heard rustling sounds behind her, but she hesitated before turning to check for the source.

"Hey, it's me," her younger brother Rashan whispered. "Why are you out here?"

She sighed in exasperation, "Just go away and leave me alone, okay?" Keyona turned away from him, thinking that she needed to find a better destination immediately, if not sooner. She would have gone farther away initially, if she could have figured out

where to go. Her temporary plan hadn't taken into consideration anyone seeking her out.

"And don't tell anyone where I am," she called to Rashan's retreating back.

Keyona took a deep breath then blew it out. Siblings were the primary cause of her departure in the first place. Mentally, she listed the reasons: six siblings were entirely too many, especially when they were all gathered together at the same time; the younger ones drove her crazy; and being the middle child left her feeling insignificant.

Hoisting her backpack, Keyona debated whether to go to her friend's house, which was three blocks over. She slumped down again to think about it. Her friend had three brothers and one sister—not exactly an oasis of peace and quiet. Often, when visiting, she missed the relative peace of home. As she pondered, her older brother stepped into the alley and, without a word, squatted next to her, his back against the fence.

Text Questions

1. What prompted Keyona's distress?
   a. Her entire family had gathered for the afternoon.
   b. She wanted time away from too many siblings.
   c. She wanted to visit her friend who wasn't home.
   d. Her brothers ganged up on her.

2. What does it mean to say Keyona had a *temporary* plan?
   a. She was running away.
   b. She hadn't thought through all the ramifications of the plan.
   c. It would last indefinitely without changing.
   d. It was a plan she had thought about carefully.

3. In what way could Keyona show perseverance in the story?
   a. She could talk to Rashan.
   b. She could talk things over with her friend.
   c. She could return home and show patience with everyone.
   d. She could insist on getting her own way.

4. Which statement best describes Keyona's feelings about her family?
   a. Being the middle child left her feeling insignificant.
   b. The younger ones drove her crazy.
   c. She hadn't planned on anyone seeking her out.
   d. She would have gone farther away initially.

5. What do you think will happen next in the story? Give reasons to support your answer.

   _____

   _____

Name_____

Morning Meal

Jorge couldn't help hovering in the doorway, absently rubbing the back of his neck while observing his mother under the comforter. He'd never seen her rise later than him, and he wondered what prompted it now.

"Mom?" he finally dared speak. "Is there anything you need before I catch the bus?"

"Mercy, what time is it?" She gave him a wan smile. "I should start my day, but it was such a horrid night. I hardly slept at all."

He twisted his hands in front of him, while attempting to reassure her. "Not to worry. I fixed breakfast and packed a lunch. Are you sure there isn't anything I can bring you?"

Mom tried to lift herself up to a sitting position but fell back on the pillows. "What an awful migraine. It left me dizzy. I'd better take this slowly." She turned her head to gaze at him. "Maybe some toast and juice, if you have enough time?"

Jorge practically bounded down the hall in his eagerness to please her. He fumbled in the kitchen, retrieving the toaster from the lower cupboard and putting a bagel down. While it toasted, he rummaged around for butter and jam, considering the options and trying to recall her favorite flavor. There wasn't any strawberry, and his dad was the one who used raspberry, so that settled it: pomegranate jam. Jorge poured juice and searched for a tray to carry everything. His preparations kept him from noticing the acrid smell of burning bread. Glancing at the clock, he hastily assembled the food and delivered the tray to Mom. He didn't have time to consider what he'd do if she didn't approve.

"Thank you, Jorge." Mom had managed to rouse herself a bit. "I'm sure the food will be just the thing to strengthen me. Don't worry about me; I'll be fine."

As he departed, Jorge marveled that she hadn't even hollered about the burnt toast!

Text Questions

1. Which word best describes the *acrid* smell of burning bread?
   a. sharp
   b. sour
   c. sarcastic
   d. stinging

2. Which statement explains a possible reason for Mom not getting up for breakfast?
   a. She usually got up later than Jorge.
   b. She slept through the alarm.
   c. She felt dizzy and lightheaded.
   d. She wanted Jorge to fix breakfast.

3. Which words best describe Jorge's feelings about his mother's unusual behavior?
   a. puzzled, surprised
   b. anxious, concerned
   c. fearful, afraid
   d. angry, resentful

4. Which of the following is best supported by evidence in the story?
   a. Jorge doesn't care about missing the bus.
   b. Jorge is willing to help.
   c. Jorge knows how to cook.
   d. Jorge isn't very independent.

5. Why might Mom have disapproved or hollered about the breakfast? Give reasons to support your answer.

_____

_____

Name_____

Kite Competition

The sight of the waves as he clambered out of the car made up for the fact Jonathon was here with his parents, missing his friend's much discussed birthday party. Family vacations didn't always make his list of preferred ways to spend a weekend, but Jonathon did love the ocean. He'd brought his skimboard, with the thought that he'd snag some time to himself.

"Hey, Jonathon," Dad motioned to him. "Here's an announcement for the kite festival this weekend. They have a competition for the best handcrafted kite, with awards based on its flying ability."

Jonathon reluctantly perused the poster tacked to a utility pole. "Honestly, Dad, I'd rather skimboard."

"Okay," Dad laid a hand on Jonathon's shoulder. "I can't force you to enter, but I can encourage you.

You've often said you wish you could express your creativity. Well, here's your opportunity."

"Huh?" Puzzled, Jonathon considered his dad's words. Maybe making a kite would be a creative way to express himself, but he had his doubts. Still, Jonathon agreed to give it a try to please him.

Carrying his kite, Jonathon advanced to the area where his fellow competitors had gathered. The wind tugged the frame, threatening to pull the canvas into the air. It felt like an extension of himself, soaring and showing everyone what he was made of, instead of feeling invisible as he so often did. Jonathon braced himself. His orange and green kite contrasted sharply to the dull brown of the sand and gray-blue of the ocean. With glee, he flung his kite skyward.

Text Questions

1. Based on what you read, what is Jonathon's decision, or dilemma, in the story?
   a. He didn't want to miss his friend's birthday party.
   b. He wanted to snag some time for himself.
   c. He couldn't decide whether to skimboard or enter the kite competition.
   d. He didn't care what his dad thought.

2. How does Jonathon's dad influence him in the story?
   a. He said Jonathon could go to the birthday party.
   b. He helped Jonathon build a kite.
   c. He forbid Jonathon from skimboarding.
   d. He gave Jonathon a suggestion and supported him.

3. What is one theme of the text?
   a. honesty
   b. self-expression
   c. insecurity
   d. fear of failure

4. What does the word *threatening* mean as it is used in the text?
   a. a warning
   b. approaching quickly
   c. frightening
   d. menacing toward another person

5. What do you learn about Jonathon in the last paragraph?

   _____

   _____

   _____

Name_____

Runner-Up

Emily checked her shoelaces and began to jog in small circles, slowly, waiting for Sierra. She didn't mind the brief delay; she was so grateful to have a running partner. Practically the first thing Emily had done after enrolling in this new school was to sign up for cross-country. Her mom said getting involved was the best way to make new friends, and Emily agreed.

"Hi, sorry I'm late. Have you checked the route? It's a good day for a run, don't you think?" Sierra arrived, talking nonstop as was her habit. Sierra ran every day, and her consistency had motivated Emily to take her own training more seriously. The regular practice had enabled both of them to improve their times over various terrains.

Continuing her warm-up, Emily asked, "Are you racing next week in the big regional meet?"

Sierra jogged a bit, bouncing in her impatience to start the course for the day. "Yeah, the coach encourages everyone to participate."

"Oh." Emily trailed behind Sierra just a bit, processing this information as they loped across the field, setting a comfortable pace. It was difficult for Emily to keep from fretting, knowing Sierra was easily the faster runner. She worried that her own time might hinder the team.

Race day arrived, and Emily gathered with the other team members to receive a colored wristband that identified their school, along with final instructions about the course. "Sierra, where's your band?"

"You're running in my place today because your times will contribute as much to the team as mine, and I want you to have the opportunity to show your stuff to the team. I'll be your water girl at the end." Sierra grinned and gave Emily a high-five.

"Wow, you'd give up a race for me?" Emily gave her friend a quick hug and determined this race would be her best performance ever.

Text Questions

1. What does it mean to give your best *performance*?
   a. to finish the race
   b. to achieve and do well
   c. to present music before an audience
   d. to function

2. Which title would <u>not</u> be a good alternative for this text?
   a. "Water Girl"
   b. "Cross-Country Race"
   c. "Friends Forever"
   d. "Running Partners"

3. Why was Emily fretting?
   a. She didn't like waiting for Sierra.
   b. She wouldn't be able to race in the regional meet.
   c. She was afraid she would lose her wristband.
   d. She was concerned her times would hinder the team.

4. Which statement best explains Sierra's reasons for her actions?
   a. "It's a good day for a run."
   b. "The coach encourages everyone to participate."
   c. "I want you to have the opportunity to show your stuff to the team."
   d. "I'll be your water girl at the end."

5. What is the theme, and how is it developed? Use evidence from the text to support your answer.

   _____

   _____

Name_____

A New Language

Bohdan took a deep breath as he scanned the crowd for someone who might be seeking him. Balancing his name card with his carry-on bag, he wandered away from the relative safety of the gate area toward the main corridor of the terminal. He hoped these few steps wouldn't be a foolish move that would result in missed connections with his host family. He'd traveled a bit in Europe before—short distances on family vacations—but nothing had quite prepared him for the vastness of America. After crossing the Atlantic, he had changed planes in Philadelphia and flown another five hours to reach his destination. He focused again on looking intently at faces as people bustled by, hoping for a face made familiar only by photographs.

"Ah, here you are," a man approached him, extending his hand for a welcoming handshake. Bohdan sighed with relief. "Jeremy," he said, in introduction. "My wife, Melissa and my daughter, Amy. Our son had football practice. Do you have checked luggage?"

Bohdan nodded as he scrambled to mentally translate the unusual sounds of English, which was so different from what he heard in his native Slovak. Eleven-year-old Amy peppered him with questions as they made their way through the airport. He attempted to answer, knowing this was only a preview of the next day when everyone would notice a new student midway through the year.

After eating his American-style sandwich with two slices of bread, Bohdan wandered outside to watch a group playing basketball. His mind spun from the effort of functioning all morning in a nonnative language. A girl came to sit next to him on the bleachers, greeting him in Slovak.

"You speak Slovak?" Shocked, Bohdan couldn't help reverting to his own language.

Smiling, she nodded. Her next words were in English, as if she was uncertain of all the vocabulary words. "I've been studying through an online language program. You can help me practice."

Text Questions ....

1. What is the significance of the girl studying language online?
   a. She wants to show Bohdan her intelligence.
   b. She shows friendship and acceptance to a newcomer.
   c. She helps Bohdan feel ill at ease.
   d. She tells Bohdan this is the best way to learn English.

2. Why might Bohdan use the term *vastness* to describe America?
   a. It is a very large country.
   b. A great number of people live in America.
   c. It has a lot of space without people.
   d. The country does not have boundaries.

3. What is the theme or moral of the text?
   a. loyalty
   b. honesty
   c. fear of failure
   d. belonging

4. What would cause Bohdan to be noticed at school?
   a. He is carrying a name card.
   b. He has never traveled before.
   c. He is a new student partway through the year.
   d. He is not speaking English at school.

5. What does Bohdan struggle with the most in his adjustment to a new country? Give evidence to support your answer.

   _____

   _____

Name_____

Return of the Aunts

Always they descended in a pair, flinging open the front door. Auntie Rachel and Auntie Cordelia arrived in a clamor, saying hello as they clunked too many suitcases on the hall floor, and the dogs howled. Auntie Cordelia headed for the kitchen, where Mother stood speechless, holding a wooden spoon. "Cordelia," Mother's voice quivered, and the spoon hit the counter.

"We're here, Mary Jane. You sit right down and rest them feet. What you got cooking—baked beans? Let's spice them up a bit." Soon, horribly strong odors colored the air. Auntie Rachel commenced to dusting—everything wood and some things that weren't. You daren't sit still too long when Auntie Rachel flung her cloth. Dad heard the ruckus and snuck in the back door, creaking up the stairwell but not quick enough.

"Robert," Cordelia crooned. "Come and taste these beans, and see if I've got enough flavor."

"How long are you staying?" Mother asked, her voice still shaky.

"Oh, maybe a fortnight. Ha! I've always wanted to say *fortnight*, ever since we traveled to England."

However, it turned out the aunts didn't stay long, once my brother, Caleb, and I decided to act. At dinner, Caleb told about the pheasant he had hanging in the barn and how he'd skin it for dinner tomorrow. Mother seemed to catch on and pondered which pot would be big enough. Auntie Rachel attempted to eat her Brussels sprouts, but imagination took over and she fled the table. Cordelia went pale. "You expect me to cook wild animals?"

"Oh, yes," Caleb said proudly. "How you gonna fix them, Auntie Cordelia? I'm sure Mother would be overjoyed to find you a recipe."

The aunts left before dessert. We could hear banging suitcases in the spare room; they didn't even mess up the comforter on the bed with sleeping. Caleb got a big dish of ice cream with chocolate sauce and whipped cream as the door slammed behind the aunts.

Text Questions

1. Which words describe Mother's response to the aunts?
   a. clamor, ruckus, banging
   b. speechless, quivered, shaky
   c. snuck, creaking, quick
   d. spice, odor, flavor

2. What was Mother doing when she *pondered* which pot would be big enough?
   a. She considered it carefully.
   b. She didn't give it much thought.
   c. She weighed each pot in the kitchen.
   d. She reflected on why she would use a pot to cook pheasant.

3. What is the main problem in the story?
   a. The aunts come to cook and clean.
   b. The aunts are unwelcome and cause a ruckus.
   c. The aunts catch Dad sneaking up the stairs.
   d. The aunts do not like to eat pheasant.

4. Which of the following did <u>not</u> happen in the story?
   a. Auntie Cordelia headed for the kitchen.
   b. Auntie Rachel commenced to dusting.
   c. Auntie Cordelia traveled from England.
   d. Auntie Rachel fled from the table.

5. How might the story change if Caleb hadn't claimed to have caught a pheasant?

   _____

   _____

Name_____

From the Depths

"You should go fishing with Dad sometime," Brett nudged his sister, Jayna. "It's great! You get to spend time with Dad, watch gentle waves lap at the boat, and eat delicious fish for dinner." He grinned, knowing Jayna loved swimming and all things water-related, including fish, but only if they were cooked. Worms and other such edibles required for fishing were not even on her list.

"Another day, okay?"

"Brett isn't just teasing." Jayna didn't realize Dad had been listening in on their conversation. "Mom's taking Brett to a swim meet, and I'd enjoy having some company—want to come along?"

The sun sparkled on the water, and Jayna had to admit the weather was just right—not blistering hot but warm enough to sit still on the surface of the lake without shivering. Dad launched the dory and maneuvered to within a quarter mile of shore, in an area with massive oaks and elms lining the bank. He cast his line into a still deep pool, hooked his rod to the edge of the craft, and settled into a daydream while waiting.

Jayna stared intently into the depths, wishing she had brought something to read. At first, she thought the dark spot drifting by was the shadow of a trout, but when it began to surface, Jayna realized it was a different creature entirely. The flat gray snout, white whiskers, flat head with wide set eyes and steel and white markings looked like a cross between a shark and a prehistoric monster. Suddenly, the fish (if indeed that's what it was) disappeared. The fishing pole jerked violently before being yanked overboard. Ripples widened as the boat bounced roughly in the water, then tipped over. Jayna struggled to find her bearings to swim to her Dad and right the craft but found her feet tangled in the fishing line. She glanced around to locate him, but he had disappeared along with the creature and the rod.

Text Questions

1. What convinced Jayna to go fishing?
   a. She would be able to go swimming.
   b. She could spend time with Dad.
   c. She liked to eat fish.
   d. She didn't want to go to Brett's swim meet.

2. Based on what you read, what kind of creature did Jayna see?
   a. a prehistoric monster   c. a mythical beast
   b. a lake fish   d. an ocean shark

3. Which characteristic did Jayna display?
   a. stubbornness   c. curiosity
   b. diligence   d. impatience

4. What did Brett do when he *nudged* his sister?
   a. He pushed her gently with his elbow.
   b. He tapped her shoulder with his finger.
   c. He shoved her roughly into the wall.
   d. He bumped into her by accident.

5. What is the unsolved mystery in the story? How would you explain what happened?

_____
_____
_____

Name_____

Green Goo

Brandon leaned his skateboard against the kitchen wall as he shrugged off his backpack, letting the screen door slam shut behind him.

"You'd better make sure the wheels are clean or Mom won't be very pleased. It doesn't belong in the house anyway." Tabitha laid a spatula on the counter and reached up to put a container of oat cereal in the pantry. Then she turned toward the hallway.

Opening the refrigerator, Brandon scanned the contents, searching for something to drink. He decided maybe he'd better start with water, so he retrieved a glass from the cupboard and went to the sink. "Ewww, what's this?" He motioned feebly to a mess of green goo in the blender perched on the counter.

His sister grinned. "Don't you like my experiment?"

"I'm guessing this will bother Mom more than my skateboard." Brandon made a face and began rummaging through the kitchen for something edible, as he assumed whatever his sister had been creating was not fit for human consumption.

"Mom said I could invent something," Tabitha retorted. "I'll clean it up soon enough."

"What's in it, anyway? It smells horrible."

Tabitha offered Brandon a spoon. "Would you like to be the first person to taste it and guess the ingredients?"

"No way." Brandon hefted his skateboard and walked through the dining room on his way to his bedroom. He had to admit, though, he was curious. More to the point, if the stuff wasn't fit to eat, what could they do with it? Hesitating, he turned. "What are you going to do with your concoction?"

"Mom said if it didn't turn out right, I could test the new garbage disposal."

Text Questions

1. Based on what you read, what might have been one of the ingredients in Tabitha's creation?
   a. green jelly beans
   b. breadcrumbs
   c. spinach
   d. orange juice

2. What does the word *curious* mean as it is used in the text?
   a. eager to know
   b. prying into her business
   c. seeking attention because it was unusual
   d. careful

3. What was Brandon's reaction to Tabitha's concoction?
   a. He thought it sounded delicious.
   b. He thought their mother would enjoy it.
   c. He wasn't sure it would be fit to eat.
   d. He was sure it would clog the garbage disposal.

4. Why might someone hesitate to consume something with mysterious ingredients?
   a. to make sure the food is not rotten
   b. to make sure it doesn't have inedible items
   c. to make sure you don't have food allergies
   d. all of the above

5. How would you add a greater element of suspense and mystery to this story?

_____

_____

Name_____

Adventure Hike

Trevor trudged up the rise, knowing the view from the top would be spectacular. He assumed Ellie was keeping pace behind him. The humidity kept his shirt clinging to his skin under the daypack he wore. The red trail dust covered his tennis shoes, and he had mud splatters on his legs from places where moisture from the last tropical shower didn't evaporate.

"Unbelievable view, isn't it?" Ellie stood alongside him, catching her breath.

"You can see all along the Na Pali coast." Trevor pointed. "How are you doing?" He felt responsible for Ellie, since he'd begged her parents to allow his younger cousin to accompany him on this adventure hike.

"I'm okay. How many more ridges?" They had studied the trail in the guidebook but weren't prepared for the steep ridges. She repositioned her water bottle in the pack.

"This is the last ridge," he said, gesturing ahead. "Below is the secluded beach we read about. We'll rest there for lunch before following the trail inland along the creek into the jungle."

Trevor and Ellie enjoyed their respite, watching surfers and crashing waves, before picking their way among the rocks, watching carefully to make sure they didn't miss the trail. They drained their water bottles as the humidity increased and insects assaulted them. Ellie's shoes rubbed blisters on her feet, but she dared not complain, knowing Trevor had to be experiencing the same. Sloshing through the stream at times, scrambling over slippery rocks, they navigated the narrow path through the jungle.

"How much farther to the falls, do you think?" Ellie gasped.

"Not sure. We should have brought more water." Trevor held back giant leaves to let her pass into a clearing of sorts. "I don't think this is it."

"This waterfall may not be our destination, but it looks good to me. Let's stop here."

Text Questions

1. What does it mean to say the beach is *secluded*?
   a. locked away
   b. withdrawn
   c. set apart for a particular purpose
   d. isolated

2. In what type of environment were Trevor and Ellie hiking?
   a. desert
   b. tropical
   c. polar
   d. temperate

3. In what ways were Trevor and Ellie unprepared for their adventure?
   a. They didn't pack enough water for the climate.
   b. They didn't allow enough time to get to their destination before dark.
   c. They didn't consult a trail guide.
   d. They didn't wear tennis shoes.

4. What is the main idea of the text?
   a. Tropical hikes have beautiful scenery.
   b. A tropical hike can be strenuous.
   c. It's important to reach your destination no matter what.
   d. Do not take someone younger than you on an adventure hike.

5. What could Trevor and Ellie have done differently to make the hike more enjoyable?

_____

_____

Name_____

Security Guards

"Where do you suppose they go?" Katrina whipped her long braid around as she rotated slowly on the metal cafeteria bench.

Perched on the end of the bench, Melinda leaned forward, crossing her long legs and swinging one foot. "I dunno. D'ya suppose they go off to sleep or something?"

Taking a bite of apple, Katrina chewed, pondering the question. "I think filling the role of security guard is just a cover for their real job. What if the security guards were actually the principal's personal agents, hired to snoop in kids' lockers, gathering information?"

Both girls giggled as they gathered up their garbage and threw it away.

"Maybe their police academy instruction was so awful that they have to train at a martial arts center." Melinda put her hands alongside her cheeks as if to restrain herself. "Maybe their alternate job is to clean the marsupial cages at the local zoo."

Tears trickled down Katrina's face, and she made a feeble attempt at swiping them away. "You're so weird. What if they're really aliens—masked aliens!"

The bell rang, signaling the end of lunch and the passing period for afternoon class. The laughing girls picked up their backpacks and headed to gym class, stopping at their lockers on the way. Behind them a boy trailed, the son of one of the security guards. He had always assumed his dad ate lunch, just as he did. But the overheard conversation made him wonder, how would anyone really know what security guards do? Neither the boy nor the giggling girls noticed the lights flickering as they walked down the corridor.

Text Questions

1. What made the boy wonder about the job of security guards?
   a. His dad was a security guard.
   b. He overheard the girls talking.
   c. He had never seen his dad eat lunch.
   d. He had seen his dad hanging around the lockers.

2. What does the word *principal* mean as it is used in the text?
   a. the head of the school
   b. the main actor in a performance
   c. the person with the most authority
   d. the person primarily responsible for an obligation

3. What is the mystery in the story?
   a. the true role of security guards at school
   b. what security guards eat for lunch
   c. where the other kids were during lunch
   d. why the lights in the corridor flickered

4. Which of the following is the <u>least</u> likely explanation for the girls' question regarding the whereabouts of the guards?
   a. personal agents
   b. additional training during the day
   c. cleaning cages at the zoo
   d. masked aliens

5. What explanation would you give for the lack of visibility of the security guards and the flickering lights?

   _____

   _____

Name_____

Island of Mystery

Christopher hesitated before descending the steps to the tarmac, uncertain as to what—or who—they might find on this isolated but inhabited island. His parents had sent him to visit his grandparents for summer vacation, and they were known for embarking on unusual adventures, this being the latest. Sometimes Christopher wondered when his grandparents would give up their wild travels and be content to stay at home, reliving their adventures through pictures or videos.

"We're here," he announced, to no one in particular. "Now what?"

Grandpa Earl ruffled Christopher's hair and grinned. "Let's go find some mystery."

Christopher raised his eyebrows. "Huh? I thought we were here to sightsee."

"You could call it that," his grandmother's soft voice didn't match her spirit of fun and adventure. "We plan to visit historical sites to learn more about the stories behind the statues."

"Statues? We flew all this way to see hunks of rock?" Shaking his head in disbelief, Christopher grabbed

Grandma's carry-on and followed Grandpa into the terminal. He gazed at the low-lying hills in the distance covered with vegetation and wondered how his grandparents had been able to afford this trip.

"Imagine that, two thousand miles from anywhere, on an island with a few people and a lot of statues." Grandpa Earl chuckled. "For years scientists presumed there weren't enough people with the skills or tools to build the statues. So how did the massive icons get here?"

Christopher humored his grandfather. "And why? And who built them?" He glanced around to make sure they still had Grandma Margie in tow.

Oblivious to Christopher's concerns, Grandpa continued on, assuming Grandma could take care of herself. "They have a few clues: signs of horrendous warfare, a population that dwindled from several thousand to just over one hundred, statutes toppled and in disrepair. Archaeologists have more questions than answers, but now they're talking with the island's inhabitants."

Text Questions

1. Which question is still unanswered about the island?
   a. who is visiting it
   b. what the geography is like
   c. why it has statues
   d. whether it is inhabited

2. How do the scientists hope to learn more about the mystery?
   a. by visiting the historical sites with statues
   b. by taking pictures and videos
   c. by researching the facts about the population
   d. by talking to the inhabitants

3. What does the word *presume* mean as it is used in the text?
   a. to plan to do something without authority
   b. to take for granted
   c. to consider the possibilities
   d. to assume something is true based on evidence

4. What is the main idea of the text?
   a. spending summer vacation with grandparents
   b. going on an island adventure
   c. learning about mysterious statues on an island
   d. what Christopher might find on the island

5. Based on the evidence in the story, what might be one possible explanation for the current state of the statues?

_____

_____

Name_____

Reaching for the Heights

Andrea took her time descending from the fifty-year-old cherry tree in the vacant lot. The leafy giant held far more intrigue for her than the abandoned building on the property. Most of her friends had outgrown tree climbing, if they had ever had an interest. Granted, the kids she knew who had climbed trees had never reached the heights she dared. Hopping down, she hurried to make it to school before the tardy bell rang.

During lunch break, Andrea had a hard time making a decision. She was sure she could get a pick-up game of Ultimate Frisbee going, but the drain pipe behind the oak tree at the end of the classroom wing had been calling to her since she'd discovered it the previous week.

"What does she think she's doing? Wonder if we should alert the janitor and let her get caught." Andrea caught snatches of conversation as she stealthily approached her latest climbing target.

"Beats me, although I wish I were that agile and good at climbing." Gavin shrugged his shoulders and sauntered toward the baseball diamond.

"Why?" Ian didn't understand his friend's needs for challenge and excitement.

Andrea found it difficult at times to ignore the boys' taunts, although at other times, they made good comrades for her adventurous spirit. Her friends didn't realize she had goals that went far beyond climbing whatever was handy. Occasionally, Andrea dreamed of the future: a time when she would climb trees and ladders and slide down poles, all to rescue people and help them in their distress.

Text Questions

1. Which phrase does <u>not</u> give you a clue to Andrea's personality?
   a. the leafy giant
   b. had outgrown tree climbing
   c. the heights she dared
   d. good comrades for her adventurous spirit

2. What does Andrea see herself doing in the future?
   a. climbing trees and ladders as a firefighter
   b. climbing poles in a circus
   c. climbing utility poles to fix telephone wires
   d. climbing trees as a tree trimmer

3. What does the word *abandoned* mean as it is used in the text?
   a. Someone was hiding in the building and watching Andrea.
   b. Someone lived on the property, and Andrea was trespassing.
   c. Someone had left some things in the building.
   d. Someone deserted the building and no longer used it.

4. What role do the boys play in the story?
   a. They prevent Andrea from reaching her goals.
   b. They help Andrea succeed.
   c. They provide conflict by sometimes teasing and sometimes joining Andrea.
   d. They give wisdom to the main character.

5. Based on what you read, what elements of danger are in the story?

   _____

   _____

Name_____

Surf's Up!

"Don't forget your lunch!"

"I won't," Koda reassured his mom, already on his way out of the house. With anticipation, he gathered up his new surfboard, sunscreen, and flippers.

"Surf's up!" his friend Zachary greeted him. Arriving at the beach, they gaped in astonishment at the huge waves sparkling and crashing in the sunshine.

They paddled out together and waited for the perfect wave. Zachary caught a wave before Koda and rode it all the way in. Finally, Koda spied his opportunity. Facing the beach, he lay on his board and paddled furiously, hoping to stand at just the right moment and catch a ride to shore.

Raising his head to scramble into position, Koda saw Zachary on the beach, a look of terror on his face. Koda turned to discover a massive wall of water bearing down on him. Paddling as fast as he could, he couldn't escape, and the wave swept Koda up. He rose with the water until his surfboard crested on top of the wave. For a brief moment, Koda entertained the hope he would just slide down the back of the wave, since he wasn't yet standing on his board. As he began to slide forward and fall with the wave, Koda panicked. The wave swallowed his board. Fortunately, he remembered the advice to swim safely behind the wave. He took a deep breath and let the swells carry him unharmed to calm waters.

Zachary hurried over. "You okay?"

Nodding, Koda glanced around for his board.

"Sorry, it's broken." Zachary offered him a hand up out of the coarse sand. "Here, borrow my board and get right back out there."

Koda wasn't sure he was ready to try again, but he thanked Zachary and paddled back out. What a good surfing buddy. Zach had managed to scare up a board and was right there with him.

Text Questions

1. Why might Zachary encourage Koda to "get right back out there"?
   a. He wanted Koda to get hurt.
   b. He wanted Koda to overcome any doubts and fears.
   c. He wanted Koda to find the pieces of his board so Zachary could have his board back.
   d. He wanted to try to catch another perfect wave.

2. What is the main idea of the text?
   a. surfing with a friend
   b. buying a surfboard
   c. surfing safety rules
   d. learning to surf

3. Why did Koda gather up his board and flippers in *anticipation*?
   a. He was preventing his brother from trying the new surfboard.
   b. He was looking forward to trying his new board.
   c. He was expecting Zachary to help him.
   d. He was waiting for the perfect wave.

4. Which sentence shows why Koda emerged unharmed from his experience?
   a. Koda turned to discover a massive wall of water bearing down on him.
   b. Paddling as fast as he could, he couldn't escape.
   c. He rose with the water until his surfboard crested on top of the wave.
   d. He remembered the advice to swim safely behind the wave.

5. What dangers did Koda face in this story?

_____

_____

Name_____

Stranded!

Derek stooped to yank his sandals off his feet, not bothering to unfasten the straps. "Come on, let's go!" he hollered to Trey. "If we hurry we can make it to the secret beach, explore a bit, and cross back over without getting stranded by the tide." Leaving the sandals perched on a boulder, Derek continued across the rocky outcropping, leaving Trey to scramble after him.

The surf pounded the rocks just off the shore, leaving the approach to the beach beyond the point unobstructed by seawater. Derek had studied the tide tables carefully, planning this excursion for days, looking forward to being able to make the trek to the often inaccessible stretch of shoreline. He jumped down from his perch to land on a thin layer of residual saltwater on the sand below.

"Right behind you!" Trey paused to balance on the jagged rocks, before leaping down to join Derek.

"Wow! Let's go investigate the caves." Both boys loped across the beach toward the caves at the base of the cliff.

Engrossed in their explorations, the boys didn't realize how far away from the access point they'd wandered, until Derek turned to watch a magnificent wave crash to shore. "Trey! We need to head back, or we'll be caught when the tide comes in."

Derek and Trey raced down the beach, setting challenges along the way to see who could outrun the other, until they arrived at the point. Seawater swirled and eddied below the rock outcropping as they clambered along the pathway over the point. Just before the descent to the main beach, they stopped to survey the situation. Rippling waves and sea foam filled the crevices between the rocks below, engulfing their access to solid sand.

Text Questions

1. What does the word *excursion* mean as it is used in the text?
   a. a military raid
   b. a round trip on a train or ship with reduced rates
   c. a short trip taken for pleasure
   d. a tour of a place of interest

2. How does the setting affect the characters in the story?
   a. The setting provides the story problem and conflict.
   b. The setting provides a way for the characters to develop and display specific traits.
   c. The characters manipulate the setting to achieve their goals.
   d. The characters do not interact with the setting.

3. What is the theme or moral of the text?
   a. Always have a buddy to swim in the ocean.
   b. Be aware of waves and tides.
   c. Wear shoes to explore beaches and caves.
   d. If you climb rocks, you will be trapped.

4. Why did Derek want to visit the secret beach?
   a. He wanted to get stranded by the tides.
   b. He had been there many times.
   c. He wanted to run races on the beach.
   d. He wanted to explore the caves.

5. What are some options Derek and Trey might have for making it safely back to shore? Give reasons to support your answer.

_____

_____

Name_____

The Case of the Missing Reed

Nicholas scooted into the band room seconds before the final bell. He hadn't intended to be tardy, as he wanted the extra time to switch gears in his thinking from schoolwork to the upcoming band festival. It would have been helpful to have a few minutes to review the music before rehearsal, as well. After opening his clarinet case, he reached for his reed guard to take out a new reed for the instrument.

"What? Where are my reeds?" Sheets of music scattered as Nicholas frantically searched the case. The reeds were nowhere to be found. He calmed down enough to quickly assemble the clarinet and check to see if he had a reed in place from the previous practice. Nicholas sighed with relief at the sight of the slim, light-colored piece of wood held in place on the mouthpiece with the ligature, or clamp. Upon looking closely, he realized the reed was split, and now he had no way to replace it.

Nicholas began to panic, the festival was tomorrow, and he wanted to keep his first-chair position.

"Mr. Lehman, have you seen my reed guard?" With effort, Nicholas kept his tone even and his voice calm. "It's not in my case, and the reed I have is split."

Mr. Lehman looked up from arranging music on his director's stand. "Did you have it yesterday?"

At the risk of having it sound like a lame excuse, Nicholas said, "Yes. It just disappeared."

Looking out over the gathering band students, Mr. Lehman posed the question to the class, asking also if anyone had a reed Nicholas could use for rehearsal.

"I'll look at home, sir, just in case," Nicholas assured his instructor. There had to be some explanation; he was conscientious with his band equipment.

Text Questions

1. What does the word *conscientious* mean as it is used in the text?
   a. He always used the right band equipment.
   b. He did not steal other people's band equipment.
   c. He took care of his equipment.
   d. He was strict about who could borrow his equipment.

2. What will happen if Nicholas doesn't find the reed guard?
   a. He will be disqualified from band.
   b. He will play with a split reed in the band festival.
   c. He will have to borrow a reed for rehearsal.
   d. He will lose his first chair position in band.

3. Why did Nicholas want to arrive early to band rehearsal?
   a. He had been tardy too many times already.
   b. He wanted to review the music before rehearsal.
   c. He wanted to search for the missing reed guard.
   d. He needed to assemble his instrument.

4. Which of the following statements does not express one of Nicholas's concerns about the missing reed guard?
   a. The reed he had was split.
   b. He didn't have any other replacement reeds.
   c. The band festival was the next day.
   d. He was conscientious about his band equipment.

5. What are some things Nicholas could do to solve the mystery?

   _____

   _____

Name_____

The Kraken

The captain breathed a sigh of relief with the dawning of the new day. All through the night, his crew had been pulling out all the stops in a race for survival. Every hand at the oars, the ship had practically flown away from the danger of that *thing*. The captain believed it was an enormous pirate ship, robbing unarmed merchant ships, and then sinking their victims. The crewmen, however, were haunted by stories told in the dark of the night at the taverns in town. The legends claimed a horrific beast roamed the seas, preying on ships, eating them whole in the night. The Kraken! The beast would appear during the worst storms, rising out of the sea, wrapping its tentacles around the ships and crushing them. Rumor had it that the previous night the ship *SeaStar* had been transporting spices from India to England when it hit. First the clouds came, then the rains, then the sleet. The sailor in the crow's nest had spotted it first. A large shape—black against the fog of the night—was gaining on them! The captain, concerned for the welfare of vessel and crew, had ordered the crew to sail northeast toward the coastline away from the storm and the phantom. They had fled in frenzy, fear feeding their speed toward the sunrise. The captain looked to the dawn again. Whether it was a pirate ship as he suspected or a large sea monster, it didn't matter. What mattered was that it never showed itself in the daytime. Now that the sun was up, the crew gave a resounding cheer. They were safe for the moment.

Text Questions

1. What does it mean to say the captain was concerned for the crew's *welfare*?
   a. He wanted them to stay healthy.
   b. He was concerned about their well-being and safety.
   c. He worked for the government to provide aid.
   d. He worked hard to provide benefits for the crew.

2. Based on what you read, which was <u>not</u> a possibility for the identity of the mysterious thing?
   a. a pirate ship
   b. a horrific beast
   c. an unidentified island
   d. a violent storm

3. Which evidence best supports the theory that the mysterious thing was a storm?
   a. The clouds, rain, and sleet came.
   b. It robbed their ship of its cargo.
   c. It had been eaten during the night.
   d. It disappeared during the daytime.

4. How do members of the crew react to the threat?
   a. They determine to fight the beast head-on.
   b. They flee in fear and cheer when the threat disappears with the dawn.
   c. They hide from the pirates to escape capture.
   d. They man the lifeboats to escape potential disaster.

5. Why do you think the mysterious thing disappears in the daytime?

   _____

   _____

   _____

Name_____

Hummock Trail

Matt grabbed Pete's arm. "C'mon, Mr. Graville is telling us about the nature walk."

"What's so exciting about that?" Pete grumbled. "Nature walks are for wimps." He trailed behind Matt, more to stay out of trouble than out of any real interest.

"When was the last time you took a hike among pieces of volcano?" Matt challenged, and took a step closer to the rest of the group gathered around their science teacher. Matt had been looking forward to this field trip, not only for the chance to be excused from other classes but also for the opportunity to see a volcano up close. They had already visited the visitor center and exhibits at the rim of the volcano, which he'd found fascinating. But this stop promised to be even more exciting: they would hike a trail through hummocks left by the last eruption. As far as Matt was concerned, this was second only to hiking the rim of the crater itself, which they had not been allowed to do.

"Does everyone have a trail guide, assignment sheet, and buddy?"

Pete confronted the instructor. "Why do we need buddies? This is middle school, not elementary."

"Good question," Mr. Graville acknowledged. "Does anyone know the answer?"

Matt didn't want to antagonize his friend any further so he kept quiet, although he knew the reasoning behind the requirement. While Mr. Graville was reviewing the questions they would investigate, Matt had gazed across the terrain and noticed the trail was barely visible among the gravelly sand and pumice. He was curious to discover the effects of the eruption on the landscape and how the environment had evolved since then.

Text Questions

1. What does the word *hummocks* mean as it is used in the third paragraph?
   a. low rounded hills
   b. heavily wooded land
   c. mounds in an ice field
   d. mounds of rock, ash, and mud

2. What danger might they face on the trail that would require the presence of a buddy?
   a. unexpected predators
   b. shifting terrain
   c. losing the trail and getting lost
   d. the volcano erupting

3. Based on what you read, which word best describes the landscape?
   a. barren
   b. icy
   c. breathtaking
   d. lush

4. What is the main idea of the text?
   a. how to talk with a science teacher
   b. exploring a hummock trail near a volcano
   c. things to do on science field trips
   d. answering questions about the volcano's crater

5. Why did Matt find hiking the hummock trail exciting? Give evidence from the story to support your answer.

   _____

   _____

Name_____

Dinner Biscuits

"Mrs. Conte, we don't have a recipe." Juan almost forgot to raise his hand. One of his home economics teacher's strict rules was students had to raise their hands so she knew who was talking to her among the chattering from the kitchen stations.

One station over, Maya rummaged through the cupboards looking for the ingredients they needed. "Flour, salt, baking soda," she muttered. Her partner, Kaitlyn, assembled a mixing bowl, measuring cups and spoons, and a pastry blender on the counter. Together, they perused the recipe for today's assignment: dinner biscuits. The group or groups whose final product had the highest score would help make biscuits for the faculty breakfast the following week and be excused from their first-period class.

During the taste test, Mrs. Conte awarded high marks to Maya and Kaitlyn's biscuits. "What's that unusual flavor I detect? And your biscuits are a bit sweeter—did you follow the recipe exactly?"

Kaitlyn smiled and nodded. She knew her biscuits were light and flaky, and she also knew how she had chosen to deviate from the recipe.

"See you at the faculty breakfast, Mrs. Conte," Kaitlyn gathered her books and waved as she left the home economics room.

After all the students had exited, Mrs. Conte rifled through the papers in the basket on the corner of her desk. She had distributed copies of the same recipe to the entire class, marking the kitchen number on each recipe copy, and requested that students leave their copies on their way out. Kaitlyn and Maya's recipe copy wasn't there. Thinking they had left it on the kitchen counter, the teacher searched their station. No recipe.

Text Questions

1. Why did Mrs. Conte search Kaitlyn's kitchen station?
   a. to discover the mystery ingredient
   b. to put the utensils away
   c. to find the recipe copy
   d. to taste the dinner biscuits

2. Based on what you read, which flavor might Kaitlyn have added?
   a. baking soda
   b. orange extract
   c. extra salt
   d. chili powder

3. What does the word *deviate* mean as it is used in the text?
   a. to turn aside from the directions
   b. to do the wrong thing
   c. to put the recipe in a different place
   d. to disobey the kitchen rules

4. Which of the following statements describes the reward for the group who made the best-tasting biscuits?
   a. They would be excused from the test.
   b. They would be excused from home economics class.
   c. They would be allowed to eat their finished product.
   d. They would be allowed to make biscuits for the faculty breakfast.

5. What might have happened to Kaitlyn's recipe? How would you explain the mystery?

   _____

   _____

   _____

Name_____

Go-Cart Adventure

Austin handed Lucas a wrench so he could tighten the last nut. "Do you think this will really go?"

Glancing at Austin, Lucas asked, "The engine runs, doesn't it? This is going to be a fantastic machine!"

The brothers had spent weeks gathering materials to build a go-cart, mostly salvage metal from their uncle's garage. Grandpa helped weld the metal parts together into a frame with his soldering gun. Then, once the frame was complete, the boys went in search of wheels. Grandpa's shop yielded two old bicycle wheels, but they needed four. The boys headed back to the garage and discovered an old lawn mower, which they raided for wheels and an engine. Grandpa's soldering gun came in handy to form an axle from scrap metal pipes.

They couldn't figure out how to make it turn until Grandpa told them to use the steering mechanism from the lawn mower. Then he helped them figure the math and angles to get the steering correct.

"How can we get it to go faster?" Austin wondered.

Grandpa chuckled. "In order to make the lawn-mower motor go faster, you'll need different gears. Motorcycle gears would be best, but why not use those since they're handy?" He gestured to the parts from the old scooter Lucas had found in the shop.

When it was ready for testing, Lucas jumped in and drove to a nearby hill. Steering frantically, he barely avoided shrubbery along the roadside. At the bottom of the hill, Lucas pressed his foot on the brake pedal, hoping it would hold and halt the vehicle. Skidding to a stop, the chain popped off the axle.

Running alongside, Austin pouted. "It's broken, and I didn't even get to try it."

"Don't worry. It was such a great ride; it's worth putting in the effort to fix it. You'll get the next turn." Lucas grabbed the tow rope and headed for the garage.

Text Questions

1. What could Austin and Lucas have done to make their experience safer?
   a. weld the chain to the axle
   b. wear a helmet
   c. add another brake
   d. made it so the go-cart wouldn't turn

2. Which event did <u>not</u> happen in the story?
   a. Lucas tightened the last nut.
   b. They gathered scrap metal from their uncle's garage.
   c. Grandpa fastened the metal parts together with wire.
   d. They got wheels and an engine from an old lawn-mower.

3. What is the main idea of the text?
   a. finding salvage materials
   b. working together with Grandpa
   c. building a go-cart
   d. being safe on a go-cart

4. What does it mean to *raid* the lawn-mower for wheels and an engine?
   a. to make away with
   b. to attack
   c. to invade
   d. to strike

5. Why might this story be called an adventure?

   _____

   _____

Name_____

State Fair

"McKenzie?" Lidia glanced around for her friend and their brothers, Eli and Fernando. The commercial exhibits were crowded, and the four of them had agreed at the outset that they should stay together. Lidia couldn't imagine how they'd disappeared during the one or two minutes she'd paused to examine a display of jewelry.

Noise echoed off the concrete floor as fairgoers and hawkers competed to make themselves heard in their individual conversations. Lidia turned around in a complete circle, slowly, scanning the crowd for a glimpse of her companions. Walking more quickly, she examined faces as she moved through the throng, hoping to see someone familiar. "Eli? Fernando?" Lidia's concern grew, as she felt particularly responsible for her younger brother, hoping he had not, in turn, become separated from the other two.

A shaft of bright light guided Lidia to the outside entrance of the building, and she stepped into the sunshine. Confused, she looked up and down the walkway, not recognizing her surroundings. "This isn't where we came in," she muttered. "Which way should I go to get back to where we started?" It appeared as though more people congregated to the left, so she headed in that direction, unsure where to begin looking. Was she decreasing her chances of finding them by leaving the building?

Lidia approached a crossroads and looked around in dismay. Streams of people were entering a building, apparently the same building she had just exited. Perhaps the others were waiting for her by the main entrance. A sense of urgency propelled her forward, but out of the corner of her eye, she noticed a vendor selling outlandish hats with feathers. "If I wasn't afraid of missing them, I'd stop and get one," she told herself. "Then this wouldn't happen again."

Text Questions

1. How did Lidia become separated from her companions?
   a. She couldn't hear them talking to her.
   b. She stopped to examine a display of jewelry.
   c. She left the building through a different door.
   d. She stopped to buy a hat.

2. Which statement gives a clue as to the setting of the story?
   a. She examined faces as she moved through the throng.
   b. Fairgoers and hawkers competed to make themselves heard.
   c. It appeared as though more people congregated to the left.
   d. Lidia approached a crossroads and looked around in dismay.

3. Which words best describe the main feeling in the story?
   a. concern, anxiety, panic
   b. excitement, enjoyment, pleasure
   c. loneliness, isolation, sadness
   d. fear, helplessness, dread

4. What does the word *exhibits* mean as it is used in the text?
   a. entertainments
   b. evidences
   c. documents
   d. presentations

5. How would you compare Lidia's experience to something similar you have experienced?

_____

_____

Name_____

The Walking Dead?

Rick slowed down for his friends to catch up. He didn't want to be by himself. It was starting to get dark, and he'd told his parents he'd be home before it did. The only way to make it in time was to take the shortcut, which was right through the middle of the cemetery.

Matthew and Phil caught up to Rick just as he opened the gate. "What are you doing?" Matthew asked.

"Taking the shortcut back. I can't be late."

"Just call your parents," Phil suggested.

"I can't. I forgot my phone, and I know you two don't have one yet, so it's either take the shortcut or we all get in trouble for being late."

None of the boys wanted that. They were all supposed to get to spend the night at Rick's house. They'd gone up to the park to play basketball for a while but had lost track of time. They knew, just like Rick did, that they'd promised they'd be back before dark. The two boys reluctantly followed Rick into the cemetery. The creaking of the gate as it closed behind them made the boys walk faster.

Halfway through the cemetery, they heard a noise. It sounded as if someone was following them. They looked over their shoulders but saw nothing. No one wanted to admit he was scared, but it was obvious in the way each of them began to move more quickly.

The sound of footsteps grew louder, and the boys didn't even bother to pretend they weren't afraid. They took off running.

"There's the gate up ahead," Phil screamed as the three boys aimed for the exit, flinging open the gate and then slamming it behind them as they stood safely on the sidewalk and just across the street from Rick's house.

None of the boys saw the gray raccoon that watched them as they ran the rest of the way to Rick's front door.

Text Questions ....

1. Why do Rick and his friends decide to take the shortcut through the cemetery?
   a. They like doing daring things.
   b. They need a quicker route home.
   c. They want to see if they spot a ghost.
   d. They are lost.

2. List three things in sequential order that happen in the story.

   a. _____

   b. _____

   c. _____

3. Which adjective best describes how the boys feel about taking the shortcut through the cemetery?
   a. excited
   b. apprehensive
   c. sympathetic
   d. apathetic

4. What is most likely the cause of the mysterious noises in the cemetery?
   a. a spirit
   b. the caretaker
   c. an animal
   d. another boy

5. What will most likely happen the next time Rick promises his parents he will be home at a certain time?
   a. He will use the cemetery for a shortcut.
   b. He will remember to be on time.
   c. He will not go anywhere again.
   d. He will be late next time.

Name_____

A Deal with a Gremlin

Gabe struggled to get the chain settled back on the sprocket of the rear wheel. It was loose again, and he didn't have time to properly fix the bike until the weekend. As he wrestled with the chain, a low-pitched growl caused him to fumble with the greasy metal. Thinking the neighbor's dog had escaped, he glanced over his shoulder. The round eyes that stared at him didn't belong to a dog.

"Trouble?" the voice grated. Gabe wasn't sure he wanted to respond to the creature, but he'd take any help he could get. He nodded and gestured toward the sagging bicycle chain.

"I'll make you a deal," the gremlin growled. He wasn't overly friendly, but he wasn't menacing either.

"Such as?" Gabe tilted his head, avoiding the gremlin's gaze.

"I'll repair your bicycle in exchange for a place to stay; I feel most at home in computers. Allow me to reside in your laptop. I'll set up a cozy compartment next to your hard drive."

"Uh, sure, but I don't think you'll fit. Laptops are very thin, you know."

The gremlin smiled, calculating. "I'll make it work." Before Gabe could reconsider, the gremlin had the chain completely off and the gears apart. He then reassembled everything correctly and in working order.

"Wow. Thanks! Gotta go." Gabe leapt on the bike and flew down the driveway, scattering bits of shale and fallen leaves in his wake.

Trudging up to his room with a stack of homework, Gabe breathed a sigh of relief at the thought that he hadn't given the gremlin his computer password. Unless gremlins are good at hacking . . . He shook his head. Gabe wasn't surprised that his room appeared exactly as he'd left it; if the gremlin truly decided to take up residence in his computer, he wouldn't see it. He deposited his backpack on the bed, grabbed his laptop, and logged on.

Text Questions

1. What happens as a result of Gabe hearing the growl?
   a. He returns the dog to the neighbors.
   b. He fumbles with the bicycle chain.
   c. He leaps on his bike and tears down the driveway.
   d. He has a conversation with a gremlin.

2. What does the word *compartment* mean as it is used in the text?
   a. enclosed space   b. cell   c. division   d. cubbyhole

3. What might be one consequence of the deal Gabe made with the gremlin?
   a. He will have to work on his bike again on the weekend.
   b. He won't be able to complete his homework on time.
   c. He will have problems with his computer.
   d. He will have to explain the gremlin to his parents.

4. Which of the following cannot be determined from the passage?
   a. where the gremlin prefers to live
   b. the deal the gremlin made with Gabe
   c. the nature of Gabe's problem
   d. details about the gremlin's appearance

5. What do you think will happen next in the story? Give evidence from the story to support your answer.

_____

_____

Name_____

Northern Night

Alisha paced before the hearth with its blazing fire, trying to warm herself. Her thermal undershirt, long-sleeve shirt, flannel shirt, and two sweatshirts hadn't warded off the chill as she trudged through drifts after school. How long would it take to acclimate to the harsh Alaskan winter? Alisha crossed to the window and glanced at the thermometer. It was twenty below outside. She wondered if her layers would be sufficient to see the display of northern lights tonight.

"Tomorrow, I'll buy a parka," Alisha promised herself, heaving the solid cedar door open. Descending the snow-covered steps, Alisha was grateful for the rain boots she'd brought with her when they moved. Eventually, her feet would numb, but the galoshes covered her ankles, so the snow didn't soak her immediately.

She caught glimpses of light flashing through a stand of hemlock. The northern lights? She couldn't be sure. She'd have to navigate through the trees to the clearing for the best view. The snow thinned where boughs sheltered the ground, and Alisha stamped on the solid ground to restore her circulation. Light still danced among the branches, and Alisha glanced up to determine its source. Before her were tiny creatures with dazzling wings. They weren't fireflies. She'd done a report once on fireflies before they moved and had discovered Alaska was not their native habitat.

Alisha paused in her trek to watch the luminescent movement—too mesmerized to feel startled as the insects circled closer until they encompassed her neck like a multicolored scarf. She snuggled into the strange glow, no longer feeling the chill of the Arctic air. Reluctant to leave, she lingered, forgetting the northern lights, knowing she should return to the safety of the cabin.

Brilliant bits of color greeted Alisha as she opened her eyes. She struggled to focus. A rainbow through the cabin window? Not likely; it hadn't rained. Her grandmother's quilt, tousled? A vague recollection flitted at the edges of her memory.

Text Questions

1. How did Alisha know the creatures were not fireflies?
   a. Fireflies don't glow in the dark.
   b. She had just moved away from Alaska.
   c. She had read that fireflies don't live in Alaska.
   d. She had read about mythical creatures in Alaskan forests.

2. Which of the following is not a meaning of *mesmerized* as it is used in the text?
   a. spellbound
   b. fascinated
   c. entranced
   d. controlled

3. Which statement does not contribute to the main idea of the text?
   a. Alisha did several things to keep warm.
   b. Alisha wanted to view the northern lights.
   c. Alisha's grandmother made her a multicolored quilt.
   d. Alisha saw unusual light flitting through the trees.

4. What role does the setting play in the story?
   a. Alisha interacts with the Arctic climate and the mysterious creatures as if they were characters in the story.
   b. The setting serves as a comparison to where Alisha used to live.
   c. Alisha must conquer the setting to obtain her goals.
   d. The setting affects the dialogue of the characters in the story.

5. How would you describe Alisha's experience? Explain your answer.

_____

_____

Name_____

Riches to Rags

Would this be the day? Tabitha had been optimistic that soon Jason would notice her. Receiving no response to her daily greeting, she slouched on a vacant seat toward the back of the bus.

Hoping to offset the persistent rejection, Tabitha exited the bus one stop early, planning to browse the windows of her favorite retro shop. A trinket caught her eye, and she ventured into the business.

"How are you today, Tabitha?" the store clerk came around the counter.

"All right." Tabitha tried to hide her disappointment. "Just wanted to see if you have anything new in your inventory."

Coming alongside Tabitha, Agnes put a hand on her shoulder. "You can't fool me. What happened?"

"Jason continues to ignore me, as if I don't exist." Tabitha took a ragged breath.

"Will you let me assist you?"

Tabitha hesitated. Granted, Agnes resembled an overgrown teenager, but Tabitha imagined her friend's days of boy-girl relationships long gone. "Well… what did you have in mind?"

"I'd like to give you something." Agnes motioned for Tabitha to follow her to the rear of the shop, where she presented the girl with a gorgeous shirt. While the fabric didn't exactly shimmer, it reminded Tabitha of her beloved aunt's mother-of-pearl pendant. She anticipated wearing it the next day, wondering if Jason would notice.

"Hey, Tabitha, are you ready for the vocabulary test?"

Tabitha stumbled in the aisle, shocked when Jason spoke. Assuming the shirt was having the desired effect, she smiled and gave him what she hoped was a coherent answer. She'd figure out a dozen ways to wear this article of clothing.

The next morning, Tabitha sifted through her clothes, searching for the shirt. Calling to her mother, she didn't wait for an answer, but hurried to the laundry room, in case it had landed in the hamper.

"This rag?" Her mother held up an iridescent piece of cloth, shredded and in tatters.

Text Questions

1. What changed in Jason's response to Tabitha?
   a. He ignored her after she visited the retro shop.
   b. He noticed her and responded when she wore the shirt.
   c. He followed her to the retro shop.
   d. He waited for her to get on the bus.

2. What does the word *inventory* mean as it is used in the text?
   a. cash register
   b. grocery list
   c. property Agnes owns
   d. goods for sale

3. Based on what you read, what can you infer about the shirt?
   a. It had magical qualities.
   b. It fit Tabitha perfectly.
   c. It made Tabitha look more attractive.
   d. It was the latest style.

4. How would you describe Agnes's relationship with Tabitha?
   a. Agnes was a busybody who meddled in other people's business.
   b. Agnes cared and wanted to help.
   c. Agnes wanted to make things more difficult for Tabitha.
   d. Agnes thought Jason was insensitive.

5. Why do you think the shirt was in tatters?

_____

_____

Name_____

The Storytellers

Adrián meandered over to sit by Zachary in the cafeteria, letting his tray clatter on the table. The heads turned of those who were curious about the new kid, but Adrián didn't care; the newness would wear off soon enough. Might as well get some enjoyment out of it while he could.

"What brought you here, anyway?" Jayden narrowed his eyes and scrutinized the newcomer.

Realizing Jayden wasn't referring to this specific lunch period, Adrián said, "My dad's company transferred him." He chomped into his burrito, which was stuffed with beans, asadero cheese, and bits of chicken.

"Tell us another of your dad's wacky stories," Zachary requested.

Jayden interrupted before Adrián could begin talking. "What stories?"

Adrián swallowed, scattering grains of rice with a fork, composing his thoughts. His dad claimed he heard the stories at work, but Adrián had never quite figured out who the storytellers were.

Sensing his comrades had settled down enough for him to get a word in edgewise, he launched into his anecdote. "He has one tale about a commander in the military. Seems the rest of his unit fled the enemy, leaving him the only remaining soldier, and he was out of ammunition. Somehow he managed to stun the general and escape. I don't remember the details," Adrián mumbled the last line and took a gulp of orange juice.

Zachary glanced at him quizzically. "What exactly does your dad do for a living?"

"Uh," Adrián stammered. "He takes care of people." That's how his dad described the lawn-mowing, flower-tending, and ground excavation that comprised his daily duties.

"Where?" Jayden taunted him.

Adrián scraped a pencil against the edge of the table, rubbing off golden flecks of paint, eyes downcast. "The cemetery."

Text Questions

1. What is Adrián's role in the story?
   a. He is trying to make friends at his new school.
   b. He is the brunt of the boys' jokes.
   c. He becomes a storyteller like his dad.
   d. He defends his dad's work.

2. What is one possible element of fantasy in the story?
   a. ghosts   b. fairies   c. dragons   d. magic

3. What is Adrián's dad's job?
   a. He takes care of people.
   b. He plans landscapes for businesses.
   c. He talks to people about their experiences.
   d. He is the caretaker of a cemetery.

4. What did Jayden do when he *scrutinized* Adrián?
   a. He looked at him carefully to notice details.
   b. He examined him to see if his answer to the question made sense.
   c. He inspected him to see if he fit in with the group.
   d. He studied him to give him a test.

5. What is the significance of the cemetery in relation to Adrián's dad's stories?

   _____

   _____

Name_____

Tick Tock

Someone was watching; Savannah felt eyes following her as she wandered through the antique shop. She glanced over her shoulder to discover her mother wasn't paying attention, and the shopkeeper was nowhere to be seen. But still, she sensed the uncomfortable heaviness of someone studying her.

She spun around and saw it—in an obscure corner sat a massive, ornate grandfather clock. The pendulum swung back and forth, keeping a perfectly steady rhythm. Not a speck of dust marred the flawless surface of the clock face. Above the case that housed the pendulum, a single, carved eye stared directly at Savannah.

She couldn't resist moving forward, the timepiece beckoning her closer until they stood face-to-face.

Tick tock, tick tock. The hands advanced, the pendulum swung, and the eye stared. Savannah shivered.

"Time to leave!" Her mom's voice called from another area of the shop.

Savannah pivoted and let out her breath. "I'm coming!" Weaving around an ancient trunk and two unusual watercolor paintings, she hastened toward the main entrance and accompanied her mother outside.

Eucalyptus trees flashed by the window of her mother's maroon sedan, their varying shades of gray-green smeared like paint. A motorcycle zoomed past, causing her mom to swerve sharply, honking the horn. The car jounced onto the shoulder and skittered to a stop.

Glancing out the window, Savannah gasped as she noticed a single eye glaring at her from between the limbs of a gnarled oak tree.

Her mom twisted the steering wheel, and their vehicle shot back onto the highway. The mysterious tree disappeared from view behind them.

Tick tock. Momentarily, the faint sound of the swinging pendulum echoed in her mind. Then, it too was gone.

Was she going insane? Savannah contemplated her mom: Mom hadn't seen the eye, hadn't heard the clock. Had it all really happened? Or was it just her imagination?

Text Questions

1. What caused Savannah to wonder if she was going crazy?
   a. The trees blurred outside the car window.
   b. She saw a single eye in two different places.
   c. She heard voices from within the grandfather clock.
   d. The case of the clock opened and beckoned her inside.

2. What does the word *ornate* mean as it is used in the text?
   a. showy   b. flowery   c. fussy   d. elaborate

3. Which of the following does <u>not</u> contribute to the mood of the story?
   a. a massive clock   c. a watercolor painting
   b. a carved eye   d. a gnarled oak tree

4. How might the story change if told from Savannah's mother's point of view?
   a. Her mother might question Savannah's behavior.
   b. Her mother might point out intriguing objects in the antique store.
   c. Her mother might ask Savannah about her interest in the clock.
   d. Her mother might have blamed a car accident on Savannah.

5. What do you think will happen next in the story?

   _____

   _____

Name_____

The Figurine

Olivia lifted the ceramic figurine—a birthday present from her parents—from its carton.

"Doesn't it look just like you?" Her mother moved closer, smiling. "We were sure you'd love her."

Love her? Granted, the figurine had the same chestnut-colored hair as Olivia, the same circle-shaped face, the same light dusting of freckles. But the resemblance stopped at the eyes. Unlike Olivia's hazel eyes, the doll's eyes were sparkling green. But that was of no consequence. What mattered was that Olivia detested figurines and always had. Her parents should have known better.

Olivia huffed and stomped into her bedroom. What a disaster this birthday had been. Why couldn't her parents have gotten her a pair of designer shoes or maybe even a new bicycle? But, no, instead she received an uninteresting doll with creepy emerald eyes.

Olivia yawned and tossed the figurine in an obscure corner before sinking onto her comforter and turning toward the wall. Green eyes stared back at her. How had the creature managed to leave the corner?

Grabbing the figurine, Olivia glared at it, throwing it into the wastebasket.

Darkness descended as Olivia slipped under the covers, fluffed her pillow, and squirmed under the sheets. She peeked at the doll to discover it head down, in the trash, right where it belonged. She smiled and rolled over. Then Olivia screamed. Once again, emerald eyes stared at her.

Snatching the figurine, Olivia leapt up and shoved it into her bureau drawer. She pressed her hands against the smooth wood surface, exhaling slowly and then opened the drawer a crack to peek. The doll hadn't budged.

Sunlight tiptoed through the window as Olivia hurried to the dresser and yanked the top drawer open. The figurine lay in repose, untouched, gazing at her with hazel brown eyes.

Olivia turned toward the mirror and winked one sparkling green eye at her reflection.

Text Questions

1. What did Olivia do when she *exhaled*?
   a. evaporated   b. sighed   c. breathed out   d. expired

2. What startled Olivia?
   a. her parents giving her a birthday gift
   b. the figurine's resemblance to Olivia
   c. the darkness of the winter night
   d. the figurine staring at her after she put it away

3. What is the main idea of the text?
   a. Things are not always what they seem.
   b. It takes perseverance to accept a gift.
   c. If you ignore your problems, they will go away.
   d. Two wrongs don't make a right.

4. From Olivia's perspective, what was the main issue?
   a. She didn't have a happy birthday.
   b. She didn't like figurines.
   c. She didn't like the doll's appearance.
   d. She didn't want anyone to know about the figurine.

5. What do you think would have happened if Olivia had accepted the figurine instead of rejecting it?

   _____

   _____

Name_____

A Twist of Fate

Anastasia tossed her ebony hair and balanced carefully, attempting to sit gracefully at the cramped desk. The heels of her gothic boots made the feat difficult. She groaned as their homeroom teacher launched into the day's announcements: It was Spirit Day tomorrow. Imagining the ruckus that would upset her carefully orchestrated routine, Anastasia scowled. She'd heard Riley, a popular girl in their grade, making elaborate plans to dye her hair in the school colors for the occasion.

After school, Anastasia pondered the thoughts that had persisted throughout the day. Tired of feeling ill at ease with people ridiculing her, she figured it was time to break out of her mold and shake up her classmates. Anastasia realized her efforts might go unnoticed in the chaos of Spirit Day, but nevertheless, she set her jaw and marched into a variety store. Perusing the array of hair products, she spotted an unusually shaped bottle on the bottom shelf. "Change the color of those tresses," the label invited. "Say the word and the color is yours." Intrigued, Anastasia carried two bottles to the register.

Anastasia considered her options; how could she best blend in? The school colors were emerald and bronze, and she definitely did not desire even a hint of blonde. Mission accomplished, Anastasia stared at her sparkling green hair in the mirror, contemplating her course of action with the second bottle.

"A small surprise for Riley," she mused. Holding the container, she briefly wondered about its permanence but said the words, "Transform Riley's hair to charcoal gray."

In disbelief, Anastasia did her best to ignore the taunts that greeted her for not wearing gothic clothing. Her only consolation was Riley's surprise. Making certain to join her for lunch, Anastasia deliberately showed Riley her drink.

"Why is it such an unusual color?" Riley took the bait.

"It's special." Anastasia smiled and offered the bottle. "Would you care to taste it?"

Text Questions

1. What will be the result of Riley tasting Anastasia's drink?
   a. She will become special and gothic.
   b. Her hair will sparkle like emeralds.
   c. Her hair will turn slate gray.
   d. Anastasia's hair will become black again.

2. What does the word *permanence* mean as it is used in the text?
   a. stability
   b. longevity
   c. dependability
   d. resistibility

3. What makes Anastasia decide to change her hair color?
   a. She wants to surprise Riley.
   b. She is tired of others teasing her.
   c. She wants to adopt a gothic look.
   d. She wants to have blonde hair.

4. Which phrase does <u>not</u> contribute to the plot development?
   a. carefully orchestrated routine
   b. making elaborate plans
   c. thoughts that had persisted
   d. break out of her mold

5. What is another way Anastasia might have accomplished her goals?

_____

_____

Name_____

The Gift of Sight

Christopher adjusted his eye patch, then shouldered his backpack for the trek home from school. He didn't need the patch, really, but it made him feel less embarrassed to wear it. Years ago, the doctor had given him a glass eye to replace his injured eye, and it didn't match the remaining good eye.

Stomach rumbling, Christopher decided to detour by the local market to pick up a snack. He contemplated his options as he approached the corner opposite the market and waited for the signal to change. Next to him, a man with a white cane stood, listening intently to the sounds of traffic.

"Hello, sir," Christopher attempted to capture the man's attention without startling him. "I'll cross with you if you'd like."

"Thank you, young man. I'd appreciate it. This is a dangerous intersection for all of us."

"Yes," Christopher agreed. "The light just turned; you have two steps before the curb." He resisted the urge to take the gentleman's arm to guide him, knowing that such an action might set him off balance.

As they reached the sidewalk on the opposite side, the man handed Christopher a small box with twine fastened around it. "You gave me your sight, I'd like to return the gift," the stranger said.

Puzzled, Christopher loosened the knot to lift the lid and reveal the parcel's contents. A thumbnail-sized, circular plastic disk lay nestled on foam; its color was an exact match to his functioning eye.

Text Questions

1. What does "decided to detour" mean?
   a. He had to go a different way because of traffic.
   b. He went a different way than his usual route.
   c. He wanted to avoid the signal light.
   d. He decided to walk instead of taking the bus.

2. Why did Christopher wear an eye patch?
   a. He was ashamed of his mismatched eye colors.
   b. He couldn't see out of his glass eye.
   c. It would force his good eye to do the work of both eyes.
   d. It was part of a costume.

3. What did the gentleman give to Christopher?
   a. a helping hand
   b. a new glass eye
   c. a colored contact lens
   d. a new eye patch

4. Why did Christopher offer to help the man?
   a. Christopher had limited sight and wanted the assistance himself.
   b. The man was completely blind, and the intersection was dangerous.
   c. Christopher wanted something in return from the stranger.
   d. The traffic signal was broken, and there was no way for the man to cross the street independently.

5. What is the significance of the gift Christopher received?

   _____

   _____

   _____

Name_____

The Statue

As the school bus came to a halt, Justin gathered up his jacket and book bag to exit. He looked forward to these days when he visited the library on the way home from school. Bounding up the steep marble staircase and entering those sacred halls always stirred up in him a sense of awe. Not that Justin was a voracious reader—quite the contrary. He was awed that anyone would naturally feel that way about books. Even so, he appreciated the library's collection of comic books that spanned the years.

Justin settled in at a table with a stack of his favorite comics, primed for some entertaining reading. Every time he got into a story, someone or something interrupted him.

"Hey, Justin," his science lab partner whispered. "Do you have notes from yesterday's experiment?"

Shaking his head, Justin frowned and looked intently at his reading. He turned a couple of pages, then felt a tap.

He tried to ignore it, but he couldn't help glancing to identify its source. Audrey's skirt rustled as she navigated the row of tables. She must have bumped him with an elbow. Sighing, he pulled out a piece of paper and wrote his frustration before attempting to focus again. Justin continued to alternate between reading and scribbling notes to vent his irritation until he had to scramble homeward.

As he left the library, Justin slipped the tightly folded piece of paper under the feet of the statue of Prometheus, a god of intellect, portrayed at the library's entrance. He knew the act was meaningless, but the small ritual made him feel more at ease.

Justin dumped his homework on his bed to sort through the evening's assignments, only to find a new book. He picked up the history of comic book art, marveling at its mysterious appearance.

Text Questions

1. Why did Justin write notes on a scrap piece of paper?
   a. to tell his partner about the science experiment
   b. to vent his irritations about interruptions when he was reading
   c. to leave a note for the statue
   d. to remind himself which comic books he had read

2. What does the word *sacred* mean as it is used in the text?
   a. The library was regarded with great respect and reverence.
   b. The library was dedicated to a Greek god.
   c. The library was used for religious gatherings.
   d. The library was set apart only for people who are voracious readers.

3. How does Justin respond to the interruptions?
   a. He ignores his partner and notices the person walking by.
   b. He reports what happened to the librarian.
   c. He makes a note and continues reading.
   d. He decides to leave the library and not return.

4. What is the theme or moral of the text?
   a. It's not a good idea to read comic books.
   b. It's not okay to whisper in a library.
   c. It's good to study the Greek gods and what they represent.
   d. It's good to find appropriate ways to express frustration.

5. How would you explain the appearance of the book in Justin's backpack?

   _____

   _____

Name_____

The Cheshire Cat*

The cat grinned good-naturedly when it saw Alice; its elongated claws and numerous teeth making her feel as if she ought to treat it with respect.

"Cheshire Cat," she said timidly, and the feline's smile widened. "Please tell me which way I ought to travel from here."

"That depends a good deal on where you desire to go," said the cat.

"I don't particularly care where—" said Alice.

The cat interrupted. "Then it doesn't matter which way you go."

"—so long as I arrive SOMEWHERE," Alice finished by way of explanation.

"In THAT direction," the cat continued, waving its right forefoot, "dwells a Hatter; and in THAT direction," waving the other talon, "lives a March Hare. Visit either you like: they're both mad. In fact, we're all insane here." Changing the subject, the cat asked, "Do you play croquet with the queen to-day?"

"I should like it very much," said Alice, "but I haven't been invited yet."

"I plan to be in attendance," said the cat and vanished.

Gazing at the place where the cat had reclined, Alice was startled to see it suddenly reappear, then vanish again.

Alice waited momentarily, half expecting to see it reappear, but it did not, and so she strolled on in the direction of the March Hare. "I've seen hatters before," she reasoned; "this will be much more entertaining, and perhaps as this is May it won't be raving mad—at least not so mad as it was in March." Looking up, she noticed the cat again, perched on a chestnut branch.

"I do wish you wouldn't keep appearing and vanishing so suddenly: your behavior makes one quite giddy." With that, Alice proceeded down the path, puzzling on the curious spectacle of the cat vanishing quite slowly, beginning with its tail, and ending with the grin, which lingered after the rest of it had disappeared.

Text Questions

1. Which creature did Alice decide to visit?
   a. the queen
   b. the Cheshire Cat
   c. the Hatter
   d. the March Hare

2. What curious sight did Alice experience?
   a. the March Hare bustling about in sheer madness
   b. the Queen playing croquet
   c. the Cheshire Cat vanishing slowly so that only its grin lingered
   d. the cat's extremely long claws and many teeth

3. What does the word *spectacle* mean as it is used in the text?
   a. a strange and remarkable sight
   b. a public exhibition
   c. a pair of eyeglasses
   d. foolish behavior

4. What effect did the cat's behavior have on Alice?
   a. It made her feel frustrated.
   b. It made her feel dizzy.
   c. It made her feel respected.
   d. It made her feel lonely.

5. What is the significance of the cat vanishing?

_____

_____

*excerpted from *Alice's Adventures in Wonderland* by Lewis Carroll (*www.gutenberg.org*)

Name_____

Thoughts From a Muse

One day, Shaggy met an owl on his afternoon walk by the river. The owl called himself Muse—an interesting name for an owl, yet Shaggy inquired no further. The owl flew alongside Shaggy on his usual solitary journey. Shaggy asked the owl his occupation, to which he replied, "I flutter over the shoulders of others, giving them tidbits for their life stories as I'm able. And in return, they give me perspective, as they allow me to see through the eyes of another."

Shaggy enjoyed his chat with the Muse. Although probably inaccurate, the latter's knowledge of the future was of particular interest. The owl predicted a world with various restrictions placed on people, yet at the same time a type of utopian society. He then stopped his narrative to ask Shaggy his opinion. Shaggy replied that the notion seemed but a crumbling dictatorship, cracking at the seams. The owl then told of a young boy who had managed to keep a treasure in that society, where such secrets, knowledge, and treasure are forbidden. Shaggy wondered what treasure the boy might have had, but the Muse declined to answer. The owl remarked how he enjoyed the conversation, complaining that most humans had little time for such things anymore. Promising to return next week to the owl's tree-top dwelling, Shaggy bid the Muse farewell and walked himself down to the meadow.

His paws tired, Shaggy flopped on the grass and idly observed some ducks trawling lazily across the pond as he contemplated the ideas the Muse had discussed. One idea flitted through his unkempt head but dissipated before he could fully identify it. Scattered thoughts drifted on the wind: people of the past who refused to back down, the boy with the forbidden treasure.

Shaggy rolled over, reveling in the feel of the tender clover, content to let such weighty thoughts pass him by.

Text Questions

1. What kind of creature is Shaggy?
   a. an owl
   b. a young boy
   c. a dog
   d. a duck

2. Why did the owl appreciate the conversation?
   a. He was able to talk Shaggy into agreeing with his point of view.
   b. He felt that people didn't have much time for conversation.
   c. He wanted to tell Shaggy what to write.
   d. He thought Shaggy could use the company.

3. What does the word *dissipated* mean as it is used in the text?
   a. disappeared
   b. scattered
   c. wasted
   d. indulged

4. Who tells the story?
   a. the owl
   b. Shaggy
   c. a narrator
   d. the Muse

5. What treasure do you think the young boy had?

   _____

   _____

Name_____

The Time Machine

The year was 2170. The pre-dawn darkness was illuminated by a small workshop adjacent to a mansion. Inside the workshop, it was as bright as day. Lights hung at intervals across the ceiling, creating a network of cables and wires.

"Nearly finished." The old man almost cackled with glee, then rubbed his eyes as if to sweep away the dark circles. Walter recalled in detail the initial conversation in which they had set the terms for this endeavor. "I promise you all the equipment you require to finish your design," Dr. Mangier, who owned the property and had hired him, had said. Walter's patched and frayed clothing bore testimony to the fact his employer conveniently forgot to provide proper wages. However, the equipment was well beyond the scope of what the old man could ever afford. He wiped the soot from his spectacles and bent over his project, which vaguely resembled a metal cell with a platform in the center.

There were wires and circuits intertwined throughout the structure and a small control panel at chest height at its core. The old man mumbled to himself as he worked to fasten his watch to the control panel, reasoning that it was worthless to construct a time machine without the ability to regulate the year of destination. Breathing a sigh of relief, he prepared to embark on a maiden voyage in the contraption. Whistling contentedly, he focused on a final review of his plans: he knew exactly where he intended to land. The machine lit up, nearly outshining the stars, and vanished . . .

The year was 2170. The pre-dawn darkness was illuminated only by a small lantern outside a mansion. Dr. Mangier, the gardener, labored in the shadows planting petunias for his master while in the interior of the house, a solitary light burned in the sitting room. An old man with dark circles under his eyes observed, whistling contentedly.

Text Questions ....

1. Which evidence supports the old man's financial position?
   a. "I promise you all the equipment you require to finish your design."
   b. Walter's patched and frayed clothes bore testimony.
   c. Wires and circuits intertwined throughout the structure.
   d. He worked to fasten his watch to the control panel.

2. What did the old man receive from his employer?
   a. valuable equipment
   b. a garden
   c. a watch for the control panel
   d. new clothing

3. What does the word *testimony* mean as it is used in the text?
   a. a statement made under oath
   b. a public declaration
   c. evidence of a fact
   d. a person who tells what happened

4. What do you notice about the old man's character during the story?
   a. He becomes angry and bitter over time.
   b. He feels defeated and gives up on the project.
   c. He plans a way to change his circumstances.
   d. He asks his employer for assistance in meeting his goals.

5. How would you describe the twist in the story?

   _____

   _____

Name_____

Dragon Games

"Hey, Zao, let's go!"

Zao opened one eye to see his friend, Areo, standing above him. He jumped up and flapped his wings to work out the kinks. "I'm ready when you are!"

"Alright then! Follow me!" Areo took off like an arrow from a bow, straight into the air, her wings glimmering in the early-morning sunlight. Zao followed, full of anticipation because they were finally old enough to compete in the dragon games, a festival held every year for young dragons. After the competition, contenders left the clan for three years on a legendary quest, with successful completion granting them Drake status. The games were designed to train young dragons for their quest.

"Come on, hurry up!" called Areo. Zao cleared his head, realizing that Areo was far ahead of him. She did a quick turning maneuver, allowing Zao to catch up.

The enormous stone coliseum accommodated over 300 dragons, and their clan had 200 Drakes—mature dragons who had passed their quests—as well as 100 dragons who had yet to become Drakes. Zao sighed as he scanned the field where everyone else had already arrived, awaiting the first event. He had expected they would compete with the younger dragons, as he and Areo were the smallest and youngest dragons by at least a full year. Shaking his head, Zao determined it didn't matter as he was ready to compete and win. He glanced at Areo to discover her expression mirrored his thoughts. They flew down to join the other dragons in the circle as an elder Dragon with silver scales and a massive wingspan addressed them. "For your first challenge, the first dragon to reach the top of the pillar of flames will win the event." He reared up on his great hind legs, took a deep breath, opened his jaws, and let loose a giant column of flame. Zao and Aero took flight, straight into the air.

Text Questions

1. Why did Zao sigh?
   a. He was exasperated with Areo.
   b. He was disappointed they were not competing with younger dragons.
   c. He was discouraged because he failed his first attempt.
   d. He was impatient to get started.

2. What is the theme or moral of the text?
   a. courage
   b. honesty
   c. kindness
   d. triumph over evil

3. What does the word *accommodated* mean as it is used in the text?
   a. adapted to
   b. reconciled
   c. supplied
   d. had enough space for

4. Which plot element indicates this is a fantasy story?
   a. competitions with challenges
   b. the desire to compete with others of similar ability
   c. anticipation at finally being old enough to participate in a desired event
   d. fire-breathing dragons

5. What kind of quest would you set forth for Zao? Give evidence from the story to support your answer.

_____

_____

Name_____

Monster Camp

"Scree! Screeee!" the harsh sounds grated on my nerves, causing me to make mistakes I would then have to scribble out.

"Will you be quiet? I'm trying to write an important letter, and I need to concentrate." Exasperated, I shut the door between our adjoining rooms and hunkered over the desk again.

When I initially signed up to attend Weeping Willows—the regional monster summer camp—my brilliant principal had assigned a banshee as my roommate. At first, I was thrilled, because not many banshees enroll in camp. Actually, there was only one banshee in the entire camp, and I was stuck with her for the duration. She's not bad as monsters go, but when she's bored, she screeches. When she is tired, she screeches. And when she's reading . . . she screeches! Unfortunately, I am a green fluffy monster with oversized, extremely sensitive ears. I can hear a bat flapping 500 feet away. Grabbing my pair of fuchsia headphones, I gingerly set them over my ears, in an attempt to block out the racket. Not completely soundproof, they deaden the highest pitches a bit. Camp had just begun, and already I was going crazy. Something would have to change immediately, or I would have no sanity left. Glancing at my paper, I couldn't help grinning at my deviousness. In truth, I was not writing a letter home; I was working on a reflector dish. My family had always said I was destined for a job in engineering, so in a manner of speaking, my endeavors did have to do with family. The metallic reflector dish would be my first metal-shop project here at camp, giving me the opportunity to prove my family correct. If I am successful, it will effectively absorb my roommate's screeches and reverberate them in any direction I choose. Quivering with anticipation, I renew my focus on the task before me. What an ideal revenge weapon!

Text Questions

1. Which of the following would be a better title for the text?
   a. "How to Make a Metal Reflector Dish"
   b. "Silencing Your Roommate"
   c. "Silent Revenge"
   d. "Weeping Willows Summer Camp"

2. What is the narrator's main feeling toward her roommate?
   a. exasperation
   b. rage
   c. friendliness
   d. boredom

3. Which statement gives an indication of why the noise is a problem?
   a. The narrator was stuck with the banshee for the duration.
   b. The narrator had oversized, extremely sensitive ears.
   c. The headphones were not completely soundproof.
   d. The narrator was working on a reflector dish.

4. What does the narrator mean when she says she is stuck with the banshee for the *duration*?
   a. for as long as the banshee continues to screech
   b. until she crossed the room to close the door
   c. during the time she was writing the letter
   d. the amount of time that camp lasts

5. What are some other ways the narrator might solve her problem?

_____

_____

Name_____

Shadows

Spencer trudged along, contemplating his ongoing dilemma: finding a sense of belonging at yet another new school. The route he traveled had fascinating shadows of trees and buildings, and he stayed in those shadows. Not having a shadow of his own usually wasn't a problem, as most of the time no one noticed, but every once in a while other students gave him strange looks. Especially in each new community, since as a military family, they relocated on a regular basis.

His absorption with shadows, though, gave him a focus during the lonely times. Not having one of his own, he adopted shadows of particular objects as his friends; it was safer than messing with the shadows of other people.

"Hey, Spencer, how's it going?" Hearing a voice behind his right shoulder, Spencer turned in surprise, as he'd never been sought out in the neighborhood before.

"Uh, fine, Hannah." Spencer found himself tongue-tied, in awe of an individual with such a looming shadow, particularly a female. This late in the afternoon, the shadow of Hannah's almost six-foot frame lengthened impressively.

Slowing her stride to match his, she said, "Why don't you ever speak to anyone? Everybody thinks you're a snob, that you consider yourself better than the rest of us."

Spencer stared at her in disbelief. "No, on the contrary, but I'm not normal—see?" He gestured toward the sidewalk.

"Amazing," Hannah shook her head. "You're obviously not transparent; have you talked with a doctor or scientist to see if they have any theories?"

"Hardly." Spencer gave her a wry smile. "It's more helpful to research and investigate this on my own. So far my assumption is that since shadows are formed when an object blocks light, somehow my body allows light to transcend it."

"Have you ever imagined what it would be like to find yourself a new shadow?" Hannah surprised him by thinking out of the ordinary with him.

Text Questions

1. Which of the following would be a better title for the text?
   a. "Learning About All Shadows"
   b. "Just Me and My Shadow"
   c. "The Most Impressive Shadow"
   d. "Shadows of Belonging"

2. What is one way Spencer dealt with his lack of a shadow?
   a. He borrowed shadows from other people.
   b. He adopted shadows from one or more interesting objects.
   c. He ignored it and lived life normally.
   d. He avoided walking in the shadows because he was afraid of them.

3. Which element makes this a fantasy story?
   a. shadows that are alive
   b. a girl with a long shadow
   c. a boy's lack of a shadow
   d. a magician

4. What does it mean to say Spencer is *not normal*?
   a. He is uncommon.
   b. He is not standard height.
   c. He is not an ordinary kid.
   d. He doesn't follow a routine every day.

5. In what ways does Spencer's explanation make sense? What other explanations—fantastical or ordinary—might there be for his lack of a shadow?

   _____

   _____

Name_____

The Electric Touch

Diego debated whether or not to assist the science teacher in her attempts to get the students' attention. Here, in science class, his ability wouldn't be quite as noticeable, and he could make a positive difference. He unobtrusively pointed a gloved finger at the light switch, and the lights went out. Wiggling his finger slightly at the switch, he turned the lights on again. As expected, the class quieted some, enough for the teacher to explain the day's experiment.

"Let's work with Diego; he really understands circuits and all that stuff." Two of three students headed toward his workstation. Diego wasn't surprised. During the entire unit on electricity, he had never lacked lab partners. He'd been very careful not to accidentally touch anyone, lest he shock them. Kids had long since quit asking questions about the gloves he wore constantly.

Thumping his books on the kitchen table, Diego set aside his speculations about when they might move on from electricity to bask in the security of his home environment, where he wasn't considered a freak.

"Those cookies smell good, Mom. What kind are they?" Diego swooped in to see if there was any cookie dough available for sampling. Her response was muffled by the sounds of his brother's electric guitar as Ricardo wandered through the kitchen, guitar not plugged in, as per usual. He grinned at the thought of the oven heating up at his mother's touch, Ricardo's unnecessary guitar cords stowed safely in their case, and his dad's truly wireless television.

Grabbing a couple of cookies fresh from the oven, Diego struggled to balance his books under his arm and tromped upstairs. His computer booted up, and his desk lamp clicked on as he entered his room, just as he intended—designed without external electricity.

Text Questions

1. Which statement gives you a clue about Diego's unusual ability?
    a. He could make a positive difference.
    b. Wiggling his finger slightly at the switch, he turned the lights on again.
    c. "He really understands circuits and all that stuff."
    d. He had never lacked lab partners.

2. What does the word *security* mean as it is used in the text?
    a. safety
    b. freedom
    c. guarantee
    d. reliability

3. What role do the gloves play in the story?
    a. They keep Diego's hands warm.
    b. They keep Diego from shocking other people.
    c. They enable him to get cookies from the oven.
    d. They are Diego's fashion statement.

4. What is the story problem?
    a. Diego's computer is broken.
    b. Diego doesn't have any lab partners.
    c. Diego tries to fit in in spite of his unusual ability.
    d. Diego gets in trouble for shocking other students.

5. How would you describe Diego's ability?

_____

_____

Answer Key

Answer Key

Nonfiction

Animals

Page 9 A Forest Secret
1. b
2. a
3. a
4. c
5. Answers will vary.

Page 10 Animal Intelligence
1. b
2. d
3. b
4. a
5. Answers will vary.

Page 11 Long-Distance Travelers
1. b
2. c
3. a
4. a
5. Answers will vary.

Page 12 The Jumping Spider
1. a
2. d
3. c
4. a
5. Answers will vary.

Page 13 Swimming with the Turtles
1. c
2. d
3. a
4. a
5. Answers will vary.

Page 14 The Rare Dolphin
1. a
2. c
3. b
4. d
5. Answers will vary.

Page 15 Blue Dragons
1. b
2. b
3. d
4. c
5. Answers will vary.

Page 16 Pippi
1. b
2. d
3. a
4. b
5. Answers will vary.

Page 17 Nature's Helicopters
1. c
2. d
3. a
4. d
5. Answers will vary.

Page 18 The African Generuk
1. b
2. c
3. d
4. a
5. Answers will vary.

Page 19 Deadly Delicacy
1. c
2. b
3. a
4. c
5. Answers will vary.

Page 20 The Climbing Rodent
1. b
2. c
3. a
4. a
5. Answers will vary.

Page 21 Panda Ants
1. c
2. b
3. c
4. a
5. Answers will vary.

Page 22 Cave Dwellers
1. d
2. a
3. c
4. a
5. Answers will vary.

Page 23 Animals and Humans
1. b
2. d
3. a
4. c
5. Answers will vary.

Biographies

Page 24 The Unknown Winston Churchill
1. c
2. b
3. d
4. a
5. Answers will vary.

Page 25 Lawrence of Arabia
1. b
2. a
3. d
4. a
5. Answers will vary.

Page 26 Sir Thomas More
1. c
2. c
3. d
4. b
5. Answers will vary.

Page 27 Olympic Inspiration
1. c
2. b
3. d
4. a
5. Answers will vary.

Answer Key *(cont.)*

Page 28 Harry S. Truman, U.S. President
1. c
2. a
3. d
4. d
5. Answers will vary.

Page 29 Man of Finance
1. d
2. a
3. c
4. b
5. Answers will vary.

Page 30 Stronger Than Steel
1. b
2. d
3. a
4. c
5. Answers will vary.

Page 31 Just an Ordinary Guy
1. b
2. c
3. a
4. d
5. Answers will vary.

Page 32 Woman of Justice
1. a
2. c
3. b
4. d
5. Answers will vary.

Page 33 The Father of Public Libraries
1. b
2. a
3. d
4. a
5. Answers will vary.

Page 34 Margaret Thatcher, Prime Minister
1. d
2. b
3. a
4. d
5. Answers will vary.

Page 35 Author of Adventure
1. b
2. a
3. d
4. c
5. Answers will vary.

Page 36 Pelé
1. b
2. a
3. c
4. d
5. Answers will vary.

Page 37 Harland David Sanders
1. c
2. c
3. a
4. d
5. Answers will vary.

Page 38 Walt Disney's Greatest Storyman
1. a
2. c
3. d
4. b
5. Answers will vary.

Page 39 Barbara McClintock, Nobel Prize Winner
1. b
2. d
3. a
4. c
5. Answers will vary.

History

Page 40 Washington's Crossing of the Delaware
1. d
2. b
3. a
4. c
5. Answers will vary.

Page 41 Animated Cartoons
1. c
2. a
3. c
4. b
5. Answers will vary.

Page 42 Handheld Calculators
1. b
2. b
3. d
4. c
5. Answers will vary.

Page 43 The Emancipation Proclamation
1. b
2. c
3. b
4. c
5. Answers will vary.

Page 44 Prohibition
1. d
2. a
3. c
4. b
5. Answers will vary.

Page 45 The Great American Dessert
1. b
2. d
3. c
4. a
5. Answers will vary.

Answer Key *(cont.)*

Page 46 The History of Airships
1. b
2. d
3. d
4. a
5. Answers will vary.

Page 47 Pirates of the South China Sea
1. b
2. a
3. b
4. c
5. Answers will vary.

Page 48 The Beginnings of Fountain Drinks
1. a
2. c
3. d
4. b
5. Answers will vary.

Page 49 The Louisiana Purchase
1. b
2. c
3. d
4. a
5. Answers will vary.

Page 50 Julius Caesar, Kidnapped
1. b
2. c
3. d
4. c
5. Answers will vary.

Page 51 That Phone in Your Pocket
1. b
2. d
3. c
4. c
5. Answers will vary.

Page 52 Livestock Reduction
1. d
2. b
3. b
4. a
5. Answers will vary.

Page 53 Salt of the Earth
1. a
2. c
3. b
4. d
5. Answers will vary.

Page 54 Claiming the South Pole for Mankind
1. c
2. d
3. a
4. d
5. Answers will vary.

Page 55 Braces
1. d
2. b
3. a
4. c
5. Answers will vary.

Science
Page 56 Microbursts
1. a
2. b
3. b
4. c
5. Answers will vary.

Page 57 Invasive Plant Species
1. b
2. b
3. c
4. a
5. Answers will vary.

Page 58 Twins
1. b
2. c
3. d
4. a
5. Answers will vary.

Page 59 "Beam Me Up"
1. d
2. a
3. c
4. b
5. Answers will vary.

Page 60 The Science of Color
1. d
2. c
3. a
4. b
5. Answers will vary.

Page 61 Audiology
1. a
2. c
3. d
4. d
5. Answers will vary.

Page 62 How Are Mountains Formed?
1. d
2. b
3. b
4. c
5. Answers will vary.

Page 63 Telling Time Without a Clock
1. b
2. a
3. d
4. b
5. Answers will vary.

Page 64 Physics for Our Amusement
1. a
2. b
3. c
4. b
5. Answers will vary.

Answer Key *(cont.)*

Page 65 Antarctic Ice Sheet
1. d
2. a
3. d
4. b
5. Answers will vary.

Page 66 Garbage to Good
1. d
2. b
3. c
4. a
5. Answers will vary.

Page 67 The Exciting Field of Engineering
1. d
2. a
3. b
4. c
5. Answers will vary.

Page 68 How We Use Corn
1. a
2. b
3. c
4. d
5. Answers will vary.

Page 69 International Space Station
1. c
2. b
3. b
4. a
5. Answers will vary.

Page 70 Geothermal Energy
1. b
2. c
3. a
4. b
5. Answers will vary.

Current Events

Page 71 Football for Kids
1. b
2. d
3. a
4. c
5. Answers will vary.

Page 72 Men on Mars?
1. d
2. d
3. b
4. b
5. Answers will vary.

Page 73 The Philippines
1. b
2. d
3. b
4. a
5. Answers will vary.

Page 74 United States Spy Agencies
1. c
2. c
3. a
4. b
5. Answers will vary.

Page 75 Word of the Year
1. c
2. d
3. d
4. a
5. Answers will vary.

Page 76 Global Warming
1. c
2. a
3. b
4. c
5. Answers will vary.

Page 77 3D Printing
1. b
2. b
3. a
4. c
5. Answers will vary.

Page 78 Is Recycling Worth It?
1. d
2. b
3. c
4. a
5. Answers will vary.

Page 79 The Homework Debate
1. a
2. b
3. a
4. d
5. Answers will vary.

Page 80 Meteorites on Earth
1. d
2. b
3. a
4. c
5. Answers will vary.

Page 81 Electric Cars
1. d
2. c
3. d
4. a
5. Answers will vary.

Page 82 Tree Climbing: Not Just for Kids
1. c
2. d
3. a
4. c
5. Answers will vary.

Page 83 Weather Is a Current Event
1. a
2. c
3. b
4. b
5. Answers will vary.

Page 84 Travel of the Future
1. d
2. a
3. c
4. b
5. Answers will vary.

Answer Key *(cont.)*

Page 85 The State of Hawaii
1. c
2. a
3. c
4. d
5. Answers will vary.

Page 86 Virtual Learning
1. c
2. c
3. b
4. d
5. Answers will vary.

Fiction

Fairy Tales/Folklore

Page 89 Bearskin
1. b
2. b
3. d
4. b
5. Answers will vary.

Page 90 Puss in Boots
1. b
2. c
3. d
4. b
5. Answers will vary.

Page 91 Felicia and the Carnations
1. c
2. a
3. d
4. b
5. Answers will vary.

Page 92 The Firebird
1. d
2. b
3. a
4. a
5. Answers will vary.

Page 93 Prince Ricky
1. b
2. b
3. d
4. c
5. Answers will vary.

Page 94 The Old Woman and the Doctor
1. c
2. d
3. c
4. a
5. Answers will vary.

Page 95 Mercury and the Woodman
1. b
2. c
3. d
4. a
5. Answers will vary.

Page 96 The Bear and the Travelers
1. a
2. d
3. b
4. c
5. Answers will vary.

Page 97 The Stag at the Pool
1. d
2. c
3. b
4. c
5. Answers will vary.

Page 98 Two Fables
1. b
2. a
3. b
4. d
5. Answers will vary.

Page 99 Samar and the Tigers
1. a
2. c
3. c
4. b
5. Answers will vary.

Page 100 The Turtle and the Lizard
1. c
2. a
3. c
4. b
5. Answers will vary.

Page 101 The Perfect Princess
1. b
2. c
3. a
4. d
5. Answers will vary.

Page 102 The Lynx and the Hare: A Chippewa Fable
1. c
2. a
3. d
4. c
5. Answers will vary.

Page 103 The Miserly Farmer
1. c
2. b
3. d
4. a
5. Answers will vary.

Historical

Page 104 Storms of Life
1. b
2. d
3. c
4. a
5. Answers will vary.

Answer Key *(cont.)*

Page 105 Held for Ransom
1. c
2. b
3. a
4. b
5. Answers will vary.

Page 106 Friend or Foe
1. c
2. d
3. c
4. a
5. Answers will vary.

Page 107 Salvage, Anyone?
1. d
2. a
3. b
4. c
5. Answers will vary.

Page 108 Space Wars
1. c
2. c
3. d
4. a
5. Answers will vary.

Page 109 Leap from the Sky
1. d
2. a
3. c
4. b
5. Answers will vary.

Page 110 Maria Isabella Boyd
1. c
2. b
3. d
4. c
5. Answers will vary.

Page 111 The Raft
1. b
2. a
3. a
4. c
5. Answers will vary.

Page 112 The Midnight Ride
1. d
2. c
3. a
4. b
5. Answers will vary.

Page 113 Bombs Away
1. c
2. d
3. c
4. b
5. Answers will vary.

Page 114 Texas Quilts
1. c
2. c
3. b
4. d
5. Answers will vary.

Page 115 Farewell at Independence, Missouri
1. c
2. b
3. a
4. d
5. Answers will vary.

Page 116 Penicillium
1. b
2. a
3. d
4. c
5. Answers will vary.

Page 117 Kit
1. d
2. a
3. b
4. c
5. Answers will vary.

Page 118 Labor for Grain
1. b
2. c
3. d
4. a
5. Answers will vary.

Page 119 Golf for Everyone
1. c
2. d
3. b
4. b
5. Answers will vary.

Contemporary Realism

Page 120 Meeting of Two Worlds
1. c
2. b
3. a
4. d
5. Answers will vary.

Page 121 Change of Plans
1. b
2. c
3. a
4. a
5. Answers will vary.

Page 122 Climb a Mountain
1. b
2. a
3. a
4. b
5. Answers will vary.

Page 123 Friendly Ferns
1. d
2. a
3. b
4. c
5. Answers will vary.

Page 124 Fast Pitch
1. d
2. a
3. c
4. b
5. Answers will vary.

Page 125 Rescue Companion
1. c
2. c
3. a
4. d
5. Answers will vary.

Answer Key (cont.)

Page 126 Perfect Planets
1. b
2. b
3. a
4. c
5. Answers will vary.

Page 127 Restart
1. d
2. b
3. b
4. c
5. Answers will vary.

Page 128 Tunnel Tour
1. d
2. c
3. a
4. b
5. Answers will vary.

Page 129 Mountains and Mushrooms
1. b
2. a
3. c
4. d
5. Answers will vary.

Page 130 Runaway
1. b
2. b
3. c
4. a
5. Answers will vary.

Page 131 Morning Meal
1. a
2. c
3. b
4. b
5. Answers will vary.

Page 132 Kite Competition
1. c
2. d
3. b
4. a
5. Answers will vary.

Page 133 Runner-Up
1. b
2. a
3. d
4. c
5. Answers will vary.

Page 134 A New Language
1. b
2. a
3. d
4. c
5. Answers will vary.

Page 135 Return of the Aunts
1. b
2. a
3. b
4. c
5. Answers will vary.

Mystery/Suspense/Adventure

Page 136 From the Depths
1. b
2. b
3. c
4. a
5. Answers will vary.

Page 137 Green Goo
1. c
2. a
3. c
4. d
5. Answers will vary.

Page 138 Adventure Hike
1. d
2. b
3. a
4. b
5. Answers will vary.

Page 139 Security Guards
1. b
2. a
3. a
4. d
5. Answers will vary.

Page 140 Island of Mystery
1. c
2. d
3. d
4. c
5. Answers will vary.

Page 141 Reaching for the Heights
1. a
2. a
3. d
4. c
5. Answers will vary.

Page 142 Surf's Up!
1. b
2. a
3. b
4. d
5. Answers will vary.

Page 143 Stranded!
1. c
2. a
3. b
4. d
5. Answers will vary.

Page 144 The Case of the Missing Reed
1. c
2. c
3. b
4. d
5. Answers will vary.

Page 145 The Kraken
1. b
2. c
3. a
4. b
5. Answers will vary.

Page 146 Hummock Trail
1. d
2. c
3. a
4. b
5. Answers will vary.

Answer Key *(cont.)*

Page 147 Dinner Biscuits
1. c
2. b
3. a
4. d
5. Answers will vary.

Page 148 Go-Cart Adventure
1. b
2. c
3. c
4. a
5. Answers will vary.

Page 149 State Fair
1. b
2. b
3. a
4. d
5. Answers will vary.

Page 150 The Walking Dead?
1. b
2. Answers will vary.
3. b
4. c
5. b

Fantasy

Page 151 A Deal with a Gremlin
1. b
2. a
3. c
4. d
5. Answers will vary.

Page 152 Northern Night
1. c
2. d
3. c
4. a
5. Answers will vary.

Page 153 Riches to Rags
1. b
2. d
3. a
4. b
5. Answers will vary.

Page 154 The Storytellers
1. c
2. a
3. d
4. b
5. Answers will vary.

Page 155 Tick Tock
1. b
2. d
3. c
4. c
5. Answers will vary.

Page 156 The Figurine
1. c
2. d
3. a
4. b
5. Answers will vary.

Page 157 A Twist of Fate
1. c
2. b
3. b
4. c
5. Answers will vary.

Page 158 The Gift of Sight
1. b
2. a
3. c
4. b
5. Answers will vary.

Page 159 The Statue
1. b
2. a
3. c
4. d
5. Answers will vary.

Page 160 The Cheshire Cat
1. d
2. c
3. a
4. b
5. Answers will vary.

Page 161 Thoughts from a Muse
1. c
2. b
3. a
4. c
5. Answers will vary.

Page 162 The Time Machine
1. b
2. a
3. c
4. c
5. Answers will vary.

Page 163 Dragon Games
1. b
2. a
3. d
4. d
5. Answers will vary.

Page 164 Monster Camp
1. c
2. a
3. b
4. d
5. Answers will vary.

Page 165 Shadows
1. d
2. b
3. c
4. c
5. Answers will vary.

Page 166 The Electric Touch
1. b
2. a
3. b
4. c
5. Answers will vary.

Tracking Sheet

NONFICTION

Animals		Biographies		History		Science		Current Events	
Page 9		Page 24		Page 40		Page 56		Page 71	
Page 10		Page 25		Page 41		Page 57		Page 72	
Page 11		Page 26		Page 42		Page 58		Page 73	
Page 12		Page 27		Page 43		Page 59		Page 74	
Page 13		Page 28		Page 44		Page 60		Page 75	
Page 14		Page 29		Page 45		Page 61		Page 76	
Page 15		Page 30		Page 46		Page 62		Page 77	
Page 16		Page 31		Page 47		Page 63		Page 78	
Page 17		Page 32		Page 48		Page 64		Page 79	
Page 18		Page 33		Page 49		Page 65		Page 80	
Page 19		Page 34		Page 50		Page 66		Page 81	
Page 20		Page 35		Page 51		Page 67		Page 82	
Page 21		Page 36		Page 52		Page 68		Page 83	
Page 22		Page 37		Page 53		Page 69		Page 84	
Page 23		Page 38		Page 54		Page 70		Page 85	
		Page 39		Page 55				Page 86	

FICTION

Fairy Tales/ Folklore		Historical		Contemporary Realism		Mystery/ Suspense/Adventure		Fantasy	
Page 89		Page 104		Page 120		Page 136		Page 151	
Page 90		Page 105		Page 121		Page 137		Page 152	
Page 91		Page 106		Page 122		Page 138		Page 153	
Page 92		Page 107		Page 123		Page 139		Page 154	
Page 93		Page 108		Page 124		Page 140		Page 155	
Page 94		Page 109		Page 125		Page 141		Page 156	
Page 95		Page 110		Page 126		Page 142		Page 157	
Page 96		Page 111		Page 127		Page 143		Page 158	
Page 97		Page 112		Page 128		Page 144		Page 159	
Page 98		Page 113		Page 129		Page 145		Page 160	
Page 99		Page 114		Page 130		Page 146		Page 161	
Page 100		Page 115		Page 131		Page 147		Page 162	
Page 101		Page 116		Page 132		Page 148		Page 163	
Page 102		Page 117		Page 133		Page 149		Page 164	
Page 103		Page 118		Page 134		Page 150		Page 165	
		Page 119		Page 135				Page 166	